TOWARD
Zero-Defect
Programming

TOWARD
Zero-Defect
Programming

Allan M. Stavely

New Mexico Tech

ADDISON-WESLEY

An imprint of Addison Wesley Longman, Inc.

Reading, Massachusetts • Harlow, England • Menlo Park, California
Berkeley, California • Don Mills, Ontario • Sydney • Bonn • Amsterdam
Tokyo • Mexico City

Publishing Partner: Peter Gordon
Associate Editor: Helen Goldstein
Production Editor: Patricia A. O. Unubun
Cover and Interior Design: Alwyn R. Velásquez
Composition: Windfall Software

Many of the designations used by manufacturers and sellers to distinguish their products are claimed as trademarks. Where those designations appear in this book, and the publisher was aware of a trademark claim, the designations have been printed in initial caps or in all caps.

The programs and the applications presented in this book have been included for their instructional value. They have been tested with care but are not guaranteed for any particular purpose. Neither the publisher or the author offers any warranties or representations, nor do they accept any liabilities with respect to the programs or applications.

This book was typset in T_EX in a Linux environment on a PC. The fonts used were Sabon, Leawood, and MathTimes for math. It was printed on Clearfield.

Library of Congress Cataloging-in-Publication Data
Stavely, Allan M.
    Toward zero-defect programming / by Allan M. Stavely.
        p.   cm.
    Includes bibliographical references and index.
    ISBN 0-201-38595-3
    1. Computer software—Quality control. 2. Computer software-
-Verification.   I. Title
QA76.76.Q35S73 1999
005.1'068'5—dc21   98-3278
                                        CIP

1 2 3 4 5 6 7 8 9 10–MA–0201009998

To my parents, Earl and Ann

Preface

This is a book for programmers who want to write programs with no bugs, or at least with as few bugs as is humanly possible with current technology.

Programmers can do this by using a particular kind of specification and verification, which I will present in the book. By verification, I mean proving, mathematically, that a program agrees with its specification.

Don't panic. You will see that this does not require great mathematical sophistication, only knowledge of a few particular techniques and ways of doing things (and then, of course, practice). There is no rigorous mathematical formalism in this book. In fact, the specifications and proofs are usually only semiformal and are sometimes quite informal indeed.

Why verify programs? Because it is a very effective way of detecting bugs. We often find that, as we attempt to verify a program, that our efforts fail because the program is not, in fact, correct. When this happens, we have found a defect. Then, of course, we fix it.

This will be our fundamental assumption:

The purpose of verification is to eliminate defects.

This is a very pragmatic view. Others may take the "all-or-nothing" position that verification is a mathematical exercise that produces mathematically perfect objects and is worthless if it can't do that, but we won't say any such thing here. You won't see any claims in this book that verified programs cannot possibly contain any defects, do not need to be tested, and can be trusted unconditionally. On the contrary, we cannot always detect all defects in a program using verification: we are human, and we make mistakes. Thus, verified programs still need to be tested carefully, and I will present methods for doing this as well.

The methods presented in this book are based on a set of interrelated techniques developed at IBM in the late 1970s and early 1980s, under the name *Cleanroom Software Engineering*. IBM has used them on a number of substantial projects since then, with impressive success, and since the late 1980s their use has been spreading to other companies and organizations.

These methods work. Cleanroom methods can reduce the number of defects in software by an order of magnitude or more. The extra time spent in specifying and verifying is more than made up in reduced debugging and reworking time, so using these methods costs nothing extra in terms of effort or schedule time. And the methods scale up well to large systems. You don't need to take my word for it: the results have been reported in the open literature. You will see some of the data, with literature citations, in Chapter 1. And I, along with my colleagues and students, get similar results.

There is no magic here. Our methods require programmers to work carefully and systematically, to check their work, and above all to understand their programs very thoroughly. But these are things that they should be doing anyway, even if many don't. You can think of methods as merely tools that help programmers to do these things.

This book presents my adaptation of Cleanroom methods and should not be taken as an official statement of what Cleanroom Software Engineering is. I do not speak for the Cleanroom community, which in any case has dispersed and expanded far beyond the original group at IBM. In my presentation, I have chosen to emphasize the parts of the Cleanroom process that seem to me to be the most valuable (other Cleanroom practitioners may well disagree), and to deemphasize or omit others. I have also introduced a few new ideas of my own.

The book was written with classroom use in mind and is based on a course that I have been teaching since 1993. Besides presenting the fundamentals of specification, programming, verification, and testing in the Cleanroom style, I have included extra explanations, hints, and examples covering parts of the process that students seem to find difficult at first. Mine is a one-semester undergraduate course for computer science students, but a similar course could be taught at the graduate level. The book is also suitable for an intensive short course in an industrial or continuing-education setting.

Programming professionals will also find this book useful for self-study. You will see in Chapter 6, however, that the recommended way to do the verification is in small groups, in review meetings, rather than on your own. Thus, if you intend to study this book outside a course, you will get the best results if you can work with at least two or three other people who already know these methods or who would like to study them with you.

As a minimum, the reader should be familiar with the basics of algorithms and data structures, as taught in the usual first course in the subject, and with the rudiments of discrete mathematics (sets, relations, functions, and so on). The reader should also, of course, have enough experience in programming and debugging to appreciate how valuable zero-defect programming would be if we could do it!

I also assume the ability to read and understand the structure, at least in general terms, of programs written in languages in the Algol family (including Pascal, C, Modula, Icon, and so on). In Section 9.4 I also use the functional languages Scheme and ML, but that section can be omitted by readers who have no familiarity at all with functional languages. Similarly, in Section 8.4 I use the object-oriented features of C++ and Python languages in my examples, but that section can be skipped by readers who have no familiarity at all with object-oriented programming or languages.

The methods of this book can be applied to programs in a wide variety of languages. To demonstrate this, extended examples of programs, parts of programs, and program development will be presented using the following languages: C, C++, Icon, ML, Pascal, Python, and Scheme. Particular features of these languages are explained where they are used, so a detailed knowledge of all these languages is not required. However, more of the examples are written in C than in the other languages, so familiarity with C would be helpful.

In many places in the text, short fragments of programming-language code are used to illustrate the ideas being presented. Most of these fragments are written in a generic, "ordinary" procedural programming language: except for trivial details such as where the semicolons are, the language of each fragment might be Pascal, or Modula, or Turning, or Icon, or Ada, or any of a dozen others. The syntax may vary, but the meaning should always be apparent. When an example is meant to be in a particular programming language, I will say so.

Literature citations and comments on related work appear in the Notes sections at the end of each chapter.

My most important source does not appear in those citations. I received my first training in Cleanroom methods at a one-week intensive workshop at the Rochester (New York) Institute of Technology in the summer of 1992. The workshop was sponsored by the (U.S.) National Science Foundation. It was a condensed version of IBM's in-house training course and was conducted by Philip Hausler, Mark Pleszkoch, and Steve Rosen, of the IBM Cleanroom Software Technology Center. I am most grateful to them and to IBM, NSF, and RIT for making the workshop possible. Although I do not cite this workshop in the Notes in specific chapters of the book, the workshop was a primary source for much of the material, particularly the material of Chapters 2 through 6 and Chapters 10 and 11.

I am also most grateful to friends and colleagues who have made valuable contributions to this book through consultation, suggestions, and corrections: Michael Deck, John Duncan, Doug Dunston, Suzanne Flandreau, Alex Kent, Ray

Piworunas, Steve Powell, John Shipman (for help on more occasions than I can count), and Laurie Williams; also to Peter Gordon at Addison Wesley Longman, for support and suggestions; and to all of the students in my classes over the past five years, for helping me to debug my presentation of this material. Many thanks to all of you.

Cleanroom methods are the best that I have found for producing high-quality software, and experience has shown that they can take us a long way toward the goal of zero defects. I am confident that they will continue to be developed and refined and reasonably sure that different but even better methods will eventually be developed. Meanwhile, Cleanroom methods have proven their worth and are ready for practical use today, and I hope that the presentation in this book of my version of them will help to promote their use.

In any case, we can begin by changing our attitude toward bugs: they are not inevitable, and they are not acceptable. *Zero defects* is the goal that we should strive for. We will not always be able to achieve it, but we should try.

A. M. S.
Socorro, New Mexico

Contents

Chapter 1 Introduction   1

    1.1 The Problem: Bugs   1

    1.2 The Cleanroom Method   3

    1.3 About This Book   6

        Notes   8

Chapter 2 The Functions Computed by Programs   11

    2.1 Computations: States and Functions   11

    2.2 Representation of Functions: Concurrent Assignments   12

    2.3 Conditional Concurrent Assignments   15

    2.4 Local Variables   17

    2.5 Specification Using Intended Functions   18

    2.6 Other Notation Conventions   20

    2.7 Writing Intended Functions   23

        Exercises   27

        Notes   29

Chapter 3 Verification   31

    3.1 The Structured Control Constructs   31

    3.2 Placement of Intended Functions   33

    3.3 The Substitution Principle   36

    3.4 Sequences of Statements   38

    3.5 Trace Tables   41

3.6 If-statements   42
3.7 Conditional Trace Tables   47
     Exercises   51
     Notes   52

Chapter 4 Verification of Iterations   53

4.1 While-statements   53
4.2 Proving Termination   55
4.3 Initialized Loops   57
4.4 Writing Intended Functions for Loops in Isolation   59
4.5 Other Forms of Indefinite Iteration   63
     Exercises   66
     Notes   67

Chapter 5 Programming with Intended Functions   69

5.1 A Pascal Program: Length of the Longest Line   69
5.2 A C Program: Counting Letters and Digits   77
5.3 An Icon Routine: Uncompressing a String   83
5.4 A Study in Abstraction: The Registrar's Program   90
5.5 Keeping Things Simple   96
     Exercises   100
     Notes   102

Chapter 6 Verification Reviews   103

6.1 Why Verification Reviews Are Necessary   103
6.2 Verification Reviews in the Cleanroom Process   104
6.3 How Verification Reviews Are Done   105
6.4 Example: Another Routine from the Registrar's Programs   108
6.5 Example: A Routine from a Test-data Generator   111
6.6 Discussion of the Examples   117
     Exercises   119
     Notes   119

Chapter 7 Definite Iteration   121

7.1 Definite Iteration Over Sequences   121
7.2 Sequence Variables   124
7.3 Other Sequence Expressions   127
7.4 Ranges of Integers   131
7.5 Other Data Structures   133
7.6 The Iteration Mechanisms   136
7.7 Sets and Sequences in Program Design   142
     Exercises   145
     Notes   147

Chapter 8 Data Abstraction and Object-oriented Programs   149

8.1 Data Abstraction and Encapsulation   149
8.2 The Abstraction Function   152
8.3 Data Invariants   155
8.4 Object-oriented Programs   161
     Exercises   166
     Notes   166

Chapter 9 Recursion and Functional Languages   169

9.1 Recursive Routines   169
9.2 Termination   174
9.3 Mutual Recursion   176
9.4 Functional Languages   178
     Exercises   184
     Notes   185

Chapter 10 Testing   187

10.1 The Role of Testing   187
10.2 Usage-based Testing   190
10.3 Test-data Generators   191

10.4 Other Forms of Testing   196
      Exercises   197
      Notes   198

Chapter 11 Incremental Development   199

11.1 Developing a Program in Increments   199
11.2 Planning and Carrying Out the Process   201
11.3 Example: Rehearsal Scheduling   203
      Exercises   207
      Notes   208

Chapter 12 Where Do We Go From Here?   209

12.1 Other Parts of the Cleanroom Process   209
12.2   Other Formal Methods   212
12.3 What Have We Accomplished?   216
12.4 Prospects for the Future   219
      Notes   222
      Hints for Selected Exercises   225
      References   227
      Index   235

TOWARD
Zero-Defect
Programming

1

Introduction

1.1 The Problem: Bugs

Computers are everywhere, and they affect our lives every day — for many of us, every hour of every day. They control our cars, watches, telephones, and electrical appliances. Shops and companies use them in doing business with us, in every activity from running cash registers to mailing bills to keeping goods on the shelves. They control the planes we ride in and the traffic signals on our roads. They keep some of us alive by controlling our pacemakers and other medical devices. And, because you are reading this book, you are probably a programmer or a student of programming, and you use computers every day in your work.

If computers are everywhere, so is the software that those computers run. And, sadly, so are defects — in plain language, bugs — in that software.

You probably notice bugs in the programs that you use. I notice them every day. There's a bug in my site's mail program that has been there for years. It causes the program to lose track of where I am in the list of messages that I'm reading; I would run into it every day if I forgot that I needed to work around it. There are bugs in our news reader; one, for example, keeps me from seeing some articles under some circumstances. There are bugs in our web browser, our spreadsheet program, our printer software, our library's automated catalog ... the list goes on and on. Most of them waste only small amounts of my time when I encounter them, but this wasted time adds up; besides, they are very annoying. And occasionally such a bug causes me to lose hours or days of work.

Some software defects are more serious, much more serious. Bugs in the programs that control medical devices have killed people. Bugs have caused aircraft

1

to crash. Bugs have shut down telephone networks, power grids, railways, and air traffic control centers; have disrupted space missions; and have caused environmental damage. Bugs have caused financial institutions and other businesses to lose large amounts of money, sometimes many millions of dollars at a stroke.[1]

Software defects can be very costly even before the software is put into service. Most large software projects are finished late and over budget, often by tens or hundreds of millions of dollars, if they are finished at all. Some projects are never finished, and are written off entirely, again costing millions. There are many reasons why this happens, including poor specifications, requirements that change before the project is done, and inadequate budgeting. But a leading cause, again, is bugs: quite simply, the programmers can't get their code to work.

We might guess that most bugs occur only in particularly poorly written programs, and that competent programmers produce bug-free code. We would be wrong. On the contrary, almost every program of nontrivial size has some bugs, perhaps many. According to data from industry, a typical program contains several bugs per thousand lines of code when it is delivered and put into service. This means that large programs such as operating systems and business transaction-processing systems are likely to contain hundreds or thousands of bugs!

This situation is not acceptable. We need to do better.

But how? Just by trying harder? There is no reason to believe that just asking programmers to be more careful will help much. Neither will asking programmers to spend more time on their work. In fact, in many companies it isn't even possible, because getting the product out the door quickly is the top priority, or because their programmers work very long hours already.

By doing more testing and debugging? Maybe. But it turns out that you can't count on even the most careful testing to detect much more than 90% of the bugs in a program. And doing even this much testing is usually very time-consuming and expensive.

The problem is in the number of bugs that are in the code before testing begins. A program that contains several bugs per thousand lines of code after testing must have contained one or more per hundred lines when testing began. That is too many. At this rate, any program of more than a few thousand lines (which is small by today's standards) will contain so many bugs that we can't expect to find them all by testing.

It's not that programmers are unskilled or sloppy workers. In fact, today's programmers are, on average, pretty good. But programmers are human, and they

---

[1] Here and in the rest of the book, references appear in the Notes sections at the ends of the chapters.

make mistakes. A good programmer can often write a hundred lines of code without making a single mistake. But not consistently, every time, week after week, month after month. I can't do it, and — be honest — neither can you.

What we seem to need is some better way of constructing our programs in the first place, so that we can avoid or detect most of our mistakes before we even start running tests. That way, we could expect the testing to detect most of the remaining defects, leaving us with a final product containing very few — perhaps none at all. Is this possible?

1.2   The Cleanroom Method

This is exactly the approach that was taken by a group at IBM's Federal Systems Division. This group, led by the late Harlan Mills, developed a group of techniques for producing very-high-quality software, in the period from the late 1970s to the early 1980s. Together, these techniques are called *Cleanroom Software Engineering.*

The term is borrowed from the field of semiconductor fabrication. Computer processor and memory chips and other integrated circuits are fabricated in *clean rooms*, which are environments as free from dust and contamination as they can possibly be made. The air is filtered; the workers wear special lint-free clothing. Every effort is made to keep the chips free from contamination while they are being fabricated.

Of course, this is the only way that such complex and delicate chips can be fabricated. Imagine trying to make them on a workbench on a dusty, dirty factory floor. The chips would end up full of dirt and contamination. And then what? There is no process that can vacuum a dirty chip clean, no special solvent that can wash away all the particles of dust. But that is the equivalent of what we hope to do with software when we rely on debugging to eliminate defects.

In the Cleanroom approach to software, special methods are used at each stage of the development to avoid errors. First, the computation that the program must produce is clearly and carefully specified in a particular way, called functional specification. Such a specification may or may not contain a lot of specialized mathematical notation, but it must be clear and precise.

Then, as the software is being designed and coded, every part of it will have its own specification of the computation that it must produce. Furthermore, at each step, the specifications and code are used to verify that all of the pieces fit together correctly, so that each part does indeed agree with its specification. If it does not, it is defective. The author of the code fixes the defect, and the verification is attempted again. The code is not considered finished until every part of it has been successfully verified.

This verification is performed by small groups of people in review meetings. The proofs are mathematical, but are often quite informal, and the group will discuss each point only as long as it takes for all of them to agree that the software is correct. This kind of correctness verification is perhaps the most radical innovation of Cleanroom.

The verifiers hope, of course, that they will successfully verify each part of the program, but they expect to find at least a few defects as they try. In fact, this is the reason for doing the verification at all. This is the central assumption in Cleanroom specification and verification:

The purpose of verification is to eliminate defects.

The value of the verification is *not* in the proofs of correctness; it is in the defects that are detected and corrected during the verification process.

Finally, after the program has been completely coded and verified, testing begins. Typically, the development group hands the program over to an independent testing group. At this time, some defects may remain, because the verification team may have overlooked them, but there should be very few. The testing has two purposes: first, to find as many of the remaining defects as possible; and, second, to act as a quality-control check on the development and verification activities. If too many errors are discovered during testing, it is a sign that some previous step is not being done properly, and steps are taken to correct the process.

Cleanroom-style testing is done in a particular way that attempts to execute the software in the same ways that real users eventually will. This way of testing is particularly good at detecting, usually early in the testing process, the defects that the users would run into most frequently. The result is that users typically encounter very few defects when the software is put into production use.

Testing of this kind involves executing the whole program as it would be executed in actual use. In a Cleanroom project, *unit testing*, or testing of individual routines, modules, or other components in isolation, is usually not done at all: the first time code is executed is as part of a whole program, in *integration testing*. This is possible because the code is almost defect-free before the first test is run; unit testing is not needed to bring it to the level of quality at which integration testing can be done effectively. Thus, the verification reviews replace unit testing in the Cleanroom process.

Still, on a large project, there are advantages to building and testing the software in stages. In the Cleanroom process, this is typically done by developing the software incrementally. The first increment may be a very minimal, stripped-down program that implements only a small amount of the functionality that will eventually be required, perhaps not even enough to be useful to a user at all. Even so, it is a complete program that can be tested using real inputs. After that, each increment is produced by adding more code and functionality to the previous increment; this can be done while the previous increment is being tested. The last increment is the final product.

Do these Cleanroom methods work? Experience has shown that they do. After code has been written and verified, it may still contain a few defects, but very few: perhaps three per thousand lines. This is before the code has ever been executed — with no testing at all! Then testing detects most of the remaining defects, perhaps 90% of them.

Furthermore, Cleanroom-style development usually costs nothing extra! If anything, it usually costs less in terms of total effort and cost and in terms of schedule time (the "time-to-market" that is critically important to many companies). Extra time is spent doing the specification and verification but, because this leads to fewer defects, much less time is spent in debugging and correcting the code. Additional time is saved by omitting unit testing, which involves not only designing and running the tests but also writing drivers, stubs, and other "scaffolding" code so that the units can be executed in isolation.

It even turns out that most of the defects that remain after verification are simple oversights, not deep design flaws. They are usually caught very early in testing and are usually very easy to find and fix. The typical Cleanroom-developed program starts working almost immediately, with very little debugging needed, and works perfectly, or almost perfectly, from then on.

Here is some data from industry. In seventeen substantial projects at IBM and elsewhere from 1987 to 1993, amounting to almost a million lines of code in all, the code contained only about 2.3 defects per thousand lines after verification, but detected during testing. Remember, this is approximately the number of defects present in the code before it has ever been tested or executed at all! This is an amazingly good result. A few of the projects:

- IBM's COBOL Structuring Facility, a program to transform COBOL programs to a well-structured form. The code was 85,000 lines of PL/1. The bug density detected in testing was 3.4 per thousand lines. In the first three years of production use, only seven minor errors were found, which is less than 0.1 per thousand lines, and each of these was easy to fix.
- A NASA satellite-control system. This was 40,000 lines of FORTRAN. The bug density in testing was 4.5 per thousand lines. About 60% of the programs compiled successfully the first time.
- A complex decision-support program written at IBM. This program was 107,000 lines of code in a mixture of languages, written by a fifty-person team. In testing, 2.6 defects per thousand lines were found; five of the eight components had none. No defects were reported by its first users in production use.

- The device controller for an IBM tape drive, 86,000 lines of C code embedded in the device. This was a complex program that handled several real-time I/O data streams. Only 1.2 defects per thousand lines were found in testing.
- The Ericsson Telecom OS32 operating system. This was a seventy-person project lasting eighteen months, producing 350,000 lines of code in assembler and C. The defect density in testing was only 1.0 per thousand lines. The project was a great success, and was honored by Ericsson as the project that had contributed most to the company in 1993.

Furthermore, on each of these projects, a substantial increase in programmer productivity was reported compared with what each organization normally experienced.

Notice that these were not toy projects or academic exercises; they were substantial, real-world projects. Furthermore, they were typical projects for each organization, not special projects that required extraordinary methods for some reason. Once, rigorous specification and verification were assumed to be too difficult and expensive to use on most projects, and were contemplated only for projects that had (for example) unusual safety or security requirements that justified the large extra cost. But these examples show that Cleanroom methods are appropriate for projects of all kinds.

1.3   About This Book

The techniques that I will teach you in this book are based on Cleanroom methods as I have adapted them to my own needs and the needs of my students and colleagues. We won't try to follow the entire Cleanroom process exactly, as a large project team in a large organization might do. That won't be necessary. The key ideas and techniques are quite adaptable and can be used on projects of all sizes, by large or small groups of programmers, using them as appropriate under the particular circumstances.

I will concentrate on the parts of the Cleanroom technology that I consider to be the most distinctive and valuable: the methods for specification and verification. Knowing these methods, you will be able to start applying them in your work right away. I will also cover incremental development and Cleanroom-style testing. There are a few aspects of the Cleanroom process that are beyond the scope of this book; I will mention them briefly in the last chapter and include suggestions for further reading for those who are interested.

You probably know quite a lot about programming already, so I am certainly not going to ask you to learn to program all over again just so that you can do it my way! Instead, I have tried to build on what you already know about programming and to present methods that you can adapt to your skills and your situation.

I assume that you will be working as part of a small group, either in a classroom setting or in the "real world". The members of the group will do the programming, and the group will conduct the verification reviews. If necessary, the group can do its own testing as well, rather than using an independent testing group. Thus you won't need to be part of a large team in a giant organization like IBM or NASA to practice what you learn here.

I have found that students, trying these techniques for the first time in my course, can write programs that are far more defect-free than any that they have ever written before. The results probably won't be quite as good, on average, as the results that professionals get, as reported in the previous section. Still, by the end of the course, my students, working in small groups, can usually write programs of a thousand or so lines with fewer than ten bugs, measured from first execution in testing. Some of the smaller programs or components that they write, of perhaps several dozen or a few hundred lines, will contain no bugs at all — in some cases, not even syntax errors. They will be completely correct the first time.

If debugging is your favorite part of programming, this book is not for you! You'll be happier writing programs in the usual way, bashing them out as quickly as possible so that you can get on with debugging, doing as much testing and debugging as you have time for, and hoping that the result is good enough.

But if you start using the methods presented here, you'll find that you will need to spend a lot less time debugging. Furthermore, when your projects are finished, they will really be finished, and you can go on to new projects rather than being chained to old ones, fixing bug after bug in them forever.

Can we really achieve a level of zero defects in our programs? No, we still don't know how to do that reliably, every time, even with Cleanroom methods. But we can come a lot closer than we have in the past.

What we can do is to adopt a zero-defect attitude toward our programming. Defects should be the exception, not the rule. We no longer need to assume that bugs are inevitable and that all code we write is full of them. Instead, our attitude should be that defect-free code is normal and that anything less is not good enough.

We will still make mistakes, because we are human, and there's no point in feeling guilty about that. But we shouldn't make many mistakes. With help from our friends, we will find and correct almost all of them before they do any damage. And, as we practice our skills and gain experience, we may even increase our chances of achieving that elusive goal of zero defects.

Notes

ACM's *Software Engineering Notes*, a monthly journal, presents in each issue a digest of accounts of computer malfunctions that have affected the public. These accounts are taken from the public press and from submissions by readers of the journal. A selection of these accounts, with additions from other sources, has appeared in book form [Neum95]. The primary causes of many of the incidents were software bugs. Some examples:

- Blockage of the nationwide AT&T long-distance network for nine hours (pp. 14–15)
- Disruption of missions of the space shuttles *Atlantis* and *Endeavour* (p. 24)
- Landing of the *Gemini V* spacecraft 100 miles off course (pp. 27–28)
- Crash of the prototype of the Swedish fighter plane *Gripen* (pp. 36–37)
- Shutdown of the Fremont, California, air traffic control center for two hours (p. 48)
- Halting of all commuter and long-distance trains in the very busy area of Clapham Junction in south London (pp. 52–53)
- Release of thousands of gallons of radioactive water from the Bruce nuclear station in Canada (p. 81)
- Power blackout in ten western states for up to an hour (p. 83)
- Thirty-two-billion-dollar overdraft on the Bank of New York, costing the bank $5 million for interest in only one day (p. 169)

Between June 1985 and January 1987, a computer-controlled radiation therapy machine delivered massive overdoses of radiation to patients on six occasions. Four of the patients were killed and the other two were severely injured. The accidents were caused by a combination of factors, including software bugs, lack of safety interlocks in the hardware, and flaws in the operator interface. See [Leve93] for a detailed account. A summary appears in [Neum95], pp. 68–70.

The latter book also describes many software projects that were drastically over budget, and very late or never completed, with losses of up to $1 billion (pp. 216–218). Other projects of this kind, including the baggage-handling system at the Denver International Airport, are reported in [Gibb94]. That article also says (pp. 86–87):

> Studies have shown that for every new large-scale software systems that are put into operation, two others are canceled. The average software development overshoots its schedule by half; large projects generally do worse. And some three quarters of all large systems are "operational failures" that either do not function as intended or are not used at all.

A word-processing program produced by Microsoft,

> Word 3.0 for the Macintosh, delivered in February 1987 after having been promised for July 1986, had approximately seven hundred bugs — several of which destroyed data or "crashed" the program. Microsoft had to ship a free upgrade to customers within two months of the original release, costing more than $1 million. ([Cusa95] p. 40)

Estimates of industry averages for bug density in delivered code vary widely. Two published estimates that are based on actual data are 10 to 50 defects per thousand non-comment lines in delivered code produced in the U.S. ([DeMa82] p. 200) and "in the vicinity of at least 4 or 5 defects per 1000 source code statements at delivery" ([Jone86a] p. 168). Most recent estimates that I have seen have been of the same order of magnitude as the latter numbers.

According to [Jone91] (p. 166):

> Most U.S. enterprises are seriously deficient in defect removal technology; they tend to depend primarily on testing . . . The actual technologies of defect removal are advancing rapidly, and leading-edge enterprises can now exceed 99 percent in cumulative defect removal efficiency. Unfortunately, the overall U.S. norms for defect removal appear to hover around 75 percent.

Figures from [Jone86a], p. 179, indicate that a typical three-stage series of testing (individual modules, groups of modules, and the whole system) will remove only about 73% of defects on average, and 90% at best.

The examples of successful Cleanroom projects are taken from [Ling94], which gives details on seven of the seventeen Cleanroom projects mentioned in Section 1.2. A table of data on all seventeen projects appears in [Haus94]. These and other important papers on Cleanroom are collected in [Poor96]. Other books that give overviews of Cleanroom and cover various aspects of it in detail are [Beck97] and [Dyer92].

2

The Functions Computed by Programs

2.1   Computations: States and Functions

Our first job will be to learn to write specifications in a way that works well with the programming and verification techniques that we plan to use eventually. This chapter will present a way of specifying programs and parts of programs in such a way, directly in terms of the functions that they compute. This first section will introduce the concept of the state of a program, and the view of a computation as a change to a new state as a function of the current state.

As a program executes, it changes the values of its variables. It produces output on a screen or printer. It may change the contents of files. It may send bits, characters, or numbers to devices that control things in the outside world, such as elevator doors, aircraft flaps, or radiation-treatment machines.

To produce these effects, the program performs computations that use the values in the variables and data received from input devices such as a terminal keyboard or mouse. The program may also take data from files, or from sensing devices that obtain data from the outside world.

Each of these variables, files, and input and output streams must be considered as we talk about the effect of the execution of a program. We will refer to each of them as a *state variable*. At any time in a program's execution, its state variables contain all of the results that the program has produced, and all of the data that it has available to it to produce further results.

The state of the program as a whole is its *data state*, which is the aggregation of all of its state variables, plus its control state, which contains information such as which statement of the program is currently being executed, which statement in one procedure called another procedure that is currently being executed, and so on.

Each step of the program's execution will cause a change in its state. In particular, the data state of the program after that step will be some function of the data state as it was before the step. We can think of the data state of a program as if it were one big variable (call it X), which is a data structure containing fields of many different types, each field being one of the state variables. Then we can represent the effect of an execution step abstractly as

$$X := f(X)$$

where f is a function that produces one such data state from another. We will say that f is the *function computed* by this execution step.

A sequence of execution steps also produces a state change of this kind. In fact, so does the entire execution of the program. In each case, we can speak of the function computed by the sequence of steps or by the whole program. As we reason about the effects of programs, we will do it by reasoning about the relationship between the function computed by a program and the functions computed by its parts.

2.2   Representation of Functions: Concurrent Assignments

We will need a notation for representing the functions computed by particular programs and parts of programs. That notation will be the subject of the next three sections.

We could, of course, define a function in terms of the value that it gives for each of the state variables. However, definitions like this are much longer and more tedious than we need. The reason is that, in many of the computations we will be talking about, many state variables have the same values in the new state as in the current state. This is especially true of a single step in the execution of a program: typically, each step changes the value of only one or a few of the program's state variables. We would rather not be required to say of every other state variable that it has the same value in the new state as in the current state. What we want is a notation in which we need to write only what happens to the state variables whose values change.

Let us start by establishing a notation for the simplest case, in which only one variable is changed. Suppose that one of the state variables of a program is the integer variable m, and consider the assignment statement

```
m := 1
```

It computes a function that produces a new state from a current state, in which the new state is the same as the current state except that the variable *m* in the new state has the value 1. We will write that function as simply

$$[\, m := 1 \,]$$

Notice that we say nothing about any other state variable in the program: it is implied that their values do not change. The square brackets distinguish functions of this kind from the statements and other pieces of programs that compute these functions.

Now suppose that the program also has an integer variable *n*, and consider the sequence of assignment statements

```
m := 1;
n := 0
```

We will write the function that it computes as

$$[\, m, n := 1, 0 \,]$$

This says that, in the new state produced by the function, *m* has the value 1, *n* has the value 0, and all other state variables have the same values that they have in the current state.

In the new state, each variable on the left-hand side of the := has the value in the corresponding position on the right-hand side. The order of the variables and values does not matter, as long as it is consistent between the two sides. For example, this represents the same function:

$$[\, n, m := 0, 1 \,]$$

Notice also that the following sequence of statements computes the same function as the previous sequence:

```
n := 0;
m := 1
```

Our notation for functions does not tell us anything about the order in which the state variables received their values; it tells us only the final result. Furthermore, any intermediate states, or intermediate values of state variables, are not shown. For example, this sequence of statements computes the same function as the first two:

```
n := 3267;
m := 1;
n := 0
```

and you can probably think of many others. Again, the function expresses only the final result.

In this notation for functions, the piece $m, n := 1, 0$ is called a *concurrent assignment*. It is intended to look like an assignment statement in a programming language, but it suggests that any number of variables are receiving new values concurrently; that is, at the same time. In fact, that is how we should interpret it. The situation is as if the new state is calculated from the current state in a single, indivisible step.

From now on, we will often use the term "concurrent assignment" even for an assignment to only one variable, just so that we can use the same terminology in all cases.

Of course, there can be functions in which the new state depends on values of state variables in the current state. Here is an example:

$$[x := x + 1]$$

This says that the value of x in the new state is its value in the current state plus 1.

Here is another example:

$$[x, \ y := x + 1, \ x]$$

We must be careful here. This does *not* mean that the value of x is incremented by 1, and then y gets that same value. Instead, it means that the value of x is incremented by 1, and also y gets the value that x had before it was incremented.

Here is a sequence of statements that computes that function:

```
y := x;
x := x + 1
```

But notice that this sequence of statements does not:

```
x := x + 1;
y := x
```

Instead, it computes

$$[x, \ y := x + 1, \ x + 1]$$

In a concurrent assignment, every use of a state variable on the right-hand side of the assignment refers to its value in the *current* state. A use of a variable on the left-hand side indicates that the variable is receiving a new value in the *new* state.

In other words, the meaning of a concurrent assignment is as if the following sequence of events occurs: First, each expression on the right-hand side is evaluated using values of the state variables in the current state. Then, a new state is created in which each state variable on the left-hand side has the value of the expression in the corresponding position on the right-hand side, and the other state variables have the same values that they have in the current state.

2.3   Conditional Concurrent Assignments

Sometimes a part of a program can perform quite different computations under different circumstances, depending on values of some of the program's state variables. When this happens, it is easiest to describe the corresponding function by cases. Consider, for example, a computation in which the variable *avg* is set to *sum/n* when *n* is greater than 0, and to 0 otherwise. We will write this function as follows:

$$[\, n > 0 \rightarrow avg := sum/n$$
$$|\, n \leq 0 \rightarrow avg := 0 \,]$$

We will call the construct between the square brackets a *conditional concurrent assignment*. In general, it contains any number (one or more) of cases, each of which contains a logical expression and a concurrent assignment. The logical expressions (called *preconditions*) are used to determine which concurrent assignment defines the function in any particular state.

We will define the meaning of a conditional concurrent assignment as follows. In the current state, the preconditions are evaluated in the order in which the cases appear. For the first precondition which has the value *true*, the corresponding conditional assignment is selected to determine the next state. Thus, a conditional concurrent assignment is much like an "if ... else if ... else if ... else ..." construct in a programming language.

Notice that this means that a precondition does not need to state that the preconditions for the previous cases are false. Thus we could have written the above example as

$$[\, n > 0 \rightarrow avg := sum/n$$
$$|\ true \ \rightarrow avg := 0 \,]$$

Because the second case has the precondition *true*, that case is selected whenever the precondition of the first case is false. In other words, *true* as a precondition acts like *else* in an if-statement. Some people even prefer to write *else* instead of *true* in this context, and we will accept that as a variation to the notation.

Here is an example with more than two cases:

$$[\, a + b < c \text{ or } a + c < b \text{ or } b + c < a \rightarrow category := \texttt{"not a triangle"}$$
$$|\ a = b = c \qquad\qquad\qquad\qquad\quad \rightarrow category := \texttt{"equilateral"}$$
$$|\ a = b \text{ or } a = c \text{ or } b = c \qquad\quad \rightarrow category := \texttt{"isosceles"}$$
$$|\ else \qquad\qquad\qquad\qquad\qquad\quad \rightarrow category := \texttt{"scalene"} \,]$$

Notice how much simpler some of the preconditions can be because they do not need to state that all of the previous preconditions are false.

What if there is no case with a precondition of *true* or *else*, and there is no precondition whose value is *true* in the current state? In this situation, the function is undefined. In mathematical terms, the current state is not in the domain of the function, and there is no next state. In the world of real programs, a program that computes such a function may crash in this situation, or go into an infinite loop, or compute a nonsensical result, or compute any result at all — what will happen is not defined.

Here is an example:

$$[\, n \neq 0 \rightarrow avg := sum/n \,]$$

Unless the definition of our programming language says that division by 0 produces some well-defined result, that is the function computed by the following statement:

```
avg := sum/n
```

In other words, this statement had better not be executed in a state in which n is 0! In the case of a computation like this, the logical expression in the conditional concurrent assignment is a "precondition" in the sense of "condition that must be satisfied for the computation to be possible".

Let us consider one more variation on this computation. The statement

```
if n > 0 then
    avg := sum/n
```

avoids the risk of dividing by 0. What function does it compute? No, not

$$[\, n > 0 \rightarrow avg := sum/n \,]$$

One way of writing the function that it does compute is

$$[\, n > 0 \rightarrow avg := sum/n$$
$$|\ true\ \rightarrow avg := avg \,]$$

where $avg := avg$ is a crude way of saying that the state does not change at all. We need a better notation for the function that does not change the state; let us use I, which is short for "the identity function". Using this notation, we can write

$$[\, n > 0 \rightarrow avg := sum/n$$
$$|\ true\ \rightarrow I \,]$$

as the function computed by the if-statement. The identity function is frequently used as shown here, in the final default case of a conditional concurrent assignment, although it can be used in other contexts as well. In any case, we must be very careful to remember the difference between a conditional concurrent assignment that ends with $true \rightarrow I$ and one in which this final case is omitted. As you can see, they define quite different functions.

2.4   Local Variables

Consider the following problem. Suppose that we want to swap the values of variables x and y. That is, we want to compute the function

$$[\, x, y := y, x \,]$$

Does the following sequence of statements compute that function?

```
temp := x;
x  := y;
y  := temp
```

Answer: No, it does not. In the function as defined above, the values of x and y are exchanged, but the value of every other state variable is unchanged. Clearly, the sequence of statements changes the value of *temp* as well. The function that it actually computes is

$$[\, x, y, temp := y, x, x \,]$$

However, in some programming languages, such as C, a sequence of statements can be turned into a "block" that can contain local variables. Here is an example in C (assuming that x and y are integer variables):

```
{                      /* beginning of a scope */
    int temp;          /* a local variable */

    temp = x;
    x = y;
    y = temp;
}                      /* end of the scope   */
```

This is another program fragment that exchanges the value of x and y. However, in this case, the variable *temp* is only part of the internal mechanism that accomplishes this swap. The effect on *temp* is not visible outside the block (the scope of its declaration). In fact, we should not even consider *temp* part of the state of the program outside of this block.

Therefore, if we have a program in which x and y are integer variables, we can use the above block to swap x and y, and the block does indeed compute precisely the function

$$[\, x, y := y, x \,]$$

The principle is that, at any point in a program, the state of the program contains only the variables (and other state variables) that exist at that point. Variables that exist only in other scopes are not part of that state. Of course, our interpretation of this principle will depend on the scope rules of the programming language that we are using. For example, a variable that continues to exist and retains its value while execution is in another scope would remain part of the program's state, even though it may not be accessible in the other scope.

2.5   Specification Using Intended Functions

In this section we will see how functions of the kind we have been describing can be used to specify the behavior of programs and parts of programs.

A *specification* of a program (or part of a program) is a statement of the behavior that we expect of it. A specification does not talk about the program's internal structure, or the algorithm it uses, or the sequence of steps that it executes. Instead, it talks only about the behavior that can be observed from outside: the inputs that the program takes, the outputs that it produces, the changes to global objects that it causes, and so on.

This should sound familiar: these are exactly the characteristics of the functions that we have been talking about. In fact, we will write our specifications in the form of functions. When we intend that part of a program should produce a particular computation, we will describe that computation in terms of a function from the current state to a new state, using the notation presented in previous sections. This function will be called the *intended function* for the code.

In this situation we will group the intended function and the code together, putting the function above the code, like this:

$$[\ intended\ function\ ]$$
```
code
```

For example:

$$[\ m, n := 1, 0\ ]$$
```
m  := 1;
n  := 0
```

When we attach an intended function to code like this, we are claiming that the code computes what the function specifies. The claim is not necessarily true just because we say so — it must be verified. In simple cases, such as this one, it is easy to see that the code computes the intended function. As you might expect, things are not always this easy. How to do the required verification will be the subject of later chapters.

In the actual source file of a program, we can include intended functions by placing them in comments. Here is how our C example might look:

```
/* [ x, y := y, x ] */
{
    int temp;

    temp = x;
    x = y;
    y = temp;
}
```

We will often put intended functions in many places in a program. The intended function will be aligned with the part of the program that it describes. Here is another example, again in C. The first intended function describes the whole if-statement, the second describes its then-part (the block), and the third describes the sequence of three assignment statements.

$$[\, y > x \rightarrow x, y := y, x$$
$$|\, true \rightarrow I \,]$$
```
if (y > x)
```

$$\qquad [\, x, y := y, x \,]$$
```
    {
        int temp;
```

$$\qquad\quad [\, x, y, temp := y, x, x \,]$$
```
        temp = x;
        x = y;
        y = temp;
    }
```

Now for a very important concept: correctness. When we write an intended function for a piece of code, we are saying, specifically, that the code must compute that function when the code is executed in any state in the domain of the function. When this is the case, we say that the combination of the intended function and code is *correct*, or that the code is *correct with respect to* the intended function.

This is not quite the same thing as insisting that the code must compute exactly the same function as its intended function. It implies that outside of the domain of the intended function (that is, in states in which the function is undefined), we don't care what the code does. For example, the following intended function and code are correct:

$$[\, n > 0 \rightarrow avg := sum/n \,]$$
```
avg := sum/n
```

It happens that the code computes $[\, avg := sum/n \,]$ not only when $n > 0$, but also when $n < 0$. The intended function, however, is a specification for code that will compute $[\, avg := sum/n \,]$ in situations in which $n > 0$, and we have success-fully written a statement that will do that. There is no point in trying to write code that does something strange when n is less than 0! The code that we have is the simplest code that does what is required by the intended function, and that is all we need.

By the way, we can say that a section of code is correct with respect to its intended function, or that a piece of program is correct when it contains an intended function and the code that implements that function, but it makes no sense to say that a section of code by itself is correct, independent of any specification. After all, to know whether code is correct, we must know what it is supposed to do.

Furthermore, notice that the word *correctness*, as we use it here, means only that the code agrees with the intended function; it does *not* mean that the code agrees with any other ideas we may have about what we would like the program to do. If there is anything that we want the program to do, we must make sure that the intended function says so. The whole point of writing explicit specifications is to separate the problem of writing a specification that reflects what we really mean (which can be the hardest part of the job!) from the problem of writing code that satisfies that specification.

2.6   Other Notation Conventions

In this section we will present several other notation conventions that can be used in describing functions. These conventions will make our specification notation a bit more expressive, and can often be used to make our specifications more concise or our intentions clearer.

We have seen that some functions are not defined in all states; that is, their domains do not include all possible program states. We have used this function as an example:

$$[\, n \neq 0 \rightarrow avg := sum/n \,]$$

Here, the precondition $n \neq 0$ is used to define the domain of the function.

In a sense, however, this precondition is redundant. Since the mathematical expression sum/n is undefined when $n = 0$, the effect of the assignment $avg := sum/n$ is also undefined in that case. The domain of the function

$$[\, avg := sum/n \,]$$

is already only those states in which $n \neq 0$.

Let us adopt the convention that our intended functions have the *implicit precondition* that all parts of them (or, at least, all of the parts of them that we need to evaluate to determine what computation they define) are well defined in the current state. With this convention, the two functions above are equivalent.

In some cases, not all parts of a function need to be well defined in the current state, only the parts of them that we need to evaluate to determine what computation they define in that state. Consider the following example:

$$[\, n = 0 \rightarrow avg := 0$$
$$|\, else \rightarrow avg := sum/n \,]$$

In a state in which $n = 0$, the expression sum/n is not well defined, but this does not matter because in such a state we do not need to evaluate that case of the conditional.

The description of some functions would be unreasonably complicated without this convention, if we really were careful to write out all of the necessary preconditions. For example, if we write the function

$$[\, sum := sum + \sum_{i=j}^{k} a_i \,]$$

we are really implicitly asserting all of the following as preconditions:

1. The variables *sum*, *j*, and *k* have all been given values.
2. The range of subscript values from *j* to *k* inclusive, if nonempty, is within the bounds of the array *a*.
3. The array elements $a_j \ldots a_k$ have all been given values.

This does not even include many facts about the structure of the system state that would be implicit in the context of a program, such as that all of the variables mentioned are accessible in the current scope, have appropriate types, and so on. We typically write such facts as explicit preconditions only under unusual circumstances. For example, in a programming language without strong typing, the type of a variable might be determined at run-time, according to the type of the value assigned to it. In this case, the variable's type is actually part of the program's state, and it might be appropriate to write (for example)

$$[\, j \text{ is an integer} \rightarrow \ldots \,]$$

But we would never write this in a strongly typed language in which the type of *j* is explicitly declared and never changes.

All this is not to say that it is a mistake to write

$$[\, n \neq 0 \rightarrow avg := sum/n \,]$$

On the contrary, in some contexts it is preferable, because it makes the precondition explicit and emphasizes it. We would define the function in this way if we wanted to be sure that someone reading this did not overlook the precondition.

Sometimes we might want to emphasize even more strongly that a function is undefined in some states. We can say so explicitly, using the word *undefined* as in the following example:

$$[\ n \neq 0 \rightarrow avg := sum/n$$
$$|\ n = 0 \rightarrow undefined\ ]$$

(Mathematically, we can think of *undefined* as a function whose value is undefined in all states; that is, its domain is empty. If we view a function as a set of ordered pairs, *undefined* represents an empty set.)

The case containing *undefined* need not be the last case in the conditional, of course. In some situations we might prefer to put it first, like this:

$$[\ n = 0 \rightarrow undefined$$
$$|\ else \rightarrow avg := sum/n\ ]$$

All of these ways of writing the definition of this function are mathematically equivalent; which one we choose in a particular situation is strictly a matter of presentation and emphasis.

Next, let us return to the example of Section 2.4, the program fragment that swapped the values of x and y. Suppose that, for some reason, we did not want to make `temp` local to the sequence of three statements. (Perhaps our programming language does not allow this, as C does.) Then the following intended function and code would have been correct:

$$[\ x, y, temp := y, x, x\ ]$$
```
temp := x;
x := y;
y := temp
```

However, it is unlikely that we would have written that intended function and then written the code to match. What we really wanted to do was simply to exchange the values of x and y. We would have realized that we would be changing the value of *temp*, but we would not have been particularly interested in its final value. A more natural way of writing the intended function would have been this:

$$[\ x, y, temp := y, x, \text{anything}\ ]$$

By "anything" we mean that *temp* will have some value, possibly different from the value that it has in the currrent state, but we do not care what its value will be. (Strictly speaking, this "intended function" is really a relation, since there are many possible next states corresponding to a given current state, but for our purposes this is unimportant.)

"Anything" is used quite frequently in intended functions for parts of programs. The reason is that programs frequently contain variables that are used as intermediate values in computations; computing their values is necessary, but is not the real object of the computation. Variables of this kind are sometimes called *incidental variables*.

Some practitioners say that incidental variables do not even need to be mentioned in intended functions. However, this would violate our notational convention that lets us assume that the value of a variable remains unchanged by a function unless the description of the function explicitly states that it is changed. This might lead to misunderstandings and mistakes in reasoning. My preference is to mention every variable whose value is changed, without exception, using "anything" where appropriate.

Finally, there are times when we might want to say that a particular variable gets any value that satisfies particular constraints, rather than any value at all. Here is an example:

$$[\ i := \text{some value } j \text{ such that } a[j] = key\ ]$$

To allow this kind of construction is to stretch our functional view of computations substantially. (Just as with "anything", we are really defining a relation rather than a function, since there may be more than one such j.) We will allow such specifications, because sometimes they are the easiest and clearest way to specify what we need. However, they should be used sparingly and with care.

Notice that the following specification is not of this kind, because it specifies a unique value for i:

$$[\ i := \text{the smallest value } j \text{ such that } a[j] = key\ ]$$

(Here, a is apparently an array, and so the range of values from which j can be taken is implicit, as in an implicit precondition.) The situation is similar in the following:

$$[\ i := \text{the value } j \text{ such that } a[j] = key\ ]$$

Here, apparently, there is only one such j. This fact would be an implicit precondition. (Notice that, in this and the previous two examples, the fact that there is any j at all such that $a[j] = key$ is also an implicit precondition.)

These are a few of the most useful notation conventions for intended functions. Some others will be introduced as needed in the examples in the rest of the book.

2.7   Writing Intended Functions

This section will present some ideas on how to write intended functions and, in particular, how to write good intended functions. As we will see, some ways of writing intended functions are better than others.

We will be using intended functions in two ways: as documentation, and as a basis for verification. When used as documentation, functions are placed in the code to explain what the code is intended to do; they can be used in place of most of the conventional comments that we normally would (or should!) be placing in the code. When used for verification, they are compared with the code to verify that the function and the code agree.

These two uses are somewhat related. For example, even if the intended functions are written only as documentation at first, they can still be used for verification later, if they are written properly. On the other hand, after intended functions have served their purpose for verification, they can (and usually should) be left in the code to serve as documentation.

However, these two uses for intended functions can lead to somewhat different criteria for what makes one intended function better than another in a particular situation. For purposes of documentation, we certainly want the following criterion:

1. An intended function should be easy to read and easy to understand.

However, for purposes of verification, we need a bit more than this. We will need to know exactly and unambiguously what function on program states is being defined, so that we can compare this with the function actually computed by the code. Therefore we have the following criterion:

2. An intended function should be precise and unambiguous.

In other words, the question of whether an intended function and its code are correct should be answerable with a clear yes or no. The intended function should be written in such a way that either the code definitely does what the intended function says, or it definitely does not. If we can't tell whether it does or not, the intended function is not adequate for verification.

As we examine techniques for verification in the chapters that follow, we will also see that some intended functions are easier to work with than others. We want to anticipate the work we will need to do when we actually do the verification, just to make life easier for ourselves. We can't say much about this yet, but we can state the criterion:

3. An intended function should be in a form that is easy to manipulate in a verification.

So far, the only notation we have seen for expressing intended functions is the one we have been using: concurrent assignments and conditional concurrent assignments. It is not the only way of describing a computation, or even the best way under all circumstances. There are many possible ways of describing a state change in a program. An extreme example of a notation that is different from our concurrent-assignment notation is plain English. The following might be a perfectly good intended function under some circumstances:

[sort *f* alphabetically]

This is certainly easy to read — probably far more so than if the concept of "sort" were written out in a more mathematical notation. (Such a specification would need to be much longer and more complicated than you might think. See Exercise 4.) It is probably precise and unambiguous enough, assuming that *f* is (for example) a file of text lines. The reader will certainly know what "alphabetically" means in such a context.

Unfortunately, this intended function might not meet our third criterion very well. We will see in the next chapter that, for purposes of verification, the most convenient form for an intended function is usually one that explicitly gives values of variables in the new state using expressions or phrases, a separate one for each variable whose value is changed. (The reason is that one common activity in verification is to substitute an expression for a variable in another expression.)

We can make a simple change to put the intended function into this form:

[*f* := *f* sorted alphabetically]

This looks like one of our concurrent assignments, except that instead of a mathematical expression on the right-hand side we have a phrase in English. As long as the phrase clearly and unambiguously denotes a value, this is perfectly good.

Here is another possibility:

[*f* := *alphabetical-sort(f)*]

Now we have the intended function in a more–or–less mathematical form, in which the right-hand side of the assignment is in the form of an expression. This form might be even easier to manipulate in a verification than the previous form, since wherever we have mathematical expressions we can use whatever mathematical methods we know. In particular, substitution of values for variables works just as it does in elementary algebra.

Here the term *alphabetical-sort* is used as the name of a function. This kind of function is called a *specification function*: a function that is used in a specification, as opposed to a programming-language function that appears in the code. A specification function might be a well-known mathematical function such as absolute value or square root, or it might be invented by the programmer.

If there may be any doubt as to the meaning of a specification function, a definition should be provided for it. This would not be necessary for well-known mathematical functions, if a commonly used name like *sqrt* is used. In our example, *alphabetical-sort* might be a borderline case, but it is best to give an explicit definition if there is any doubt at all. A definition is certainly necessary in the following case:

[*masterlist* := *sort-by-name(masterlist)*
    where *sort-by-name(a)* = *a* sorted alphabetically using a key formed from the last-name field followed by the first-name field and the middle-initial field, separated by spaces]

The definition can be placed either in the intended function itself, as shown here, or somewhere else as a separate part of the documentation. The latter way is probably better if the definition is as long and verbose as this one, or if the same specification function is used in more than one place (as it almost always is when we do verification, as we will see.)

These are some principles that we can keep in mind when writing intended functions and for choosing the best form of an intended function for a particular purpose. However, we will see that the choice of one form over another depends very much on the context: the code that implements the function, the surrounding code and its intended functions, the vocabulary that the reader is likely to understand, and other factors.

For practice, let us look at six different ways of writing the same intended function.

$$[a > b \rightarrow a, b := b, a$$
$$| \; true \; \rightarrow I \,] \tag{1}$$

$$[\, a, b := min(a, b), max(a, b) \,] \tag{2}$$

$$[\, a, b := \text{the minimum of } a \text{ and } b, \text{ the maximum of } a \text{ and } b \,] \tag{3}$$

$$[\, a, b := \text{the minimum and maximum of } a \text{ and } b \text{ respectively }] \tag{4}$$

$$[\, a, b := a < b \, ? \, a : b, \; b > a \, ? \, b : a \,] \tag{5}$$

$$[\, \text{rearrange } a \text{ and } b \text{ so that } a \leq b \,] \tag{6}$$

Which is the best? There is no single right answer, but here are some of the good and bad features of each of these forms.

Form 1 is certainly precise and unambiguous. Many people will probably find it less readable than some of the other forms, however, and it may take someone a bit longer to decipher it and deduce the big picture. Is it in a suitable form for manipulation in a verification? As far as we can tell now, yes.

Form 2 is shorter and simpler, and therefore probably more readable. It contains no conditional, so the reader has to understand only one case instead of two. It is also precise and unambiguous, assuming that we know what is meant by the specification functions *max* and *min*, but anyone who is likely to read such a specification will almost certainly interpret these terms correctly. (If there is any doubt, definitions can be provided.) Also, this form contains easily manipulated expressions. It will turn out that the verification will be easier than with form 1 in some circumstances and harder in others. For now, we have no reason to prefer one over the other based on that criterion.

Form 3 is almost the same as form 2, except that it uses English phrases instead of functional notation. This may improve readability a bit, for some readers, but other readers will find it more verbose than necessary.

Form 4 does not have much to recommend it. It is no shorter than form 3, although some people might find it a bit simpler. Its biggest disadvantage is that it combines the values of a and b into a single phrase, which can't be substituted directly for a or b in another phrase or expression.

Form 5 is as precise and unambiguous as form 2, and may be as easy to manipulate, but it is certainly not as readable. It is more complicated, and not everyone will understand the ? notation (taken from the C programming language). When there is a simple and well-understood abstract way of representing a complicated expression, it should usually be used instead of writing the expression out in full. Here, for example, why write $a < b \,?\, a : b$ when you can write $min(a, b)$?

Some readers may find form 6 the easiest to understand, since it is entirely in English and contains no mathematical notation. However, the meaning of the word *rearrange* might not be entirely clear and unambiguous in the context. Also, this form does not give explicit values for a and b as expressions or phrases that can be manipulated in a verification.

On balance, without knowing the context we would probably consider form 2 somewhat better than the others, but in some circumstances form 1 will be easier to work with. Even form 6 might be the most appropriate in some cases. It will depend very much on the context.

Exercises

1. What is the function computed by each of the following sections of code? Express each function using a concurrent assignment or conditional concurrent assignment.

   a.
   ```
   sum := sum + a;
   n := n + 1;
   avg := sum/n
   ```

   b.
   ```
   if n > maxsize then
       n := maxsize;
   avg := sum/n
   ```

c.
```
    if x > y then
        if x > z then
            max := x
        else
            max := z
    else
        if y > z then
            max := y
        else
            max := z
```

d.
```
    if x > y and y > z then
        max := x
    else if y > z then
        max := y
    else
        max := z
```

Does this code compute the same function as in Exercise 1c?

2. For each of the following intended functions, write a section of code that computes it. (If your instructor does not specify a programming language, use the one that you use most frequently.)

a. $[\, x, y, z := y, z, x \,]$

b. $[\, x, y := x + y, y - x \,]$

c. $[\, i := i$ rounded down to the nearest even number $]$
(assuming that i is an integer variable)

d. $[\, sum := sum + \sum_{i=1}^{n} a_i \,]$

3. What is wrong with each of the following intended functions?

a. $[\, a \geq b \rightarrow b := a$
$\mid b \geq a \rightarrow a := b$
$\mid true \;\; \rightarrow I \,]$

b. $[\, masterlist \;\; := \;\; sortByName(masterlist)$
where $sortByName(a) = a$ sorted alphabetically
on the last-name field and then on the first-name field
and the middle-initial field $]$

c. $[\, backgroundcolor, textcolor \;\; :=$
an attractive shade of blue,
a color that contrasts with $backgroundcolor \,]$

4. Express the following function without using "sort" or "sorted" or similar words:

$$[\text{ sort } a \text{ in ascending order }]$$

Write it as a concurrent assignment of the form

[$a :=$ an array b such that ...]

For simplicity, assume that a and b are integer arrays with subscripts from 1 to n. (Be careful not to leave out anything important!)

5. In the last set of examples in the text, can you think of a way of phrasing form 6 that is better than "rearrange a and b"? Suggest one or more alternatives, and compare them with the original using our three criteria for goodness.

6. Before you started reading this book, what did you mean when you said that a program was correct? How did you judge whether or not a program was correct? How trustworthy are such judgments, in your experience?

Notes

The style of specification presented here, called the functional style, was introduced by Harlan Mills [Mill75]. A similar mathematical formulation, in which specifications can be relations that are not necessarily functions, is presented in [Mill89]. The notation for concurrent assignments and conditional concurrent assignments comes from an early textbook based on Mills' ideas [Ling79].

There are a number of other styles of specification. Most of the ones that are commonly known are based on *assertions*: logical statements or predicates that state properties of the results of computations. This is somewhat less direct than stating what the results actually are, as is done in functional specification.

Floyd, in his pioneering work [Floy67], attached assertions about a program's state to points in the program's flowchart. Perhaps the most influential style of specification has been the axiomatic style of Hoare [Hoar69], in which assertions called preconditions and postconditions are attached to statements and control constructs. A variant is Dijkstra's weakest-precondition style [Dijk75], [Dijk76].

It has been shown [Dunl82] that functional specifications and axiomatic specifications are logically equivalent, in the sense that they say what are essentially the same things although in different ways. Speaking of the verification of loops in particular, the authors conclude that "there is no theoretical justification for selecting one method over the other" (p. 243).

However, I once heard Harlan Mills say at a conference [Mill84] that he didn't know how to do axiomatic proofs successfully; he used functional proofs instead. As Mills was a brilliant computer scientist, this is a strong statement! My experience agrees with his: I find proofs based on functional specifications much easier to do than proofs based on assertions.

3
Verification

3.1 The Structured Control Constructs

In this chapter, we begin the presentation of techniques for verifying the correctness of code with respect to its intended functions. In this first section, we will describe the programming-language constructs that we will use in code that we intend to verify.

It is assumed that you are already very familiar with the standard structured control constructs used in most programming languages:

1. The simple statement that produces a state change in a single step. Examples are assignment statements, input and output statements, and procedure calls.
2. Sequences of statements in forms such as "... ; ... ; ...", in which the statements are executed one after another, unconditionally.
3. Conditional statements, such as if- and case-statements.
4. Looping statements, which have forms such as "while ... do ..." and "for each ... do ..."

We will concentrate on these control constructs from now on. The reason is that if we use only these constructs, verification is far easier than it would otherwise be.

There are two kinds of control constructs that we will avoid. The first is the kind of statement that many programming languages provide for terminating the execution of a loop, procedure, or other construct. Some of the common types are exit-, break-, return-, and stop-statements.

Statements like these do not necessarily produce bad control flow. The trouble is that if they can be used anywhere in the code, they can produce control flow in which (for example) control can leave a construct from several places, or from within several levels of nested constructs. Such situations tend to be hard to reason about.

Second, there is the goto-statement, which can be used to jump from one place in the code to another in almost arbitrary ways. Not only can goto-statements be used to jump out of a control construct, like the exit- and similar statements do, but they can be used to jump into the middle of a construct, such as a sequence of statements or even (in some languages) a conditional or loop! This can lead to some very confusing code, and other uses of the goto-statement can be even worse.

The programming community has learned, through many years of experience, that verification is significantly harder when exits from a control construct can be made anywhere, and unreasonably hard when goto-statements can be used freely. Therefore, we will avoid exit- and similar statements in most cases, allowing only a few simple special cases such as an exit-statement in the middle of a while-loop. Even then, the exit-statement will be treated not as a control construct in itself, but as part of the larger control construct in which it is embedded. We will not even discuss verification of programs containing goto-statements.

Constructs such as exit- and goto-statements are not really necessary: any computation that is written using them can be written without them. If you learned to program within the last twenty years, you probably don't use them much anyway (except perhaps where your programming language is deficient and you need to use them to simulate the standard structured constructs). Code that uses them can be rewritten so that they are removed, but it is usually far easier to write code using only the standard structured constructs in the first place.

There is one more important restriction that we will place on the language constructs we use: in the control constructs, all of the Boolean expressions that determine which path is taken must be free of side effects. That is, the evaluation of them must not change the value of any state variable. For example, code such as the following example (in C) is not acceptable: the assignment operation should be removed from the heading of the while-statement.

```
while ((c = getchar()) != EOF)
        ...
```

Actually, verification will be easier if we avoid side effects in expressions everywhere in the program, but some are hard to avoid. For example, even in the C statement

```
c = getchar();
```

the evaluation of the expression on the right-hand side has a side effect, because it changes the state of the input stream. Realistically, we need to be able to handle some cases of side effects such as this one, but we need to be very careful to notice them and account for them where they occur. Still, it is best to avoid them altogether wherever possible.

3.2   Placement of Intended Functions

In this section we will show where intended functions should be placed in a program when the program is to be verified.

When intended functions are meant to be used merely as documentation, they can be attached to whatever statements and control constructs the programmer chooses. However, when verification is to be done, we will require that intended functions be attached to the code in particular places, because our verification methods will depend on them being there. The result will be a large number of intended functions distributed throughout the code, probably more of them than a programmer would write for documentation alone.

In most cases, the intended function for a simple assignment statement would look just like the statement itself (except possibly for minor syntactic details, such as the use of := instead of = as an assignment operator). If so, the statement probably does not need an intended function; it can serve as its own intended function.

If the intended function would be significantly different from the statement itself, it should be shown explicitly. For example, we would certainly want to do this for assignment statements containing expressions with side effects. Here is an example:

$$[\, c, input \;\; := \;\; \text{first character of } input, \text{ all but first character of } input \,]$$
```
c = getchar();
```

For statements whose execution may fail in some states, we would use a conditional concurrent assignment with a precondition that specifies the states in which execution will succeed, as in the following example:

$$[\, \text{input stream } f \text{ is open} \rightarrow$$
$$c, f \;\; := \;\; \text{first character of } f, \text{ all but first character of } f\,]$$
```
c = getc(f);
```

A procedure call should always have an intended function. We will have more to say about procedure calls in later chapters.

The placement of intended functions in control constructs is particularly important. The control constructs that we allow have the property that they can be *nested*; that is, they can have components that are themselves control constructs. The principle for placement of intended functions in such constructs is this: there should be an intended function for the construct as a whole, and another intended function for each of the components.

Let us see how these principles apply to sequences, while-statements, and if-statements; the situation will be similar for other structured control constructs. A sequence of statements should have an intended function, which will be placed before it like this:

> [*intended function for statement1 ... statement3*]
> *statement1* ;
> *statement2* ;
> *statement3*

Where sequences are components of sequences themselves, spacing can be used to make it clear which statements are described by each intended function, like this:

> [*intended function for statement1 ... statement3*]
> *statement1* ;
> *statement2* ;
> *statement3*
>
> [*intended function for statement4 ... statement5*]
> *statement4* ;
> *statement5*

Also, whatever constructs the programming language provides for grouping, such as `begin ... end` or `{ ... }`, can be used, like this:

> [*intended function for statement1 ... statement5*]
> `begin`
>> [*intended function for statement1 ... statement3*]
>> *statement1* ;
>> *statement2* ;
>> *statement3*
>>
>> [*intended function for statement4 ... statement5*]
>> *statement4* ;
>> *statement5*
>
> `end`

A while-statement should have an intended function for the statement as a whole, and another for the loop body, like this:

> [*intended function for while-statement*]
> `while ... do`
>> [*intended function for loop body*]
>> *loop body*

An if-statement should have an intended function for the statement as a whole, and an intended function for each branch, like this:

```
[ intended function for if-statement ]
if ... then
        [ intended function for then-part ]
        then-part
else
        [ intended function for else-part ]
        else-part
```

If there is no else-part, the second intended function is omitted:

```
[ intended function for if-statement ]
if ... then
        [ intended function for then-part ]
        then-part
```

When are the intended functions written? They can be written after the code is written. If you did this, you would use the intended function for each construct to document what you had in mind when you wrote it, and what purpose it is serving in the program as a whole. Sometimes you might need to look at the construct itself, derive the function that it actually computes, and use that as the "intended" function.

Experienced programmers would probably do things in the opposite order most of the time. They would first write the intended function, according to the computation that needed to be done, then write code that implemented the function. Where this code is a control construct, they would first represent the components of the construct as intended functions, then write the implementation of the components. To return to an example from the previous chapter, suppose that the computation that needed to be done in a particular place in a program is

$$[\, y > x \rightarrow x, y := y, x$$
$$|\, true \;\rightarrow I\,]$$

Since the function is expressed in terms of a conditional, an if-statement appears to be an obvious choice to implement it, and so we would write

$$[\, y > x \rightarrow x, y := y, x$$
$$|\, true \;\rightarrow I\,]$$
```
if (y > x)
        [ x, y := y, x ]
```

Then, under the function $[\, x, y := y, x\,]$ we would write the implementation of that function. The implementation might contain lower-level intended functions;

if so, we would continue in the same way. This is precisely the idea of stepwise refinement or top-down development that you probably learned in your earlier programming courses.

3.3   The Substitution Principle

In this section we will see how to break the verification of a large program into smaller parts.

We assume that the program has been annotated with intended functions as described in the previous section. This means that there are intended functions for all of the control constructs and also for their components, so that there are many instances of the following sort of pattern:

> [*intended function for construct*]
> *beginning of construct*
>
>   . . .
>
>   [*intended function for component*]
>   *component*
>
>   . . .
>
> *end of construct*

Suppose that the component computes exactly the function that is given as its intended function. Or suppose that we can determine what function is actually computed by the component, whether or not its intended function is present. Then any other section of code that computes exactly that function can be substituted for it without changing the function computed by the larger construct. In fact, so can a mechanism that produces the same state change in one step.

This means that we can substitute the function itself for the component! It may not be in the same notation as the component, but it defines the same state change, so the function computed by the larger construct is unaffected. Furthermore, if the larger construct was correct with respect to its intended function before the substitution, it is still correct after the substitution. By this reasoning we obtain the following valuable principle:

Substitution Principle (version 1). If a component computes a particular function, the function can be substituted for the component in a larger construct without affecting the computation produced by the construct or the construct's correctness.

For example, consider the following piece of program:

```
[ y > x → x, y := y, x
| true → I ]
if (y > x)
    [ x, y := y, x ]
    {
        int temp;
        temp = x;
        x = y;
        y = temp;
    }
```

Suppose that we know that the block which is the then-part of the if-statement does indeed compute the function [$x, y := y, x$]. Then, in proving the correctness of the if-statement, we can use the function in place of the block. We do not even need to look at the code in the block in this step of the verification.

There is another version of this principle that is perhaps even more useful. Often, components do not compute exactly the same functions as their intended functions, because they have larger domains. We saw an example in the previous chapter:

$$[n > 0 → avg := sum/n]$$
```
avg := sum/n
```

Furthermore, as we shall see, components are often verified not by determining what functions they actually compute, but by other means.

But suppose we can verify, by any means at all, that a component is correct with respect to its intended function. Then we can substitute the intended function for the component in the larger construct, and attempt to verify that construct. If we are successful, that means that the larger construct, as it was before the substitution, is correct with respect to its intended function, assuming that the component computes its intended function in all states in the domain of that function; but we have already proven that it does. To summarize:

Substitution Principle (version 2). If a component is correct with respect to its intended function, and the larger construct containing it is correct with respect to its intended function when the component's intended function is substituted for the component, then the larger construct, as it was before the substitution, is correct with respect to its intended function.

Consider this example, which is slightly different from the previous one:

$$[\,y > x \rightarrow x, y, temp := y, x, \text{anything}$$
$$|\ true\ \rightarrow I\,]$$

```
if (y > x)
```
$$[\,x, y, temp := y, x, \text{anything}\,]$$
```
    {
        temp = x;
        x = y;
        y = temp;
    }
```

If we can prove that the block (the then-part) is correct with respect to its intended function, we can use the function in place of the block in verifying the if-statement. We can verify the block first, then the if-statement; or, if we prefer, we can verify the if-statement first. This proves that the if-statement is correct, assuming that the block is correct; of course, it leaves us with the obligation to prove that the block is indeed correct. But we can do the proofs in either order.

By this principle, we can break the verification of the construct into two steps: the verification of the construct using the intended function in place of the component, and the verification of the component. Repeating this reasoning for every nested component in a program, we see that we can break the verification of a large program into as many pieces as there are constructs with intended functions! Furthermore, the verifications are independent of each other and can be done in any order: bottom-up, top-down, easiest first, hardest first, or in any other order at all. Also, where an intended function is not provided for a component of a construct, we can use the function actually computed by the component, if we can derive it, and then use version 1 of the Substitution Principle rather than version 2 to justify using the function in place of the component in the verification of the construct.

3.4   Sequences of Statements

This section and the next will present techniques for verifying sequences of statements.

Consider a sequence of statements of the form

$$S_1;$$
$$S_2$$

Suppose that S_1 computes the function f_1 and S_2 computes the function f_2. That is, the sequence of statements can be represented as

$$X := f_1(X);$$
$$X := f_2(X)$$

where X is the entire state of the program, as in Section 2.1. Then the state change produced by the sequence of statements can be written as

$$X := f_2(f_1(X))$$

In other words, the function computed by the sequence of statements is the *composition* of the functions computed by the individual statements. The same is true for a sequence of three statements, or any larger number.

Therefore, if we know the functions computed by the individual statements in a sequence, we can determine the function computed by the whole sequence. This is how we will verify that a sequence of statements is correct with respect to its intended function: we will determine the function that is actually computed by the sequence, by function composition, and compare it with the intended function.

Suppose that the intended function for our sequence $S_1; S_2$ is f. Then what we must verify is that

the composition of f_1 followed by f_2 is correct with respect to f.

That is, the composition is the same as f on the domain of f. Let us call this the *verification condition* for the sequence. (A sequence of more than two statements has a similar verification condition, which speaks of the composition of more than two functions.)

More informally, we can phrase this verification condition as a question:

Does doing S_1, followed by doing S_2, do f?

We will call this the *correctness question* corresponding to the verification condition. It is perhaps more memorable than the verification condition. We must keep in mind, however, that in this context "doing f" means correctness with respect to f, which (as you will recall) is a bit less restrictive than saying it must compute the function f.

We will see that the other structured control constructs have their own verification conditions as well as corresponding informal correctness questions.

To determine the function that is the composition of f_1 followed by f_2, we evaluate $f_2(f_1(X))$, using the program's actual state variables for X. We would first find the value of $f_1(X)$; suppose it is Y. We would then substitute Y for $f_1(X)$ in the expression $f_2(f_1(X))$, giving $f_2(Y)$, and evaluate that. If f_1 and f_2 are represented in the form of concurrent assignments, we can do this easily by substituting values of individual variables.

For example, in the sequence of statements

```
n := n + 1;
y := x*n - 1
```

the function that the first statement computes is obviously [$n := n + 1$]. We substitute $n + 1$ for n in $x * n - 1$ and get $x * (n + 1) - 1$. The function computed by the sequence of statements, then, is

$$[\, n, y := n + 1, x * (n + 1) - 1 \,]$$

What we are doing can be viewed as taking the values that all of the program's state variables have (in other words, the entire data state) after the execution of the first statement, and substituting these values on the right-hand side of the second statement. However, since the value of x has not changed, the substitution for that variable has no effect. We need only substitute for variables whose values have changed.

Notice that we do the substitution symbolically, rather than starting with a particular numeric value for n, such as 200, and actually doing the arithmetic when we substitute. The latter is similar to what we would be doing if we tested the program using particular input values. Such a test, of course, only gives us information about what happens with those particular input values; the advantage of symbolic reasoning is that it tells us what happens regardless of the particular values.

The statements in the sequence might themselves be sequences or other control constructs. If so, they should have their own intended functions. The Substitution Principle tells us that, in calculating the composition, we can use the intended functions for the statements in the sequence, rather than the statements themselves, where intended functions have been provided. However, in the example above, the intended functions have been omitted, since the statements are simple assignments, so we use the functions that the statements actually compute, which are identical in form to the statements themselves.

Here is an example of a verification of a sequence. The intended function and code are

```
[ n ≥ 0 → sum, n, avg := sum + a, n + 1, (sum + a)/(n + 1) ]
sum := sum + a;
n   := n + 1;
avg := sum/n
```

First, we derive the function actually computed by the code. After the first statement, sum has the value $sum + a$, in terms of the values that all of the variables had at the beginning of the sequence. We would substitute this value into the right-hand side of the second statement if sum appeared there, but it does not, so the value that n has after that statement is just $n + 1$. For the third statement, we must use the function that it computes rather than the statement itself, because the execution of the statement does not succeed in all states. As we saw in a previous section, that function is

$$[n \neq 0 → avg := sum/n]$$

We substitute the values of sum and n into this function. Since variables that appear in the precondition refer to their values in the current state, we must substitute in the precondition as well as on the right-hand side of the assignment. The result is

$$[n + 1 \neq 0 → avg := (sum + a)/(n + 1)]$$

Then the function computed by the sequence of statements is[1]

$$[\, n+1 \neq 0 \rightarrow sum,\ n,\ avg := sum + a,\ n+1,\ (sum+a)/(n+1)\,]$$

Now we compare this with the intended function. They are not identical, but the only difference is in the preconditions, and we see that all states that satisfy the precondition of the intended function also satisfy the precondition of the function actually computed by the code. Therefore, the function computed by the code is the same as the intended function for all states in the domain of the intended function, and so the code is correct with respect to the intended function.

3.5   Trace Tables

In the example of the previous section, the sequence of statements was simple enough that the function it computed could be determined by inspection. In more complicated situations, it is helpful to use a *trace table*. This is a table that shows, symbolically, the value of each state variable that is changed in the sequence of statements, after each statement in the sequence.

A trace table contains one row for each statement in the sequence, and one column for the statements plus one column for each state variable whose value is changed in the sequence. In the column for the statements, the statements themselves (or the functions computed by the statements) appear if all of them are short enough so that this is convenient; otherwise, the statements can be numbered and the statement numbers placed in the table.

The table entries for the values of the state variables are filled in one row at a time, in the order in which the statements are executed. In the row corresponding to each statement, the new value of each state variable whose value is changed by that statement is entered in the column for that variable. The value is taken from the right-hand side of the concurrent assignment for that statement. Each state variable appearing there is replaced by the current value of that variable, which is obtained by taking the most recent entry in the variable's column. If there is none, no substitution is made for that variable.

As these substitutions are made, symbolic expressions for the values of the state variables at each step are built up, and these expressions are always expressed in terms of the values that all of the state variables had at the beginning of the sequence. Here is an example:

---

[1] Is this the answer you got for Exercise 1a of Chapter 2?

statement	x	y	z
x :=x + 1	$x + 1$		
y :=2*x		$2(x + 1)$	
z :=x*y			$(x + 1) \cdot (2(x + 1))$ $= 2x^2 + 4x + 2$
x :=x + 1	$x + 2$		
y :=3*x		$3(x + 2)$	

Please examine the table, one row at a time, and make sure that you see where all the entries come from.

It is usually helpful to simplify the expressions in the table where possible. The simplification can be shown explicitly, as was done for the value of z in the third row of this example, or the simplification can be done before the expression is entered into the table, as was done for the value of x in the fourth row.

When all rows have been filled in, the most recent entry in each column is the final value of the corresponding state variable. Thus, in the example above, the function computed by the sequence of statements is

$$[x, y, z := x + 2, 3(x + 2), 2x^2 + 4x + 2]$$

Trace tables of the kind presented here are adequate when the functions computed by statements in a sequence are free of conditionals. The following sections will present methods for dealing with conditional statements and conditional concurrent assignments.

3.6   If-statements

This section and the next are devoted to conditionals, both conditional constructs in code (such as if-statements) and conditionals in intended functions. If-statements are the subject of this first section.

We need techniques for verifying each of the control constructs that we intend to use in our programs. It turns out that the techniques for sequences, conditionals, and loops will all be somewhat different from each other.

We could, if we wished, verify conditionals in much the same way we verify sequences: derive the function actually computed by the code and compare it with the intended function. However, there is another way of doing it that, in practice, is usually more convenient: verification by cases.

Specifically, for a statement of the form

$$[f]$$
```
if B then
    S₁
else
    S₂
```

we need to verify that the if-statement is correct with respect to the intended function f in both cases: when B is true and when B is false. We will verify each case separately. Thus, the verification is broken into two steps: verifying that

1. in a state in which B is true, S_1 is correct with respect to f; and that
2. in a state in which B is false, S_2 is correct with respect to f.

These, then, are the verification conditions for if-statements, and both of them must be proved for each if-statement in the program. More informally, we can phrase the verification conditions as correctness questions:

1. When B is true, does doing S_1 do f?
2. When B is false, does doing S_2 do f?

Here is a simple example of a verification:

$$[\, y := \, \mid b - a \mid /t\,]$$
```
if b > a then
    y := (b - a)/t
else
    y := (a - b)/t
```

First, we verify

$$[\, y := \, \mid b - a \mid /t\,]$$
```
y := (b - a)/t
```

under the assumption that $b > a$. But this is immediate, since in this case we can see that

$$\mid b - a \mid = b - a$$

Second, we verify

$$[\, y := \, \mid b - a \mid /t\,]$$
```
y := (a - b)/t
```

under the assumption that $b \leq a$. Again, this is immediate, since in this case

$$\mid b - a \mid = a - b$$

By the way, notice that we could have represented the two verifications that we needed to do as follows, incorporating the assumptions into the intended functions as preconditions:

$$[\, b > a \rightarrow y := \; |\, b - a\,|\, /t\,]$$
```
y := (b - a)/t
```

and

$$[\, b \leq a \rightarrow y := \; |\, b - a\,|\, /t\,]$$
```
y := (a - b)/t
```

Now let us consider the form of the if-statement in which the else-part is omitted, so that the statement has the form

$$[\, f\,]$$
```
if B then
      S₁
```

We should remember that this means

$$[\, f\,]$$
```
if B then
      S₁
else
      do nothing
```

Therefore, there is nothing new in the rules for verifying this kind of if-statement, except that "do nothing" (in other words, $[\, I\,]$) is used in place of S_2. Thus, the verification conditions become:

1. In a state in which B is true, S_1 is correct with respect to f.
2. In a state in which B is false, the identity function I is correct with respect to f.

The corresponding informal correctness questions can be written as follows:

1. When B is true, does doing S_1 do f?
2. When B is false, does doing nothing do f?

We must be careful to remember that there are still two cases to consider! It is easy to overlook the "do nothing" case.

Here is an example of a verification:

$$[\, a, b := min(a, b), max(a, b)\,]$$
```
if a > b then
      [ a, b := b, a ]
```

The two cases of the verification are as follows:

1. When $a > b$, we see that $b = min(a, b)$ and $a = max(a, b)$, so that the function $[\, a, b := b, a\,]$ computes what the intended function specifies.
2. When $a \leq b$, a is already $min(a, b)$ and b is already $max(a, b)$, so that doing nothing does what the intended function specifies.

There are a few other kinds of conditional statement that appear in programming languages; they can be verified by varying the methods for if-statements appropriately. For example, the Modula statement

$$[f]$$
$$\texttt{if } B_1 \texttt{ then}$$
$$S_1$$
$$\texttt{elsif } B_2 \texttt{ then}$$
$$S_2$$
$$\texttt{else}$$
$$S_3$$
$$\texttt{end}$$

could be verified as if it were written as nested if-statements, like this:

$$[f]$$
$$\texttt{if } B_1 \texttt{ then}$$
$$S_1$$
$$\texttt{else}$$
$$\quad\texttt{if } B_2 \texttt{ then}$$
$$\quad\quad S_2$$
$$\quad\texttt{else}$$
$$\quad\quad S_3$$
$$\quad\texttt{end}$$
$$\texttt{end}$$

However, it can just as well be treated directly as a three-way conditional, with three correctness questions:

1. When B_1 is true, does doing S_1 do f?
2. When B_1 is false and B_2 is true, does doing S_2 do f?
3. When B_1 is false and B_2 is false, does doing S_3 do f?

You can probably work out the correctness questions that would apply if there were more cases, if the final else-part were omitted, or for a case-statement. The principles are the same for all such conditional constructs.[2]

By the way, it very often happens in practice that the intended function on a conditional statement is itself expressed as a conditional, with the cases in the statement corresponding exactly to the cases in the intended function. (This can easily happen when the programmer writes the obvious code to implement the intended function, or derives the function from the code in the obvious way.) Here is an example:

---

[2] For C programmers: remember that a switch-statement in C is not a true case-statement unless each case ends with a break-statement (and break-statements occur nowhere else). We will not discuss verification of the switch-statement in the general case: it is another control construct that is just too complicated to reason about.

$$[\, a > b \;\; \to a, b := b, a$$
$$|\; true \;\; \to I \,]$$

```
if  a  >  b  then
        [ swap  a  and  b ]
```

It is easy to see that all that must be verified here is that [swap a and b] does [$a, b := b, a$] and that doing nothing does [I]. The conditions do not need to be manipulated further in the verification. Things are not so simple when the conditions do not match, as in this version:

$$[\, a \geq b \;\; \to a, b := b, a$$
$$|\; true \;\; \to I \,]$$

```
if  a  >  b  then
        [ swap  a  and  b ]
```

This time there are more cases (in fact, combinations of cases) to consider; in particular, the verifier must think about the case in which $a = b$.

The first version is certainly preferable from the point of view of any verifier who does not want to do more work than is necessary! Furthermore, since the situation in the first version is more obvious, we are less likely to make a mistake in the verification. As a general rule, we should always try to write our code and intended functions so that the relationship between them is as clear and obvious as possible.

By the way, where the conditions are the same in the intended function and the if-statement, experienced programmers sometimes omit the intended function on the if-statement because it seems redundant. This is especially true when the state changes are the same as well. For example, if the previous example had been written as

$$[\, a > b \;\; \to a, b := b, a$$
$$|\; true \;\; \to I \,]$$

```
if  a  >  b  then
        [ a, b := b, a ]
```

it would have been reasonable to omit the intended function for the if-statement, and to write simply

```
if  a  >  b  then
        [ a, b := b, a ]
```

It is also reasonable to omit the intended function on the then-part or the else-part, or both, in such situations. Here is an example (which happens to use the syntax of the Icon language):

```
[ a > b  → a, b := b, a
| true  → I ]
if a > b then
    [ a, b := b, a ]
    {
        local temp

        temp := x
        x := y
        y := temp
    }
```

Here, an experienced programmer might write simply

```
[ a > b  → a, b := b, a
| true  → I ]
if a > b then
    {
        local temp

        temp := x
        x := y
        y := temp
    }
```

It is clear enough that $a, b := b, a$ is meant to be the intended function for the then-part of the if-statement.

For now, you should probably write intended functions everywhere. As you gain experience, you will notice situations in which you can conveniently omit a few of them without introducing errors or inaccuracy into your work.

3.7   Conditional Trace Tables

When the functions computed by statements in a sequence contain conditionals, we must use a slightly different kind of trace table. A *conditional trace table* is like an ordinary trace table, except that there is an additional column for conditions.

A conditional trace table is filled in just like an ordinary trace table is, until a computation that contains a conditional is reached. Then, the following steps are taken:

1. A copy of the table is made for each case in the conditional. In each copy, a row is added to the table, with the condition under which that case is chosen in the statement column, and with the condition with the current values substituted for all variables in the condition column. If it happens that

the condition, after this substitution, can be reduced to *false*, this copy of the table is discarded: this path through the code cannot be taken.

2. After the row for the condition, each table is filled in with rows corresponding to the computation done in the case in which the condition holds. If another conditional is reached, each table is copied and filled in just as for the first conditional, applying these three steps recursively.

3. After this, each table is filled in corresponding to those statements in the sequence after the conditional, if any. Again, if another conditional is reached, it is treated in the same way as the first one.

Here is an example, in the C language:

$$[\, c, input \; := \; \text{first character of } input,$$
$$\text{all but first character of } input\,]$$

```
c = getchar();
```

$$[\, c = \text{ ' ' } \rightarrow blanks := blanks + 1$$
$$|\; true \rightarrow I\,]$$

```
if (c == ' ')
```

$$[\, blanks := blanks + 1\,]$$

```
blanks++;
```

Here is the table for the case that $c = $ ' ' in the second statement.

statement	condition	c	input	blanks
c =getchar();		first character of *input*	all but first character of input	
$c = $ ' ' $\rightarrow \ldots$	first character of *input* = ' '			
blanks := blanks + 1;				*blanks + 1*

For the if-statement, we use only its intended function and not the code; remember that verification of that code against its intended function is a separate step. In the first line of the table, the code rather than the intended function has been used to identify the statement, just for brevity.

Now we form a conditional concurrent assignment that shows the contribution that this case makes to the function computed by the sequence. We take the precondition from the condition column. If there is more than one condition there, because there was more than one conditional in the sequence, we take the conjunction (*and*) of the conditions. We form the concurrent assignment from the most recent values of all the state variables, as in an ordinary trace table. From the above table, we get

[first character of input = ' ' →
    c, *input*, *blanks* := first character of *input*,
                all but first character of *input*,
        blanks + 1]

Here is the table for the case in which $c \neq$ ' '. (Notice that this is what we use for the condition, rather than *true*. In all but the first case of the conditional, we must include the negations of the preconditions of the earlier cases.)

statement	condition	c	input	blanks
c =getchar();		first character of *input*	all but first character of input	
$c \neq$ ' ' → ...	first character of *input* $\neq$ ' '			
I				

Here is the conditional concurrent assignment that we get from that table:

[first character of input $\neq$ ' ' →
    c, *input* := first character of *input*,
           all but first character of *input*]

Finally, we obtain the function computed by the sequence, taking into account all possible paths through the conditionals in the sequence. We do this by forming a conditional concurrent assignment whose cases are all of the conditional concurrent assignments obtained from the tables. (In mathematical terms, recall that each function is a set of ordered pairs; here we are taking the union of these sets.)

[first character of input = ' ' →
    c, *input*, *blanks* := first character of *input*,
           all but first character of *input*,
        blanks + 1
| first character of input $\neq$ ' ' →
    c, *input* := first character of *input*,
           all but first character of *input*]

Of course, if we like, we can now simplify preconditions by assuming the negation of earlier preconditions:

[first character of input = ' ' →
　　c, input, blanks := first character of *input*,
　　　　　　　　　all but first character of *input*,
　　　　　　　　　blanks + 1
| *true* →　　c, input := first character of *input*,
　　　　　　　　　all but first character of *input*]

There is one other thing that we need to watch out for: the cases of the conditional, if there are any, in which the computation is undefined. When this happens, there will be such a case in the function computed by the sequence as well, unless the condition for that case reduces to *false* after substituting the current values of the state variables.

Especially, we need to watch out for the situation in which there is no *true* or *else* case in the conditional. Unless we can see that the preconditions of the cases of the function cover all possibilities, we should proceed as if the function ended with the case *true* → *undefined* and construct the conditional trace table accordingly.

Of course, in many situations we don't want the computation ever to be undefined: we want to make sure that the *true* → *undefined* case can't happen. Consider this function one more time:

$$[\, n \neq 0 \rightarrow avg := sum/n \,]$$

We probably would not want to do this computation in any situation in which the precondition could be false. Thus, when we do it as part of a sequence, we don't expect a case split; instead, we want to prove, if possible, that $n \neq 0$. We will be able to do so in a context like this, for example:

$$[\, n := max(count, 1) \,]$$
$$[\, n \neq 0 \rightarrow avg := sum/n \,]$$

When we begin to construct the trace table, this is what we get:

statement	condition	n	avg
$n := max(count, 1)$		$max(count, 1)$	
$n \neq 0 \rightarrow \ldots$	$max(count, 1) \neq 0$ $\equiv true$		

As soon as we see that the condition is equivalent to *true*, we know that no other case is possible. We can immediately proceed as if this were an ordinary truth table, and get:

statement	n	avg
$n := max(count, 1)$	$max(count, 1)$	
$avg := sum/n$		$sum/max(count, 1)$

Exercises

1. What is the function computed by each of the following sections of code? Express each function using a concurrent assignment or conditional concurrent assignment. Use trace tables to calculate them.

    a.
    ```
    x := x + y
    y := x - y
    x := x - y
    ```

    b.
    ```
    if a > b then
         b := a
    else
         a := b;

    if a > c then
         c := a
    else
         c := b;

    if b > c and c > a then
         b := a;
    ```

2. Repeat Exercise 1 of Chapter 2, using trace tables and conditional trace tables this time.

3. For each of the following sections of program, verify it or show where it is incorrect.

    a.
    ```
    [ a ≥ b  → a, b := b, a
    | true  → I ]
    if a > b then
         [ swap a and b ]
    ```

    b.
    ```
    [ sort x, y and z so that x ≤ y ≤ z ]
    if x > y then
         [ swap x and y ];
    if y > z then
         [ swap y and z ]
    ```

4. Verify (or prove incorrect!) your answers to Exercise 2, parts a–c, of Chapter 2.

Notes

The principles of verification presented here were introduced in [Mill75]. The Substitution Principle is presented in [Ling79], Sections 5.2.2 and 6.2, where it is called the Axiom of Replacement. Trace tables and conditional trace tables are presented in [Ling79], Section 6.4. An introductory programming textbook that incorporates these concepts is [Mill87a].

Stepwise refinement was first presented in [Wirt71], and has become common practice in programming.

4

Verification of Iterations

4.1   While-statements

The subject of this chapter is the verification of indefinite iterations, of the kind produced by while-statements, repeat-until statements, and so on. This first section will present rules for verifying while-statements.

You will recall that, to verify a sequence, we derived the function actually computed by the code and compared it with the intended function. For conditionals, we could have done the verification that way, but we chose to do it by cases instead. It happens that, for while-statements, we have no choice: we must use special methods designed specifically for iteration. The reason is that there is no way, in general, to derive the function computed by a while-statement. It is not just that we don't know any way to do it: there are good theoretical reasons for believing that there *can't be* any completely general way of doing it.[1]

Instead, we proceed a bit more indirectly. We notice that the statement

$$\begin{array}{l} \texttt{while } B \texttt{ do} \\ \qquad S \end{array}$$

produces the same sequences of state changes as the following:

---

[1] If you have studied the theory of computation, you may already know that whether a given while-loop computes a given function (assuming no bound on storage) is an undecidable problem, like the problem of whether a given Turing machine computes a given function.

```
if B then
    S;
    while B do
        S
```

Therefore, if both terminate, they both compute the same function.

Now suppose that we must verify the following:

```
[f]
while B do
    S
```

We can think of expanding the loop using an if-statement, as above, except that in place of the inner while-statement we use the intended function [f] itself! This give us

```
[f]
if B then
    S;
    [f]
```

Using this as a guide, it can be shown that we need to prove the following to verify that the while-statement is correct with respect to [f]:

1. The loop will eventually terminate when started in any state in the domain of f.
2. In a state in which B is false, the identity function I is correct with respect to intended function f.
3. In a state in which B is true, the sequence of S followed by f is correct with respect to intended function f.

These, then, are the verification conditions for the while-statement. Or, phrased informally as correctness questions:

1. Does the loop terminate?
2. When B is false, does doing nothing do f?
3. When B is true, does doing S followed by doing f do f?

It may not be immediately obvious that it is legitimate to use [f] as a replacement for the loop itself in the third of these verification conditions. However, Harlan Mills has proved that the above verification conditions are indeed what must be proved to show that the loop is correct with respect to [f]. Essentially, the proof is by induction on the number of times that the loop body is repeated.

Here is an example of a verification:

$$[\, sum, i := sum + \sum_{j=i}^{n} a_j, \text{ anything }]$$
```
while i <= n do
```
$$[\, sum, i := sum + a_i, i + 1 \,]$$

This intended function has no precondition, so its domain is the set of all possible states of the program in which the values of all of the relevant variables are defined.

Thus, when we do this verification, we will actually be showing that the loop computes exactly that function.

First, we verify that the loop terminates when started in any state. In this case, the proof is easy. At every repetition of the loop body, the value of i is increased by 1. Therefore, regardless of its initial value, i must eventually be greater than n, and then the loop will terminate.

Second, we must show that when $i > n$, doing nothing computes the intended function. This is also easy. If $i > n$, the range of integers from i to n is empty, so $\sum_{j=i}^{n} a_j = 0$. Therefore, the intended function reduces to

$$[\ sum, i := sum, \text{anything}\ ]$$

and the identity function is correct with respect to this specification.

Third, we must show that the composition of the function computed by the loop body with the intended function for the loop is correct with respect to that intended function. This takes a bit more work than verifying the first two verification conditions (as is usually the case). To derive the function computed by the sequence, we construct a trace table, as follows:

statement	i	sum
body	$i + 1$	$sum + a_i$
loop	anything	$(sum + a_i) + \sum_{j=(i+1)}^{n} a_j$
		$= sum + \sum_{j=i}^{n} a_j$

We see that the result is exactly the intended function for the loop as a whole. This completes the verification.

4.2   Proving Termination

For most loops that programmers write in actual programs, the termination argument is no harder than the one we used in the example of the previous section, and it does not need to be presented any more formally than that. Usually, there is a counting variable whose value increases at each repetition, and the loop terminates when it reaches some limit; or one whose value decreases at each repetition until it reaches 0 or some other limit; or a list that grows shorter at each repetition until it is empty; or some similar situation.

For a loop of the form

```
while not eof do
```
$$[\,c, input, \ldots \;\; \rightarrow$$
$$\text{first character of } input,$$
$$\text{all but first character of } input, \ldots \,]$$

we would argue that it is the input stream that grows shorter at each repetition until it is empty. We must assume that the input stream is finite in length. One way or another, this is always the case in the real world.

In other loops, we can identify some value that increases or decreases until it reaches some limit, even though that value is not the value of a state variable. In the case of a list that grows shorter, we could say that the value is the length of the list. Or consider a loop of the form

```
while high > low do
```
$$[\, \ldots \rightarrow \ldots, high := \ldots, high - 1$$
$$|\; true \rightarrow \ldots, low := \ldots, low + 1\,]$$

Here, either *high* decreases or *low* increases at each repetition. Fortunately, we do not need to consider which happens under what circumstances, if we notice that *high* − *low* is a value that decreases by 1 at each repetition. We can simply argue that eventually *high* − *low* must become 0 (if it is not already less than or equal to 0), and then the condition *high* > *low* will be false.

Another example is a loop that uses a pointer variable to step down a linked list. In C, the form of such a loop might be

$$[\,p \text{ is the head of a linear linked list}$$
$$\text{terminated by NULL} \rightarrow \ldots \,]$$
```
while (p != NULL && ...)
```
$$[\, \ldots, p := \ldots, p\text{-}\!>\!next\,]$$

The easiest termination proof would be to consider only the first part of the condition (p != NULL) and ignore the rest, whatever it might be. We would argue that the list is finite, and that *p* eventually reaches the end and becomes NULL. We cannot say that the value of *p* necessarily increases or decreases, but we would consider the linked list that is obtained by following the pointers starting from where *p* currently points, and argue that its length decreases by 1 at each repetition and eventually reaches 0, at which time the loop terminates.

Of course, when the situation is less regular than this (for example, when there is no obvious value that increases or decreases at every iteration), proof of termination can be harder. In the general case, this is another theoretically undecidable problem (assuming no bound on storage), like the halting problem for Turing machines. This suggests strongly that proving termination can be very hard in practice. Here is a loop whose termination is not obvious at all:

```
while n > 1 do
```
$$[\ n \text{ is even} \to n := n/2$$
$$|\ n \text{ is odd} \to n := 3n+1\ ]$$

In fact, as of the time of this writing, it is an unsolved mathematical problem whether this loop always terminates! Fortunately, cases as hard as this don't occur often in actual programs.

For complicated or sophisticated algorithms, such as those studied in courses on algorithms, the reason that the algorithm terminates is often an important part of the explanation of how and why the algorithm works. When such an algorithm is coded, especially when the algorithm may not be familiar to those who are likely to be reading or verifying the program, it is a very good idea to put this explanation, including the termination argument, in comments in the code.

4.3   Initialized Loops

When we design programs, we seldom use a while-loop by itself to compute a particular result, because a while-loop by itself seldom computes exactly the function that we want. Instead, most while-loops are preceded by an initialization. It is the initialization and the loop together that compute something useful.

For example, to compute the sum of the values in an array, we might have the intention of using a while-loop, and also of using a counting variable i to index the array. We would want the loop to compute a function something like this one:

$$[\ sum, i := \sum_{j=1}^{n} a_j, \text{anything}\ ]$$

However, we cannot simply use the loop

```
while i <= n do
    sum := sum + a[i];
    i := i + 1
```

to do it. As we have seen, what this loop actually computes is

$$[\ sum, i := sum + \sum_{j=i}^{n} a_j, \text{anything}\ ]$$

But, of course, we would precede the loop with an initialization step:

```
sum := 0;
i := 1
```

Then the composition of the initialization and the loop computes the function that we want, as we see by substituting 0 for *sum* and 1 for *i* into the function computed by the loop and simplifying.

One way of looking at what is happening here is that the loop computes a function that is more general than the one we actually want. By providing particular initial values for some of the variables used by the loop, we are specializing the function that the loop computes into the one that we actually want for this particular purpose.

We can reason further than this. Recall that we verify a while-loop

$$[f]$$
```
while B do
     S
```

as if it were

$$[f]$$
```
if B then
     S;
    [f]
```

In other words, after executing the body of the loop once, we are computing the same function as when we started! The only difference is that the state of the program has changed (at least, it should have changed, or it is certain that the loop will not terminate!). The situation is exactly as if we had initialized the program's variables to the values they now have, then executed the while-statement from the beginning.

For example, suppose we took our loop that sums an array and changed the initialization to

```
sum := a[1];
i := 2
```

Assuming that $i \geq 1$, the loop will compute the same sum as before, and pass through the same states in doing so. Furthermore, this initialization puts the program into a state through which the loop would have passed if we had initialized *sum* to 0 and *i* to 1.

Let us return to the general case:

$$[f]$$
```
while B do
     S
```

We can picture the sequence of states that the program moves through, as it repeatedly executes S, as

$$\dots \xrightarrow{S} \circ \xrightarrow{S} \circ \xrightarrow{S} \circ \xrightarrow{S} \circ \xrightarrow{S} \circ \xrightarrow{S} \odot$$

ending in a state in which *B* is false and the loop terminates. Here are some of the observations that we can make:

- For each of the states in the sequence, the loop takes that state to the same final state. This is equivalent to saying that, if that final state is *Y*, $f(X) = Y$ for each such state *X*.
- We could have taken any of these states, initialized the program's variables so that the program started in that state, then executed the loop from the beginning. The effect would be exactly the same as if the program had reached this state from a state earlier in the sequence. Our choice of initialization merely determines where, along this sequence of states, the computation starts.
- The final state is a state *Y* such that $f(Y) = Y$. This is another way of saying that, when *B* is false, doing nothing computes the intended function. The fact that *B* is false is an indication that there is nothing more to do. If we are in state *Y*, it may be either because we reached that state by having executed the while-loop, possibly doing *S* some number of times, or because we started in that state and there is nothing to do.

But the most important points are these:

- A while-loop doesn't *do* a computation; it *completes* a computation.
- The initialization of the loop determines where the computation starts.
- It is the combination of the start and the completion — the initialization and the loop — that does the job.

4.4 Writing Intended Functions for Loops in Isolation

The purpose of this section is to provide some hints on how to write intended functions for while-loops in isolation, without their initialization. Students sometimes find this a bit difficult at first.

As observed in the previous section, while-loops are often preceded by initialization, and it is the sequence of the initialization and the loop that does the job we want. When this is the case, we often start by writing the intended function for the initialized loop, then writing the initialization and the loop so that the sequence of the two computes that intended function. When all of the intended functions and code for the sequence have been written, this part of the program will have the following form:

[intended function for the initialized loop]

   [intended function for the initialization]
   ...

   [intended function for the loop]
   ```
while ... do
```
    ...

Here is the example from the previous section, written out in this form:

$[\ sum, i := \sum_{j=1}^{n} a_j, \text{anything}\ ]$

```
    sum := 0;
    i := 1;
```

    $[\ sum, i := sum + \sum_{j=i}^{n} a_j, \text{anything}\ ]$
    ```
while i <= n do
```
      $[\ sum, i := sum + a_i, i + 1\ ]$

To verify the sequence, we need the functions for both the initialization and the loop. Often, as in the example above, the initialization is simple enough that we can omit writing an intended function for it and simply use the function that it computes. However, as we have seen, we cannot do this for the loop in the general case, so we must provide an appropriate intended function for the loop before we can verify the sequence. Furthermore, we will need this function to verify the loop itself.

We can view what we need to do here as "taking apart" the intended function for the sequence into two parts, in such a way that the composition of the parts is correct with respect to the intended function for the sequence. In a sense, this is the reverse of the process of deriving the function computed by the composition. However, it cannot be done so mechanically: it requires thought and insight.

We know that the intended function for a loop in isolation should be a generalization of the intended function for that loop with its initialization. It is not always easy to find the appropriate generalization. There are no rules for constructing one that will work in all cases, but here are some suggestions that may help, and some questions that you might ask yourself in the process of discovering an appropriate intended function.

- Perhaps you have some idea of the sequences of values that you want the program's variables to get as the loop iterates. Remember that the intended function must specify what the loop should compute, not only when executed from the beginning, but from a state resulting from some arbitrary number of repetitions of the loop body. In such a state, what does the loop need to compute to complete the desired computation, in terms of the values of the variables in that state?

Let us use the example shown above. Perhaps you know that you want to compute the sum of the elements of array a, and you have decided that you will use i as an incidental variable, for values of the array subscript. This would suggest this as the intended function for the initialized loop:

$$[sum, i := \sum_{j=1}^{n} a_j, \text{anything}]$$

Now, suppose you decide to do this computation by adding the value of each a_i to *sum* for each i, starting with 1 and continuing in increasing order, with i always containing the index of the next element to be added. After you have done this for some values of i, you still need to do it for the rest of them. This reasoning alone might lead you to an appropriate intended function for the uninitialized loop:

$$[sum, i := sum + \sum_{j=i}^{n} a_j, \text{anything}]$$

- Perhaps you have an idea of what the code of the initialized loop will look like, and you have tentatively written the initialization for the loop. Look at the intended function for the whole initialized loop, then look at the initialization. What is special about the values to which the variables are initialized? Do those values appear in the intended function for the initialized loop? If so, perhaps you can get an appropriate intended function for the loop by substituting the names of variables in place of the values to which they were initialized.

In the above example, i is initialized to 1 and *sum* is initialized to 0. We see that 1 appears in the initialized loop's intended function as the lower bound of the summation. Perhaps substituting i for 1 is one step in constructing the generalization we need. As it happens, that guess is correct.

It is less easy to see why 0 is special, since 0 does not appear in the intended function explicitly. However, we may happen to notice that the initialized loop's intended function can be rewritten as follows:

$$[sum, i := 0 + \sum_{j=1}^{n} a_j, \text{anything}]$$

If so, we might try generalizing by substituting *sum* for 0. Again, this happens to be the correct guess.

Of course, 1 and 0 are values that may appear in several places in an intended function and can be made to appear in many more places by using manipulations like the one we used here. In this example, it is rather easy to find the generalization of 1 to i, but it requires more insight (or a lucky guess) to introduce 0 as we did and then generalize it to *sum*.

- Look to see whether the intended function for the initialized loop, or the tentative generalization of it that you have so far, specifies doing nothing (the identity function) when there really is nothing left to do; that is, when the loop will terminate. If not, see if you can discover a way to modify it so that it does.

In the above example, suppose that we have already tentatively generalized 1 to i, using the previous hint. Then, in a state in which the loop will terminate, $i > n$ and the range of subscripts from i to n is empty. Then the function reduces to

$$[\, sum, i := 0, \text{anything} \,]$$

Clearly, the identity function is not correct with respect to this function as it stands. Doing nothing does set i to "anything", as required, but it does not set *sum* to 0.

But suppose we rewrite the function as

$$[\, sum, i := sum, \text{anything} \,]$$

We can see immediately that this function, preceded by an initialization of *sum* to 0, reduces to the previous function. This is a hint that we may be on the right track, and it also suggests an initialization value for *sum* if we have not already discovered it. We may now be able to find the generalization that introduces *sum*+ into the intended function in the general case.

- Try to adapt an intended function that you have successfully used in a similar situation or that you have seen someone else use. Especially, look for patterns of intended functions and code that commonly occur in your work; they will help you find solutions that resemble solutions that worked for you before.

It happens, for example, that the initialized loop that we have been considering is an example of a very common pattern: a variable is used to accumulate a value, which on each repetition of the loop body is combined with another value using some operation. The initialization of the loop sets that variable to the identity value for that operation (0 for addition, 1 for multiplication, the empty string for string concatenation, and so on). For loops that fit this pattern, the intended functions tend to be similar. (See Exercise 3 for an example.)

- It is sometimes easier, at least for beginners, to write the loop first, then write its "intended" function to agree with it. The above hints might be easier to apply if you can see what the initialization and the loop actually are. Once you have had more experience, you may not find this necessary, but it is a reasonable tactic for a beginner.

- Finally, you will get better at writing these intended functions as you gain experience. Writing intended functions is an acquired skill, like many of the skills that you have learned in your years of programming.

Of course, the test of whether you have found an appropriate intended function is whether you can use it successfully in the verification: both the verification of the uninitialized loop itself, and the verification of the sequence of the initialization and the loop. If either of these verifications fails, it may be that the code is incorrect, or it may be that you have not found the right intended function. You will have to use your insight and understanding of the program to decide which.

4.5   Other Forms of Indefinite Iteration

This section will present verification conditions for other forms of indefinite iteration: those in which the exit is at the bottom or in the middle, rather than at the top as in while-loops.

First, let us consider a loop with the exit at the bottom. An example is the repeat-until loop, as in Pascal and several other programming languages. One possible syntax is as follows:

```
repeat
    S
until B
```

The iteration terminates when B is true after executing S. An important difference between this and a while-loop is that S, the body of the loop, must be executed at least once.

Expanding the loop using a conditional, as we did for while-loops, we obtain the following equivalent:

```
S;
if not B then
    repeat
        S
    until B
```

As we did with while-loops, we can see how to verify that this construct is correct with respect to a function [f] by substituting the function for the inner loop:

```
[f]
S;
if not B then
    [f]
```

Using this as a guide, and reasoning as we did for while-loops, we obtain the following as the verification conditions for the repeat-until construct:

1. The loop will eventually terminate when started in any state in the domain of f.
2. In a state in which B is true after executing S, S is correct with respect to intended function f.
3. In a state in which B is false after executing S, the sequence of S followed by f is correct with respect to intended function f.

The corresponding correctness questions can be phrased informally as:

1. Does the loop terminate?
2. After doing S, if B is true, have you computed f?
3. After doing S, if B is false and you now compute f, has the whole computation computed f?

In both forms, the phrasing is a bit awkward because we must express the fact that B is evaluated not in the current state, but in the state obtained by executing S. Other than this, the verification of a repeat-until loop is not much harder than the verification of a while-loop.

Here is an example:

```
[ input contains at least one ';' →
      clause, input, c :=
            clause || the prefix of input up to and including the first ';',
            input advanced past the first ';',
            anything ]
repeat
      [ c, input := first character of input, all but first character of input ]
      read(c);

      [ clause := clause || c ]
      append(clause, c)
until c = ';'
```

In the intended functions, || is used to represent string concatenation and appending a character to a string. We must demonstrate each of the three verification conditions, assuming that the precondition of the loop's intended function is true.

The termination argument is that c will get successive characters from *input*. Since, by the precondition of the loop's intended function, *input* contains at least one semicolon, c will eventually equal ';' and the loop will terminate.

The second verification condition is demonstrated by noticing that, if $c = $ ';' after executing the loop body, *clause* has had a semicolon appended to it and *input* has had its first character, which was a semicolon, removed. This satisfies the intended function of the loop.

For the third verification condition, we notice that, if $c \neq$ ';' after executing the loop body, the input still contains at least one semicolon. Therefore, the precondition of the loop's intended function is still satisfied. We have read and appended to *clause* one character; now doing the loop's intended function reads and appends the rest, up to and including the first semicolon. By doing this sequence of computations, we have computed what the loop's intended function specifies.

Finally, let us consider the form of indefinite iteration in which the exit is from some arbitrary point within the sequence of statements inside the loop. A possible syntax is as follows:

```
loop
    S₁;
    exit when B;
    S₂
end
```

This form is sometimes called a *do-while-do loop* or a $n\frac{1}{2}$ *times loop*.

It is not too hard to see that we can adapt the verification conditions for repeat-until loops to fit this more general construct:

1. The loop will eventually terminate when started in any state in the domain of f.
2. In a state in which B is true after executing S_1, S_1 is correct with respect to intended function f.
3. In a state in which B is false after executing S_1, the sequence of S_1 followed by S_2 followed by f is correct with respect to intended function f.

Or, informally,

1. Does the loop terminate?
2. After doing S_1, if B is true, have you computed f?
3. After doing S_2, if B is false and you now compute S_2 and then f, have you computed f?

We can see that verifying these exit-in-the-middle loops is a bit more difficult than verifying a repeat-until loop, but not much. Past this level of generality, however, the situation rapidly grows more complicated. We could find the appropriate verification conditions for loops with two exits, or even more, but it is probably easiest to avoid writing such loops if possible. The case in which the conditional exit-statement occurs not in the top-level sequence of statements of the loop body, but buried within other levels of control constructs, can be so complicated that we will not even consider it.

We will examine definite iterations, which are written in forms such as "for each ... do ...", in Chapter 7.

Exercises

1. For each of the following sections of program, verify it or show that it is incorrect.

    a. [$m \geq 0 \rightarrow m :=$ remainder after dividing m by n]
        ```
        while m > n do
            m := m - n
        ```

    b. [$m, i :=$ maximum of m and $\mathbf{max}_{j=i}^{n}\, a_j$, anything]
        ```
        while i <= n do
            if a[i] > m then
                m := a[i];
            i := i + 1
        ```
        (end of the loop)

    c. [$n \geq 0$ and n is even $\rightarrow n := 0$
        | $n \geq 0$ and n is odd $\rightarrow n := 1$]
        ```
        while n > 1 do
            n := n - 2
        ```

    d. [$m \geq n > 0 \rightarrow n, m :=$ greatest common divisor of m and n, anything]
        ```
        while m mod n > 0 do
            [ n, m := m mod n, n ]
        ```

    (m mod n is the remainder after dividing m by n.) This is Euclid's Algorithm. This proof is not just a matter of substituting and simplifying, but requires a bit of insight.

2. Give a section of program that contains a while-loop and computes

    $$[\, factorial := n!\,]$$

    Verify it. What did you use for the intended function of the while-loop?

3. Construct an appropriate intended function for the loop in the piece of program below. Verify both the loop and the sequence of the initialization and the loop. Here *allnames* and *n* are strings, and *nameset* and *S* are sets of strings.

    [*allnames, S, n* :=
         the concatenation of the elements of *nameset* in alphabetical order,
         anything, anything]
    ```
    allnames := "";
    S := nameset;
    while S is nonempty do
    ```
         [*n* := the first element in alphabetical order of *S*];
         [*allnames* := *allnames* ‖ *n*];
         [*S* := *S* − *n*]
         (end of the loop)

4. Give the appropriate verification conditions for loops of the following forms.

   a. A while-loop with an additional exit in the middle:

   ```
   while B₁ do
       S₁;
       exit when B₂;
       S₂
   end
   ```

   b. A loop with two exits at arbitrary places:

   ```
   loop
       S₁;
       exit when B₁;
       S₂
       exit when B₂;
       S₃
   end
   ```

5. Show that this loop does not compute its intended function:

   $$[\,x,\ flag := x+1,\ anything\,]$$
   ```
   while flag = true do
       x := x + 1;
       flag := false
   (end of the loop)
   ```

   What function does it actually compute?

6. Show that there is no while-loop that computes (by itself, without initialization) the function

   $$[\,x := x+1\,]$$

   The situation does not change if there are other variables that the loop can set to particular values or to anything.

Notes

The verification conditions for while-loops were first presented in [Mill75]; [Ling79], Section 6.3, contains a proof that they are valid. That section also presents the verification conditions for repeat-loops and exit-in-the-middle loops.

In the hints for constructing intended functions for uninitialized while-loops, I have been inspired by Polya's classic treatment of mathematical problem-solving, [Poly45]. Polya gives many useful hints, many of them in the form of questions:

> Do you know a related problem? Have you seen the same problem in a slightly different form? Here is a problem related to yours and solved before. Could you use its result? Could you use its method?

Should you introduce some auxiliary element...?

Could you solve a part of the problem? Keep only a part of the condition, drop the other part; how far is the unknown then determined, how can it vary?

Check each step.

The problem of finding intended functions for uninitialized loops is discussed in [Dunl82], where it is shown that the problem is, in theory, equivalent to the problem of finding loop invariants in axiomatic verification. Among the journal papers that discuss the mathematical derivation of intended functions for particular patterns of loops are [Misr78] and [Dunl85]. In particular, the first of these papers discusses the pattern in which a variable accumulates a value, and the second discusses a generalization of this pattern.

Soloway and his colleagues have done interesting research on patterns of code that beginning programmers commonly use [Solo83], [John84].

The loop in which n gets either $n/2$ or $3n + 1$ is known as the Collatz $3n + 1$ Algorithm, and the conjecture that it terminates for any initial value of n is known as the Collatz $3n + 1$ Conjecture. The problem has been studied extensively; for a list of selected references in the mathematics literature, see [Guy94] pp. 215–218.

5

Programming with Intended Functions

5.1   A Pascal Program: Length of the Longest Line

In this chapter we will present the development of several complete routines and small programs, starting with an overall intended function and developing the code by stepwise refinement while verifying each step. Each example illustrates how our techniques of specification and verification can be adapted to accomodate the characteristics of particular programming languages and other practical considerations. The complete programs are typical of small utility programs that one might write to perform simple but useful tasks. The other examples are routines like those that might appear in application programs of any size.

The first example is a program that merely reads its input stream and prints the length of the longest line. It might be used (for example) to see whether a file (such as a program source file) can be printed on an output device without causing any line to be truncated or wrapped, spoiling the appearance of the output. The program will be written in Pascal. The specification is quite simple:

> [*input* is nonempty → *output* := length of longest line in *input*
> | *true* → *output* := "0"]

We could have left the behavior of the program unspecified in the case that the input is empty, but 0 is a sensible output in that case, and it takes little extra effort to add this to the specification. Furthermore, we can guess that it will probably require little extra effort in programming. A good maxim is that, all other things being equal, a program that does something well-defined and sensible for all inputs is more useful than one that works only when given certain inputs.

Strictly speaking, the specification should probably also say that the program consumes all of its input, since the input stream is a state variable, and the consumption of the input may be visible from outside the program (if the user of the program is typing the input at a keyboard, for example). However, external specifications for programs do not commonly say this sort of thing. We should probably assume, as part of the specification of any program that reads input, either *input* := empty (if the program will read all of its input) or perhaps *input* := anything (if the program may read only enough of its input to determine what the output should be).

For purposes of illustration, we will develop the program in more detail than an experienced programmer would do, taking smaller steps and using intended functions everywhere. An obvious first step in the development is to decide to compute the maximum line length first, keeping its value in a variable, then print the value of that variable. We can write the skeleton of the program immediately, choosing an obvious name for the program:

```
program maxlinelength(input, output);

var
    maxlength: integer;          (* length of the longest line *)
```

[*input* is nonempty →
       output, input, maxlength :=
            length of longest line in *input*, empty, anything
| *true* → *output, maxlength* := "0", anything]
```
begin
```
    [*input* is nonempty →
          maxlength, input := length of longest line in *input*, empty
    | *true* → *maxlength* := 0]

    [*output* := *maxlength*]
```
end.
```

Notice that the intended function on the body of the program does say that *input* is set to empty, if it is not empty already. Inside the program, the input stream is definitely a state variable whose value is observable, and we will need to account for changes in the input stream as input is being read. Notice also that *maxlength* is an incidental variable, and so we specify that it will be set to "anything". We could have said that it would be set to a particular value (and, by looking at the sequence of steps that implement this intended function, we can see what that value will be), but we do not need to do so.

Inside the body of the program are the steps that first calculate *maxlength* and then print it. It is easy to verify this sequence with respect to its intended function. In fact, it is correct almost by inspection; it is probably not even necessary to construct a trace table.

The next step is to develop the computation that computes *maxlength*. Let us suppose that we can guess that the main part of that computation will be a loop of the form

> while *input* is not exhausted
>> read a line of input and update `maxlength` accordingly

We know that this loop will compute *I* if it is executed when *input* is already empty. Therefore, it will not do the required computation by itself, since the intended function says that *maxlength* must be set to 0 if *input* is empty. However, if we initialize *maxlength* to 0 and let the loop change it if necessary, we will get this part of the computation right.

With this initialization, what should be the intended function for the uninitialized loop? We know that we need an intended function that also specifies what the loop should do after it has already executed the loop body one or more times. If we plan to use *maxlength* to hold the running maximum, so that after reading some lines it contains the maximum length of the lines read so far, it is not too hard to arrive at the following:

> [*input* is nonempty →
>> *maxlength, input* :=
>>> maximum of *maxlength* and length of longest line in *input*,
>>> empty
>
> | *true* → *I*]

Fortunately, the initialization that we have chosen is compatible with this intended function, as we can see by putting together the pieces:

> [*input* is nonempty →
>> *maxlength, input* := length of longest line in *input*,
>>> empty
>
> | *true* → *maxlength* := 0]
>> `maxlength := 0;`
>
>> [*input* is nonempty →
>>> *maxlength, input* :=
>>>> maximum of *maxlength* and length of longest line in *input*,
>>>> empty
>>
>> | *true* → *I*]

For this sequence, as for the previous one, the verification is quite easy. The breakdown of cases is the same in the two intended functions. For the first case, the verification is just a matter of substituting 0 for *maxlength* and simplifying, using the fact that the length of a line cannot be less than 0.

We already knew the general form of the loop, and now that we have its intended function we can write and verify it:

```
[ input is nonempty →
      maxlength, input :=
            maximum of maxlength and length of longest line in input,
            empty
| true → I ]
while not eof do
    [ maxlength, input :=
          maximum of maxlength and length of first line in input,
          all but first line of input ]
```

This verification is as follows:

1. Termination: the loop body consumes one line of input every time. Assuming that the input is finite, it will eventually become empty, and then eof will become true. (That is the meaning of the parameterless function eof in Pascal.)
2. False case: when the loop condition is false, the input is empty, and doing *I* is exactly what the loop's intended function specifies.
3. True case: when the loop condition is true, *input* contains a first line, so the loop body's intended function is defined in the current state. Computing the composition of that function and the loop's intended function, we obtain

```
[ (all but first line of input) is nonempty →
      maxlength, input :=
            maximum of (maximum of maxlength
                  and length of first line in input)
            and length of longest line in  (all but first line of input),
            empty
| true → I ]
```

which, under the assumption that the loop condition is true, is the same as the loop's intended function.

Now we develop the loop body from its intended function. As before, we first calculate an intermediate value and then use it:

[*maxlength, input* :=
    maximum of *maxlength* and length of first line in *input*,
    all but first line of *input*]
      `var linelength: integer;     (* length of the current line *)`
[*linelength, input* :=
    length of first line in *input*, all but first line of *input*]
[*maxlength* := maximum of *maxlength* and *linelength*]

Reading the first line and calculating its length is a simple programming task. Let us simply write down the solution, combining several development steps into one, as an experienced programmer would probably do:

> [*linelength, input* :=
>   length of first line in *input*, all but first line of *input*]
> `linelength := 0;`
>
> [*linelength, input* :=
>   *linelength* + length of first line in *input*,
>   *input* without the chars before the first end-of-line]
> `while not eoln do`
>   [*linelength, input* :=
>   *linelength* + 1, all but first character of *input*]
>   `begin`
>   `linelength := linelength + 1;`
>   `get(input)`
>   `end;`
>
> [*input* := *input* advanced past the first end-of-line]
> `readln`

There are several verification steps to do here, but they are easy; they are left as exercises. (The Pascal function `get` advances the input stream by one character; the parameterless function `eoln` is true when the input stream is at an end-of-line marker; the procedure `readln` does indeed advance the input stream past the first end-of-line marker.) We have two more functions to write code for, but they are very easy:

> [*maxlength* := maximum of *maxlength* and *linelength*]
> `if linelength > maxlength then`
>   `maxlength := linelength`

and

> [*output* := *maxlength*]
> `writeln(maxlength)`

Now we can put all of the pieces together. There is one small complication. We have introduced the variable *linelength* as an incidental variable in the body of the outer loop. However, Pascal does not allow local variables in compound statements, as C and some other programming languages do. We must move this declaration outside of the body of the main program. This means that we must also modify several of the intended functions to say that, in several of the steps, *linelength* can be set to anything.

The resulting program, fully annotated with intended functions, is shown in Figure 5.1.

Now that the program is complete and verified, we can produce the actual source file for the program. We should do this in such a way that future readers will find it as clear and readable as possible.

We will want to leave many of the intended functions as comments in the code, as documentation. However, some of them may now seem redundant, because they repeat what is obvious in the context of the code and other intended functions. These can be removed, to make the source file less cluttered and verbose. This may be a good idea, especially if the program is to be read and maintained by people who may not be familiar with our techniques of verification.

Which intended functions to retain is a matter of taste, but we should leave enough so that the reason the program works is still easy to see. In particular, a reader who understands the techniques of verification should be able to see in the comments at least a sketch of the verification of each part, and should be able to fill in the missing steps if desired.

In the intended functions, it is probably a good idea to edit them to remove, where possible, any notation that a reader unfamiliar with our specialized notation will not understand. An uninitiated programmer will probably understand most of the conditional concurrent assignment notation, but it would probably be helpful to rewrite *true* → as *else* → . Similarly, we might rewrite *I* (representing the identity function) as "do nothing." In case any reader might not interpret this notation as a conditional at all, some practitioners even insert the word "if" at the beginning of the first case of each conditional concurrent assignment.

We might also choose to relax our rule about incidental variables, omitting mentioning that they can be set to "anything" where this does not seem immediately relevant. And, of course, we should adjust indentation and spacing to conform to any other changes that we have made. The final result might be as shown in Figure 5.2 on page 76.

[*input* is nonempty → *output* := length of longest line in *input*
| *true* → *output* := "0"]
```
program maxlinelength(input, output);
var maxlength: integer;        (* length of the longest line *)
    linelength: integer;       (* length of the current line *)
```
[*input* is nonempty → *output*, *input*, *maxlength*, *linelength* :=
        length of longest line in *input*, empty, anything, anything
| *true* → *output*, *maxlength* := "0", anything]
```
begin
```
    [*input* is nonempty → *maxlength*, *input*, *linelength* :=
        length of longest line in *input*, empty, anything
| *true* → *maxlength* := 0]
```
    maxlength := 0;
```
    [*input* is nonempty → *maxlength*, *input*, *linelength* :=
            maximum of *maxlength* and length of longest line in *input*,
            empty, anything
| *true* → *I*]
```
    while not eof do
```
      [*maxlength*, *input*, *linelength* :=
            maximum of *maxlength* and length of first line in *input*,
            all but first line of *input*, anything]
```
        begin
```
        [*linelength*, *input* :=
                length of first line in *input*, all but first line of *input*]
```
            linelength := 0;
```
        [*linelength*, *input* :=
                linelength + length of first line in *input*,
                input without the chars before the first end-of-line]
```
            while not eoln do
```
          [*linelength*, *input* := *linelength* + 1,
                    all but first character of *input*]
```
                begin
                    linelength := linelength + 1;
                    get(input)
                end;
```
        [*input* := *input* advanced past the first end-of-line]
```
            readln;
```
        [*maxlength* := maximum of *maxlength* and *linelength*]
```
            if linelength > maxlength then
                maxlength := linelength
        end;
```
    [*output* := *maxlength*]
```
    writeln(maxlength)
end.
```

Figure 5.1 The fully annotated program "maxlinelength"

```
(* [ input is nonempty ->
            output := length of longest line in input
   | else -> output := "0" ] *)
program maxlinelength(input, output);
var
   maxlength: integer;          (* length of the longest line *)
   linelength: integer;         (* length of the current line *)

begin
   maxlength := 0;

   (* [ if input is nonempty ->
           maxlength, input := maximum of maxlength and length
                                     of longest line in input,
                               empty
      | else -> do nothing ] *)
   while not eof do
      (* [ maxlength, input := maximum of maxlength and
                                  length of first line in input,
                               all but first line of input ] *)
      begin
         (* [ linelength, input :=
                 length of first line in input,
                 all but first line of input ] *)
         linelength := 0;
         while not eoln do
            begin
               linelength := linelength + 1;
               get(input)
            end;
         readln;

         (* [ maxlength :=
                 maximum of maxlength and linelength ] *)
         if linelength > maxlength then
            maxlength := linelength
      end;

   writeln(maxlength)
end.
```

Figure 5.2 The source file for the program "maxlinelength"

5.2 A C Program: Counting Letters and Digits

The next program is a simple utility that counts the number of letters, digits, and other characters in the input. It will be written in C, and will illustrate (among other things) some techniques for dealing with some peculiarities of C input. Most of the verification steps are quite obvious and will be mentioned only where there is something interesting to point out; the interesting parts will be the intended functions. This is the program's specification (*stdin* and *stdout* are the C terms for the "standard" input and output streams, respectively):

[*stdout* := a line containing the number of letters, digits, and other characters in *stdin* respectively, separated by single blanks]

As in the previous program, the obvious algorithm is to read the input and keep running counts in variables, then print the counts. Here is the corresponding program at the highest level:

```
[ stdout :=  a line containing the number of letters, digits, and other
             characters in stdin respectively, separated by single blanks ]
main()
{
    int letters, digits, others;    /* counts of these in input */

    [ letters, digits, others, stdin :=
             number of letters in  stdin,
             number of digits in  stdin,
             number of other characters in  stdin,
             empty ]
    [ stdout := letters ‖ ' ' ‖ digits ‖ ' ' ‖ others ‖ end of line ]
}
```

In the first intended function in the body of the routine, notice how the right-hand-side values are aligned in a vertical column. For intended functions that specify that many state variables are changed, this is a reasonable formatting convention to help make the intended functions readable. A convention that some people prefer is to put each left-hand-side variable and its right-hand-side value on a separate line, like this:

[*letters* := number of letters in *stdin*,
  digits := number of digits in *stdin*,
  others := number of other characters in *stdin*,
  stdin := empty]

This is reasonable too, except that it breaks away from our notation for concurrent assignments and starts to look like a sequence of assignments as in a programming language. If we use this notation, we must be very careful to remember that this is still a concurrent assignment!

As before, ‖ represents string concatenation or appending a character to a string. In the last intended function, we have explicitly mentioned the end-of-line marker, since in C a special character (`'\n'`) is used for that purpose. Here is how the output operation is written in C:

$$[\ stdout := letters\ \|\ '\ '\ \|\ digits\ \|\ '\ '\ \|\ others\ \|\ \text{end of line}\ ]$$
```
printf("%d %d %d\n", letters, digits, others);
```

Here, the verification consists of reading and understanding the C statement and making sure that all of the details are present and correct.

Now let us develop the step that reads input and counts characters. From the start, we must take into account some of the properties of C input. The end of the input is marked by a distinguished value, called *EOF*. The way to read input character-by-character is to use the function *getchar*(), which returns an integer value: either a character code or the distinguished value *EOF*, which has a value different from any character code. If the value returned is not *EOF*, it may be used as a character value; conversion is implicit.

Therefore, we must keep a one-character buffer for the input and test the value in that buffer to see whether the input has been exhausted. If not, we can go on to process that character and then any input that may remain. If we use a variable called *c* as that buffer, we can see that, at any time after the first character of the input is put into *c*, the part of the input that we have not yet processed is contained in *c* followed by what remains of *stdin*.

Let us write this combination as ($c \| stdin$) and treat it as if it were a composite data structure. Then we can use this notation in our intended functions, treating this structure as if it were a single variable. Thus, we can refer to (for example) the number of letters in ($c \| stdin$), and we can express the computation that advances the input, reading the next character into *c*, as

$$[\ (c\ \|\ stdin) := stdin\ ]$$

which is a short way of saying

$$[\ c, stdin := \text{first character of } stdin, \text{all but the first character of } stdin\ ]$$

Then when we say "($c \| stdin$) is empty," we mean that $c = EOF$; the value *EOF* does not count as a character.

Using this notational technique, we can start to develop the computation as follows:

[*letters, digits, others, stdin* :=
            number of letters in *stdin*,
            number of digits in *stdin*,
            number of other characters in *stdin*,
            empty]
{
    int c;   /* input buffer: a character or EOF */

    [*letters, digits, others* := 0, 0, 0]

    [(*c* ∥ *stdin*) := *stdin*]
    c = getchar();

    [*letters, digits, others, (c* ∥ *stdin)* :=
            letters + number of letters in (*c* ∥ *stdin*),
            digits + number of digits in (*c* ∥ *stdin*),
            others + number of other characters in (*c* ∥ *stdin*),
            empty]
}

As you might guess, this has been written in such a way that the last intended function in the sequence will be the intended function for a while-loop that reads the rest of the input and counts characters. In fact, it will be another instance of the "accumulating variable" pattern mentioned in Section 4.4. The form of the loop is now quite obvious:

[*letters, digits, others, (c* ∥ *stdin)* :=
        letters + number of letters in (*c* ∥ *stdin*),
        digits + number of digits in (*c* ∥ *stdin*),
        others + number of other characters in (*c* ∥ *stdin*),
        empty]
while (c != EOF)   /* while (c ∥ stdin) is nonempty */
    [*c* is a letter → *letters, (c* ∥ *stdin)* := *letters* + 1, *stdin*
    | *c* is a digit → *digits, (c* ∥ *stdin)* := *digits* + 1, *stdin*
    | *else*   → *others, (c* ∥ *stdin)* := *others* + 1, *stdin*]

Notice that, in the intended function for the loop body, every case contains the assignment (*c* ∥ *stdin*) := *stdin*. A notational technique that some people prefer in situations like this is to separate out the common part, as shown on the following page:

$[$ *letters, digits, others,* $(c \parallel stdin) :=$
    letters + number of letters in $(c \parallel stdin)$,
    digits + number of digits in $(c \parallel stdin)$,
    others + number of other characters in $(c \parallel stdin)$,
    empty $]$

```
while (c != EOF)    /* while (c || stdin) is nonempty */
```

    $[$ c is a letter $\rightarrow$ *letters* := *letters* + 1
    $|$ c is a digit $\rightarrow$ *digits* := *digits* + 1
    $|$ *else* $\rightarrow$ *others* := *others* + 1,
    and in any case, $(c \parallel stdin) := stdin$ $]$

The verification of the loop is simple and will not be shown in detail, but suppose we wanted to write out the trace table for the composition of the loop body and the loop's intended function, to help in checking the verification condition corresponding to the case of $(c \neq EOF)$ being true. Rather than having separate columns for c and *stdin*, it is sufficient in this case to continue to treat $(c \parallel stdin)$ as if it were a single variable, obtaining the following table (the columns for *digits* and *others* are omitted for brevity):

statement	*letters*	$(c \parallel stdin)$
body	*letters* + (1 if c is a letter, else 0)	*stdin*
loop	*letters* + (1 if c is a letter, else 0) + number of letters in *stdin* = *letters* + number of letters in $(c \parallel stdin)$	empty

The implementation of the loop body is obvious, and can probably be written out immediately, in one step. (The functions `isletter` and `isdigit` are in one of the standard C libraries; the **++** operator is the C idiom for incrementing a variable by one.)

    $[$ c is a letter $\rightarrow$ *letters* := *letters* + 1
    $|$ c is a digit $\rightarrow$ *digits* := *digits* + 1
    $|$ *else* $\rightarrow$ *others* := *others* + 1;
    in any case, $(c \parallel stdin) := stdin$ $]$

```
{
    if (isletter(c))       letters++;
    else if (isdigit(c))   digits++;
    else                   others++;

    [ (c || stdin) := stdin ]
    c = getchar();
}
```

Putting all of the pieces together, we obtain the program (let us call it "letter-count") shown in Figure 5.3.

As in the previous example, we may wish to edit this program somewhat when preparing the actual source file. The variable *c* can be left as a local variable in an inner scope, if we prefer, but it will make the program a bit shorter if we eliminate this scope and move *c* out one level, making it an incidental variable in the overall program.

We can also make use of the fact that integer variables in C are initialized to 0 by default. Therefore, the initialization of our counters is redundant and can be deleted; the declaration of the variables, by itself, computes this initialization. It is a good idea to put the intended function

$$[\ letters, digits, others := 0, 0, 0 \ ]$$

on the declaration itself, to make explicit the fact that we depend on this initialization. We do not put such an intended function on the declaration of *c*, because we do not care what its initial value is.

We will convert the program's intended functions into comments in the source file, after deleting some that appear redundant, as we did in the previous example. In doing this, we might use one other notational convention that some programmers prefer: to omit the square brackets around the intended functions. In a program that is developed using intended functions as we have done, we almost always find that most of the comments in the program are intended functions. Writing

```
/* some computation */
```

instead of

```
/* [ some computation ] */
```

gives the program a less cluttered appearance. We can, if we choose, adopt the convention that all comments are assumed to be intended functions unless indicated otherwise. A possible convention for ordinary, "parenthetical" comments is to enclose their contents in parentheses!

Using these conventions for comments, and making all of the other changes, we obtain the source program shown in Figure 5.4.

This was a very simple program, and any experienced C programmer could easily have written it without the elaborate formal development shown here. The reason for including it in this chapter is to illustrate some useful notational conventions for intended functions, and the (*c* ‖ *stdin*) idiom for representing C character-by-character input in particular.

[*stdout* := a line containing the number of letters, digits, and other
              characters in *stdin* respectively, separated by single blanks]

```
main()
{
    int letters, digits, others;    /* counts of these in input */
```

  [*letters*, *digits*, *others*, *stdin* :=
              number of letters in *stdin*,
              number of digits in *stdin*,
              number of other characters in *stdin*,
              empty]

```
    {
        int c;                          /* input buffer: a character or EOF */
```

      [*letters, digits, others* := 0, 0, 0]

```
        letters = digits = others = 0;
```

      [(*c* ‖ *stdin*) := *stdin*]

```
        c = getchar();
```

      [*letters*, *digits*, *others*, (*c* ‖ *stdin*) :=
           letters + number of letters in (*c* ‖ *stdin*),
           digits + number of digits in (*c* ‖ *stdin*),
           others + number of other characters in (*c* ‖ *stdin*),
           empty]

```
        while (c != EOF)      /* while (c || stdin) is nonempty */
```

        [*c* is a letter → *letters* := *letters* + 1
        | *c* is a digit → *digits* := *digits* + 1
        | *else*   → *others* := *others* + 1;
        in any case, (*c* ‖ *stdin*) := *stdin*]

```
        {
            if (isletter(c))        letters++;
            else if (isdigit(c))    digits++;
            else                    others++;
```

          [(*c* ‖ *stdin*) := *stdin*]

```
            c = getchar();
        }
    }
```

  [*stdout* := *letters* ‖ ' ' ‖ *digits* ‖ ' ' ‖ *others* ‖ end of line]

```
    printf("%d %d %d\n", letters, digits, others);
}
```

Figure 5.3 The fully annotated program "lettercount"

```
/* stdout := a line containing the number of letters, digits,
             and other characters in stdin respectively,
             separated by single blanks */
main()
{
    /* letters, digits, others := 0, 0, 0 */
    int letters, digits, others;   /* (counts of these in input) */
    int c;               /* (input buffer: a character or EOF) */

    /* (c || stdin) := stdin */
    c = getchar();

    /* letters, digits, others, (c || stdin) :=
            letters + number of letters in (c || stdin),
            digits + number of digits in (c || stdin),
            others + number of other characters in (c || stdin),
            empty */
    while (c != EOF)    /* (while (c || stdin) is nonempty) */
    {
        if (isletter(c))       letters++;
        else if (isdigit(c))   digits++;
        else                   others++;

        /* (c || stdin) := stdin */
        c = getchar();
    }

    printf("%d %d %d\n", letters, digits, others);
}
```

Figure 5.4 The source file for the program "lettercount"

5.3 An Icon Routine: Uncompressing a String

The example in this section will be a routine written in the Icon programming language. It will illustrate some aspects of the specification and verification of routines and of the treatment of type information in languages without strong typing. It will also illustrate the use of specification functions.

The problem is to decode a string that has been encoded using run-length encoding. In this form of data compression, where there is a character repeated many times, it is replaced by a three-character sequence consisting of the following:

1. A special character, which will be called RunLengthCharacter below.
2. The repeated character.
3. The number of times that the repeated character occurred.

Let us call such a sequence a "run-length sequence." A run-length-encoded string, then, is a string that may contain run-length sequences.

The decoding routine will reverse this compression to produce the original string. It will be a procedure contained within a larger program; documentation elsewhere in the program will define which character in the Icon character set is RunLengthCharacter.

As usual, we begin by writing an intended function. The intended function for a procedure definition specifies the computation that will occur when the procedure is called. It is placed above the heading in the procedure definition, and is written in terms of the parameters that are named in the heading. Here is an example of a procedure annotated in this way:

```
[ s is a string and n is an nonnegative integer →
        return the concatenation of n copies of s ]
procedure copies(s, n)
  ...
end
```

(Actually, it would be unusual to see this particular procedure defined in an Icon program, because Icon contains a built-in procedure repl that does the same thing, but it is included here for the sake of this example.)

Icon is not a strongly typed language, so the types of the parameters are not given in the procedure heading, nor is the type of the result that the procedure returns. Types are associated with values at run-time, so the type of a variable, parameter, etc. must be considered part of the program's state. For this reason, the intended function for the procedure contains a precondition that says that the parameters are of appropriate types. As a general rule, whenever the code is in a language in which type information does not appear in declarations, the type information should be incorporated into intended functions as preconditions.

By the way, this intended function uses the syntax

$$\text{return } x$$

(rather than an assignment) to specify the value returned by the procedure. Variations that some people prefer are

$$\textit{returned value} := x$$

and

$$\textit{copies} := x$$

Here is the intended function that we might write for the procedure of this example:

```
[ s is a run-length-encoded string → return run-length-decoding(s) ]
procedure uncompress(s)
```

Here, *run-length-decoding* is a specification function, which is defined as follows:

> *run-length-decoding(RunLengthCharacter $\parallel c_1 \parallel c_2$) =*
> concatenation of n copies of c_1, where n = integer coding of c_2

> *run-length-decoding(c) = c*
> for any other character c not part of a run-length-sequence

> *run-length-decoding($x_1 \parallel \ldots \parallel x_n$) =*
> *run-length-decoding(x_1) $\parallel \ldots \parallel$ run-length-decoding(x_n)*
> for a run-length-encoded string $x_1 \parallel \ldots \parallel x_n$,
> where each x_i is a run-length-sequence
> or a character not part of a run-length-sequence

In the precondition of the intended function, what we might consider type information about s is of two kinds: the programming-language type of s (the fact that s is a string) and application-specific information about what kind of structure we are building using that programming-language type (the fact that s is a run-length encoding). Even when the programming language that we are using is strongly typed, it is appropriate to include type information of the second kind in intended functions.

We would, of course, provide a definition of the phrase "run-length-encoded string" elsewhere in the program's documentation. This definition would include a statement that RunLengthCharacter is being used in the program as the special character that indicates an encoding of a repeated character.

We can now start to develop the procedure. The obvious approach is to iterate through the characters of s from left to right, building up the decoded string in another variable. This iteration can take the form of an initialized while-loop, in which we use an incidental variable to index the characters of s. The initialized loop will be another instance of the accumulating-variable pattern, which should be quite familiar to us by now. We should be able to construct something like the following, in which the loop itself is still represented as an intended function, without much difficulty. (In Icon, # is the comment character and, as the comment implies, * is the operator that produces the length of a string.)

```
[ s is a run-length-encoded string → return run-length-decoding(s) ]
procedure uncompress(s)
    local len, i, result

    result := ""
    len := *s        # the length of string s
    i := 1

    [ result, i := result ‖ run-length-decoding(sᵢ...s_len), anything ]

    return result
end
```

You may notice that the intended function for the loop does not contain the precondition "*s* is a run-length-encoded string." This type information is assumed to apply throughout the procedure.

As usual in a sequence, the verification of the procedure at this level is by substituting and simplifying. Substituting into the return-statement, we obtain

$$\text{return } "" \parallel \textit{run-length-decoding}(s_1 \ldots s_{*s})$$

which can be simplified to

$$\text{return } \textit{run-length-decoding}(s_1 \ldots s_{*s})$$

and then

$$\text{return } \textit{run-length-decoding}(s)$$

Notice that we do not even need to know what *run-length-decoding* means to do this; this is one benefit of defining a specification function as an abstraction and using it in many places in the program.

The obvious thing to do in the loop body is the following: if the next character is RunLengthCharacter, decode the run-length sequence that it is the first character of; otherwise, take the character unchanged. The loop, using an intended function to represent the loop body, would then look like the following:

$$[\, \textit{result}, \; i := \textit{result} \parallel \textit{run-length-decoding}(s_i \ldots s_{len}), \text{anything} \,]$$
```
while i <= len do
```
$$[\, s_i = \textit{RunLengthCharacter} \rightarrow$$
$$\textit{result}, \; i := \textit{result} \parallel \textit{run-length-decoding}(s_i \ldots s_{i+2}), \; i+3$$
$$|\; \textit{else} \rightarrow \textit{result}, \; i := \textit{result} \parallel s_i, \; i+1 \,]$$

The verification of the loop, briefly, is as follows:

1. Termination: the value of i increases by at least 1 each time around the loop, so it must eventually be greater than len.
2. False case: when the loop condition is false, the sequence $s_i \ldots s_{len}$ is empty. The decoding of the empty string is the empty string (we infer this from the definition of *run-length-decoding*), so that doing nothing computes the correct function.
3. True case: the loop body, whichever case of the conditional applies, decodes a prefix of $s_i \ldots s_{len}$, appends the decoding to *result*, and (by incrementing *i*) removes that prefix from $s_i \ldots s_{len}$; we refer to the definition of *run-length-decoding* to verify that the correct prefix is decoded

in each case. Then the intended function on the loop decodes what is left of $s_i \ldots s_{len}$. This sequence of computations decodes $s_i \ldots s_{len}$ as the loop's intended function specifies.

The code for the loop body is now easy to write. We can use the procedure `copies` that we saw at the beginning of this section. (In Icon, `==` is a string-comparison operator; `=` is used only for comparison of numeric values.)

```
[ sᵢ = RunLengthCharacter →
      result, i := result ‖ run-length-decoding(sᵢ ... sᵢ₊₂),  i + 3
| else → result, i := result ‖ sᵢ,  i + 1 ]
if s[i] == RunLengthCharacter then
    {

        [ result := result ‖ n copies of sᵢ₊₁
              where n = integer coding of sᵢ₊₂ ]
        result ||:= copies(s[i+1], ord(s[i+2])

        i +:= 3

    }
else
    {

        result ||:= s[i]
        i +:= 1

    }
```

To verify this statement, we refer to the definition of *run-length-decoding* again and check that the cases in the definition match the cases in the code. (In Icon, `a +:= b` is the idiom for $a := a + b$, and similarly `a ||:= b` is the idiom for $a := a \, ‖ \, b$.) There is only one more part to verify:

```
        [ result := result ‖ n copies of sᵢ₊₁
              where n = integer coding of sᵢ₊₂ ]
        result ||:= copies(s[i+1], ord(s[i+2])
```

This is verified by substituting, for the call to `copies`, the value that `copies` returns. To find this, we take the intended function on the declaration of `copies` (as shown at the beginning of this section), substituting values for the parameters in the actual call. We obtain

$$[\; result := result \; ‖ \; \text{the concatenation of } ord(s_{i+2}) \text{ copies of } s_{i+1} \;]$$

The intended function is the same as this, except with slightly different wording.

Putting all of the pieces together, we obtain the program shown in Figure 5.5.

The corresponding source file might be as shown in Figure 5.6. Notice the big block comment at the beginning, which helps to make the procedure and its meaning easy to find by eye in a large source file. Many programmers use some such device.

```
[ s is a run-length-encoded string → return run-length-decoding(s) ]
procedure uncompress(s)
    local len, i, result

    result := ""
    len := *s          # the length of string s
    i := 1

    [ result,  i := result ‖ run-length-decoding(s_i ... s_len),  anything ]
    while i <= len do
        {
            [ s_i = RunLengthCharacter →
                 result,  i := result ‖ run-length-decoding(s_i ... s_{i+2}),  i + 3
            | else → result,  i := result ‖ s_i,  i + 1 ]
            if s[i] == RunLengthCharacter then
                {
                    [ result := result ‖ n copies of s_{i+1}
                          where n = integer coding of s_{i+2} ]
                    result ‖:= copies(s[i+1], ord(s[i+2]))

                    i +:= 3
                }
            else
                {
                    result ‖:= s[i]
                    i +:= 1
                }
        }

    return result
end
```

Figure 5.5 A routine that performs run-length-decoding

```
#----------------------------------------------------------+
#                                                          |
#    uncompress(s):                                        |
#        [ s is a run-length-encoded string ->             |
#                return run-length-decoding(s) ]           |
#                                                          |
#----------------------------------------------------------+
procedure uncompress(s)
   local len, i, result

   result := ""
   len := *s        # the length of string s
   i := 1

   # [ result, i := result || run-length-decoding(s[i] ... s[len]),
   #              anything ]
   while i <= len do
      {
          # [ s[i] = RunLengthCharacter ->
          #      result, i :=
          #          result || run-length-decoding(s[i] ... s[i+2]),
          #          i+3
          # | else -> result, i := result || s[i], i+1 ]
          if s[i] == RunLengthCharacter then
             {
                 # [ result := result || n copies of s[i+1]
                 #      where n = integer coding of s[i+2] ]
                 result ||:= copies(s[i+1], ord(s[i+2]))

                 i +:= 3
             }
          else
             {
                 result ||:= s[i]
                 i +:= 1
             }
      }

   return result
end
```

Figure 5.6 The source file for the program of Figure 5.5

5.4   A Study in Abstraction: The Registrar's Program

This example will show how specification and verification can work in larger and more complex programs. The key idea is the use of procedures, stereotyped English phrases, and similar techniques for reasoning about complex concepts and computations abstractly. The example will also illustrate the use of nested conditionals in intended functions. As it happens, the program is written in C, but particular characteristics of the C language are not the main point this time.

The program in this example was written for the registrar of a college, to help her detect conflicts in the college's schedule of classes for a semester. The program is a real application, written and verified using the methods of this book. We will consider one routine from that program, simplified a bit for presentation here.

We begin with the intended function and header for the routine. These are already written, to match the needs of the routine that calls this one.

```
[ who1 and when1 are nonempty →
        return the record of some class in instructor_schedules
        which has a conflict with any of the given instructors and times,
        or NULL if there is none ]
char *instructor_conflict_with(Instructor who1, Instructor who2,
                                Times when1, Times when2)
```

A few parts of this are concrete, in the sense that we can see their implementation in terms of C constructs, but most parts are more abstract. We can see that the routine returns a pointer to a "record", which is apparently a string, but we don't know what it contains. Instructor and Times are apparently types defined elsewhere; we have no way of telling how they are implemented. The object *instructor_schedules* is apparently a global table that holds the schedules of the instructors, but we don't know its structure.

Perhaps even more important, the intended function uses the word *conflict* without defining precisely what it means in this context. We can guess its meaning in general terms by knowing its common meaning in English but, again, we don't know how it relates to the implementation of such things as the Times data type.

Fortunately, we can do most of the development and verification of this routine without knowing much more than we do now about these abstractions, as we shall see.

From documentation elsewhere in the program, we discover that an Instructor value can be one of three kinds:

- It may denote an actual person.
- It may represent "Staff", meaning that the actual instructor for the class has

not yet been chosen. This implies that this is not an instructor for whom we need to check the schedule for conflicts.

- It may be empty. (The schedule data allows a class to have two instructors scheduled for it, but the second is optional. Most classes have only one.)

We also discover that a `Times` value may denote actual class meeting times (a set of days of the week, a starting time, and an ending time), or it may be empty. (Again, the schedule data for a class allows for an optional second value, to handle assorted special cases.)

Knowing all this, we can begin to develop the routine, by writing out the intended function in more detail, by cases. We will make this the routine that determines which combinations of instructors and times actually need to be checked for conflicts; we plan to do the actual checking in another routine called by this one. Here is how the breakdown of cases might be done:

```
[ who1 and when1 are nonempty →
        return the record of some class in instructor_schedules
        which has a conflict with any of the given instructors and times,
        or NULL if there is none ]
char *instructor_conflict_with(Instructor who1, Instructor who2,
                               Times when1, Times when2)
{
        [ who1 not "Staff" and schedule of who1 conflicts with when1
                → return some conflicting record
        | who1 not "Staff" and when2 nonempty and
                        schedule of who1 conflicts with when2
                → return some conflicting record
        | who2 nonempty and not "Staff" and
                        schedule of who2 conflicts with when1
                → return some conflicting record
        | who2 nonempty and not "Staff" and when2 nonempty and
                        schedule of who2 conflicts with when2
                → return some conflicting record
        | else → return NULL ]
}
```

We could begin writing the code for the routine directly from this, but we might prefer to prepare for this by doing one more small step in the development of the logic. We notice that common parts of the preconditions can be factored out (so to speak) in a couple of places, so it might make sense to break the intended function into pieces accordingly.

Our approach will be to find a conflict with *who*1 if there is one; then, if not, to find a conflict with *who*2 if there is one. We use an incidental variable, which is initialized to NULL. Each test sets this variable to a conflicting record if a conflict is found and leaves its value NULL otherwise.

To represent the testing steps, we can use a notational technique that has not been presented before now: nested conditional concurrent assignments. These are very much like nested if-statements in code. Essentially, we allow a conditional concurrent assignment to appear within another conditional concurrent assignment, where the assignment part would otherwise appear. Nested conditionals in intended functions can be obscure and clumsy to manipulate, so some programmers avoid them, but for some purposes they are ideal.

Here is the intended function for the routine body, rewritten as a sequence of steps, two of which are nested conditionals:

```
char *conflicting_record = NULL;
```

[*who*1 not "Staff" →
    [schedule of *who*1 conflicts with *when*1
        → conflicting_record := some conflicting record
    | *when*2 nonempty and schedule of *who*1 conflicts with *when*2
        → conflicting_record := some conflicting record
    | *else* → *I*]
| *else* → *I*]

[conflicting_record = NULL and *who*2 nonempty and not "Staff" →
    [schedule of *who*2 conflicts with *when*1
        → conflicting_record := some conflicting record
    | *when*2 nonempty and schedule of *who*2 conflicts with *when*2
        → conflicting_record := some conflicting record
    | *else* → *I*]
| *else* → *I*]

```
return conflicting_record;
```

Reasoning by cases, we can verify that the two intended functions are equivalent.

Now we implement the conditionals in the specification with if-statements having the same structure. In the process, we can rewrite the inner conditionals so that the tests for conflicts are done in sequence. Also, in anticipation of the next step of the development, we rewrite the *else* → *I* cases to show *conflicting_record* being (redundantly) set to NULL. In this form, the routine body appears as shown in Figure 5.7.

In this code, three predicates (Boolean-valued functions) are used to determine properties of Instructor and Times values. They are is_Staff, is_empty_Times, and is_empty_Instructor, and they have the obvious meanings: !is_Staff(who1) means that *who*1 is not 'Staff' , and so on (! is the negation operator in C). Their implementations are defined where the corresponding data types are defined, but we do not need to see the implementations

```
char *conflicting_record = NULL;

if (!is_Staff(who1))
    {
```
[schedule of *who*1 conflicts with *when*1
    → conflicting_record := some conflicting record
| *else* → conflicting_record := NULL]
;
```
        if (conflicting_record == NULL && !is_empty_Times(when2))
```
    [schedule of *who*1 conflicts with *when*2
        → conflicting_record := some conflicting record
    | *else* → conflicting_record := NULL]
```
    }

if (conflicting_record == NULL &&
        !is_empty_Instructor(who2) && !is_Staff(who2))
    {
```
[schedule of *who*2 conflicts with *when*1
    → conflicting_record := some conflicting record
| *else* → conflicting_record := NULL]
;
```
        if (conflicting_record == NULL && !is_empty_Times(when2))
```
    [schedule of *who*2 conflicts with *when*2
        → conflicting_record := some conflicting record
    | *else* → conflicting_record := NULL]
```
    }

return conflicting_record;
```

Figure 5.7 The body of the instructor-conflicts routine

to verify this step of the development; we simply need to use the meanings of the predicates. The verification is straightforward.

There are four intended functions that still must be implemented, and they all have the same form. The obvious thing to do is to use another routine, called in these four places, to implement them. In fact, this was our plan all along.

Since the program will also need to check schedules of classrooms for conflicts, we can use the same routine for that purpose too. Instructor schedules and classroom schedules will be kept in separate structures, called `instructor_schedules` and `room_schedules` respectively, and the appropriate schedule will be passed as a parameter to the routine. Accordingly, we can write the specification for this routine as follows:

> [*key* is an appropriate key for *sched* →
>   return the record of some class in *sched*[*key*] which has
>   a conflict with *when*, or NULL if there is none]
> conflict_with(Week_schedules sched, Key key, Times when)

In the intended function, the precondition is the kind of type information discussed in the previous section. The concept "appropriate key" is defined elsewhere; all we need to know here is that an Instructor (which is apparently a special case of the type Key) is an appropriate key for instructor_schedules.

Actually, now that we have added nested conditionals to our notation for intended functions, we can write the intended function for conflict_with so that it more closely matches the form that we are expecting. We leave the precondition as it is, but we rewrite the phrase "return ..." as an explicit conditional. Here is the result:

> [*key* is an appropriate key for *sched* →
>   [some class in *sched*[*key*] has a conflict with *when* →
>   return the record of some such class
> | *else* → return NULL]]
> conflict_with(Week_schedules sched, Key key, Times when)

With this definition, we can implement each of the inner conditional assignments as a call to conflict_with. For example, the first of the inner conditionals will be implemented like this:

> [schedule of *who*1 conflicts with *when*1
>   → conflicting_record := some conflicting record
> | *else* → conflicting_record := NULL]
> conflicting_record =
>   conflict_with(instructor_schedules, who1, when1);

The verification of each of these is performed, as usual, by comparing the intended function on the call with the intended function on the routine definition, after substituting for the arguments and returned value in the appropriate places.

The final routine might be as shown in Figure 5.8. This time, only the final source code is shown. The intermediate forms of the intended function for the body are omitted, since they are now rather redundant.

The important thing to notice in this example is that we have done the entire development using high-level abstractions, without having to make any use at all of the details of their implementations. In the specifications, we used the English phrases "is 'Staff' ", "is empty", and "conflict". In some places we needed to think about their meaning, but in other places we manipulated these as if they were mathematical constructs, merely copying and comparing them from one place to another. In other words, we used them as "formal" terms, in the sense that we made use only of their form and not their meaning. The corresponding constructs

```
/*--------------------------------------------------------------
|
|       instructor_conflict_with(who1, who2, when1, when2):
|           [ who1 and when1 are nonempty ->
|               return the record of some class in
|               instructor_schedules which has a conflict
|               with any of the given instructors and times,
|               or NULL if there is none ]
|
+--------------------------------------------------------------*/
char *instructor_conflict_with(Instructor who1, Instructor who2,
                               Times when1, Times when2)
{
    /* [ who1 not "Staff" and
                schedule of who1 conflicts with when1
            -> return some conflicting record
       | who1 not "Staff" and when2 nonempty and
                schedule of who1 conflicts with when2
            -> return some conflicting record
       | who2 nonempty and not "Staff" and
                schedule of who2 conflicts with when1
            -> return some conflicting record
       | who2 nonempty and not "Staff" and when2 nonempty and
                schedule of who2 conflicts with when2
            -> return some conflicting record
       | else -> return NULL ] */

    char *conflicting_record = NULL;
    if (!is_Staff(who1)) {
        conflicting_record =
            conflict_with(instructor_schedules, who1, when1);
        if (conflicting_record == NULL && !is_empty_Times(when2))
            conflicting_record =
                conflict_with(instructor_schedules, who1, when2);
    }
    if (conflicting_record == NULL &&
            !is_empty_Instructor(who2) && !is_Staff(who2)) {
        conflicting_record =
            conflict_with(instructor_schedules, who2, when1);
        if (conflicting_record == NULL && !is_empty_Times(when2))
            conflicting_record =
                conflict_with(instructor_schedules, who2, when2);
    }
    return conflicting_record;
}
```

Figure 5.8 The source code for the instructor-conflicts routine

in the code were `is_Staff`, `is_empty_Times`, `is_empty_Instructor`, and `conflict_with`, and we used these abstractly in similar ways.

Proceeding in this way, and creating abstractions and terminology as needed for the problem at hand, we can use our techniques of specification and verification at all levels of programs of all sizes. In other words, this is how to make our techniques "scale up".

5.5   Keeping Things Simple

Sooner or later we will need to face the problem of intended functions that get too long and complicated to be manageable. You may have noticed that some of the intended functions in the previous examples are already rather long and complicated. Look in particular at this intended function from the example of the registrar's program, in the previous section:

> [*who*1 not "Staff" and schedule of *who*1 conflicts with *when*1
>   → return some conflicting record
> | *who*1 not "Staff" and *when*2 nonempty and
>   schedule of *who*1 conflicts with *when*2
>   → return some conflicting record
> | *who*2 nonempty and not "Staff" and
>   schedule of *who*2 conflicts with *when*1
>   → return some conflicting record
> | *who*2 nonempty and not "Staff" and *when*2 nonempty and
>   schedule of *who*2 conflicts with *when*2
>   → return some conflicting record
> | *else* → return NULL]

It is twelve lines long, and this is the specification of a rather short sequence of code. Furthermore, it seems rather tedious and repetitive.

The total quantity of intended functions in some programs may also seem cumbersome and excessive. In some of our examples in this chapter and previous chapters, there have been approximately as many lines of intended functions as lines of code. This is not too unusual in practice. But we have also seen cases in which it takes several lines of intended function to specify one line of code, as in this example from the registrar's program:

> [schedule of *who*1 conflicts with *when*1
>   → conflicting_record := some conflicting record
> | *else* → conflicting_record := NULL]
> conflicting_record =
>   conflict_with(instructor_schedules, who1, when1);

If there are very many lines of code like this in a program, there can easily be twice as many lines of intended functions as lines of code.

What will happen when our programs get larger and more complex than the ones shown in these examples? Will there be five times as many lines of specification as code, or ten times, or a hundred? Will the intended functions grow to be so long and complicated that they are completely unmanageable?

This is a very real danger if we are not careful. In writing intended functions as in many other aspects of programming, keeping things simple is something that requires effort, and the ability to do it is one of the characteristics of a good programmer.

One thing that can help considerably is the use of specification functions, such as *run-length-decoding* in the example of Section 5.3. We saw several other ways of using abstract terms to keep intended functions simple and concise in the routine from the registrar's program in the previous section. Using techniques like these, so that definitions of complex terms are put elsewhere and kept out of the intended functions, certainly helps to keep the length and complexity of intended functions down.

But the use of complex concepts is only one cause of long and complicated intended functions. Two others are quite common: computations that modify many state variables, and specifications that contain many different cases.

In the "lettercount" program of Section 5.2 we saw examples of intended functions that specify changes to several different state variables. Here is one of them, the intended function for the loop that does most of the work:

$$[letters, \quad digits, \quad others, \quad (c \parallel stdin) :=$$
$$\text{number of letters in } stdin,$$
$$\text{number of digits in } stdin,$$
$$\text{number of other characters in } stdin,$$
$$empty]$$

Sometimes, as in this case, we seem to have little choice. To satisfy the specification for the program, we need to count all three kinds of characters. It makes sense to count them all at the same time, while reading the input. Any other design would be more complicated and much less efficient.

Apparently, the person who wrote the specification for this program wants to see all three counts. However, if we could question this person, we might find that, in any given run, the user will actually need only one of the counts, and the other counts will be ignored. Or we might find that the user will never really need anything but the count of letters, and that printing the other counts is a feature that is not really needed at all. Then we might be able to argue that it would be better to revise the requirements for the program and rewrite the intended functions accordingly. These issues are hardly worth discussing for a program this small and simple, but in a larger program this sort of simplification of requirements might be worth many hours or days of negotiation. In this case, as far as we know, we are stuck with this specification for the program, and it is the direct cause of some of the unavoidable complexity of the program's intended functions.

But suppose that a computation like this were inside a larger program, so that (for example) we had to count letters, digits, and other characters in the contents of a string variable s. We might design the computation to use a loop like the one in the "lettercount" program that counted all three kinds of characters at once and modified a number of global variables, as in the above intended function. However, we might choose to organize the program quite differently: we might decide that it would be better to use a routine that only returns the number of letters in a string, and other routines to count the other kinds of characters. We might sacrifice a small amount of efficiency with this approach, but each intended function would be short and simple enough to comprehend at a glance:

$$[\textit{letters} := \text{the number of letters in } s]$$

A critical aspect of a program's organization is the way that it is broken up into major pieces. These pieces may be abstract data types or *modules* or *objects*, in programming languages that support such constructs; we will discuss such things in Chapter 8. For now, let us assume that we are talking about the routines of the program.

All other things being equal, a routine that does only one job is usually easier to work with than a routine that does several related jobs. We often say that its interface with the rest of the program is *cleaner*. It is easier to understand informally. It is easier to reuse in a different context, and is likely to be easier to modify slightly if this should be necessary in the future. But, in all of these ways, a routine that does several related jobs is better than a routine that does several completely unrelated jobs! A good programmer will seldom consider writing a routine of that kind.

To judge whether a routine really does only one job rather than several, we can ask the following question: Can we describe informally what the routine does in one short phrase or sentence, without using the word *and*? If not, perhaps it is really doing several jobs, and we might consider dividing it into several routines.

More concretely, a routine that changes the value of only one state variable, or returns only one value, is easier to work with than a routine that changes the values of many state variables. Similarly, a routine that has many parameters is likely to be more difficult to work with than a routine that has only one or two.

Now that we are programming with intended functions, we have another indicator of how clean a program is — the length and complexity of the intended functions in it. As we try to write intended functions for routines and other sections of code, we are likely to notice something very important: that the sections that we consider cleanest tend to be the ones that have the shortest and simplest intended functions. This suggests that, if we start to notice that our intended functions are becoming excessively long and complicated in places, the problem might be in the way we have broken our program into routines or other major pieces. Then we might want to consider how we might reorganize the program, to break it into pieces in a cleaner way and make the interfaces among these pieces simpler.

For example, let us return to the case in which the complexity is caused by computations that modify many state variables. It may be that this is necessary to achieve the computation that we want, but we often have a choice as to how and where to do it. Perhaps we can make some variables local to one routine, so that the changes in their values are not reflected in intended functions outside of this routine. Or perhaps we can group several related variables into a data structure, so that most of the program passes around and manipulates the structure as an indivisible whole; then most intended functions will not need to specify what happens to the individual components of the structure.

What about specifications containing many different cases? We can often deal with them in a similar way. Let us look again at the big intended function from the registrar's program, including more of the context this time:

```
[ who1 and when1 are nonempty →
        return the record of some class in instructor_schedules
        which has a conflict with any of the given instructors and times,
        or NULL if there is none ]
char *instructor_conflict_with(Instructor who1, Instructor who2,
                               Times when1, Times when2)
{
        [ who1 not "Staff" and schedule of who1 conflicts with when1
              → return some conflicting record
        | who1 not "Staff" and when2 nonempty and
                    schedule of who1 conflicts with when2
              → return some conflicting record
        | who2 nonempty and not "Staff" and
                    schedule of who2 conflicts with when1
              → return some conflicting record
        | who2 nonempty and not "Staff" and when2 nonempty and
                    schedule of who2 conflicts with when2
              → return some conflicting record
        | else → return NULL ]
        char *conflicting_record = NULL;
        if (!is_Staff(who1))
            ...
}
```

Notice that the routine's overall intended function is not broken down by cases, but is phrased in a way that covers all cases. The breakdown into cases is confined to the inside of the routine. This simplifies the intended function on any call to the routine.

Also notice that the outermost intended function that is broken down by cases is the one attached to the part of the code that handles the different cases separately. We have avoided the detailed breakdown by cases in most places in the program, expressing it in the intended functions only where we need to consider each case separately. This is a strategy that often helps to reduce the overall quantity of intended functions.

In situations like this we usually cannot get rid of the complexity entirely. In the registrar's program, for example, we really must check for each kind of conflict. This is an externally imposed requirement: the program would be useless to the registrar otherwise. What we can do is to limit the scope and visibility of the complexity, so that in most places in the program it doesn't affect us.

In any case, the main point of this section is that if we find our intended functions becoming excessively long and complicated, it may be that the program's computation really needs to be complex for reasons outside our control. But it may be an indication that we have not found the most concise way to write the intended functions, or it may be an indication that the design of the program is not as clean as it should be. In either of the latter cases, rewriting may help.

Exercises

1. The following are some possible programming assignments; your instructor can suggest others. In each case, the assignment is to develop and verify the routine or program, starting with an appropriate intended function. Your instructor may specify a programming language; if not, make your own choice.

    a. A program that converts each tab character in the input to the appropriate number of space characters. (This is what the Unix utility expand does.) Assume that tab stops are at every n columns, numbering the columns in a line from 0, and that the effect of a tab character is to insert between 1 and n space characters to reach the nearest tab stop forward. If a main program can take a parameter in your programming language, make n a parameter; otherwise, define n as a constant in the program.

    b. A program that fills in a form with lines from the input. The form is read from a file. Wherever the form contains an instance of the character sequence XX, a line from the input is inserted in its place. (Only the contents of the line are inserted, not the line break at the end of it!)

      As a variation, instead of XX, let the character sequence to be replaced be an arbitrary nonempty string. Make this string a parameter of the program if possible, as in the previous assignment.

c. A program similar to the "lettercount" program of Section 5.2, which counts characters, words, and lines in the input. (This is what the Unix utility wc does.) Be sure to define carefully what you mean by *word*. Depending on your programming language and operating system, you may also need to define what you mean by *line*.

d. A version of the uncompress procedure of Section 5.3, in which the argument is not necessarily a correctly encoded string. Choose what you think is a sensible way to specify the handling of any error conditions.

e. A compression routine that is the inverse of the uncompress procedure. Sequences of three or fewer identical characters should be left unchanged, since there is no gain in compressing them. For RunLengthCharacter, choose a character that is likely to be infrequent in the input. Where RunLengthCharacter does appear in the input, it can be encoded as a sequence of length one: RunLengthCharacter, followed by RunLengthCharacter, followed by the character whose coding is one. (As a refinement, sequences of RunLengthCharacter of any length, including those of two or three characters, can be encoded just like longer sequences.) Notice that there is a maximum number of characters that can be represented in a single run-length sequence!

2. For one or more of the routines and programs that you developed for Exercise 1, choose a classmate or find another friend who understands functional specification and verification. Together with that person, go over all of the steps of the verification again. Don't be surprised if you find a few mistakes. If there are any, are they mistakes in the specification, bugs in the code, or some combination of these? Why do you think that you did not notice them when you verified the code by yourself?

3. Compile your solutions to Exercise 1. (Where these are isolated routines, write simple driver programs.) Test each program thoroughly. Did you find any bugs? Why do you think that these bugs remained even after the programs had been verified? Did it help to have your verifications checked by another person (Exercise 2)? For the programs that were checked in this way, were there fewer bugs found in testing? What percentage of the bugs were detected by checking the verification, and what percentage by testing?

4. For the programs that you wrote with intended functions (Exercise 1) and tested (Exercise 3), count the total number of bugs that you found in verification and testing. How does this compare with the number of bugs that you usually find in programs of this size, written the way you used to write programs? Do you think that programming with intended functions helps you to avoid making mistakes as you write the code?

5. Can you see any way to simplify the intended functions or code of the routines in Sections 5.3 and 5.4? In each case, think of what the rest of the program must look like, and be sure that your changes don't just shift the complexity to some other part of the program!

Notes

The Cleanroom method includes a notation called *box structures* [Mill87b], [Mill88b] for stepwise refinement of programs; box structures will be introduced briefly in Chapter 12. A programming textbook based on box structures is [Mill86]. However, my students and I have obtained good results without using box structures, developing programs by ordinary stepwise refinement as shown in this chapter.

Good reference manuals for the Pascal, C, and Icon programming languages are [Coop83], [Kern88], and [Gris90] respectively.

Run-length encoding is covered thoroughly in [Held91], along with many other data-compression techniques.

Two helpful qualitative indicators of the quality of a program's organization are the cohesion of modules and the coupling between modules. Cohesion (also sometimes called strength or binding) is a categorization of a module according to whether it does one job or several, and how closely the jobs are related in the latter case; high cohesion is generally good. Coupling is a similar classification according to the kinds of interfaces and interactions among modules; strong coupling is generally bad. These notions were introduced in [Stev74], and appear more fully developed in books by Myers (see, for example, [Myer76] Chapter 6). They are also presented in many software engineering textbooks (see, for example, [Pfle87] pp. 143–149 or [Scha90] pp. 219–233.)

Brooks, in [Broo87], distinguishes two reasons why building software is hard: its essence and its accidents. The essence is the software's inherent complexity, caused largely by externally imposed requirements and the complexity of the interfaces to which the software must conform. The accidents are the current limitations of our programming languages, programming environments, programming techniques, and other technology for representing and building our software. Brooks concludes that the essence is the hardest part, and therefore that building software will always be hard.

6

Verification Reviews

6.1   Why Verification Reviews Are Necessary

In this section I will argue that verification by a single programmer is not good enough, and that programs should be verified by groups of people, in verification review meetings.

You will recall the following statement, from the first chapter:

The purpose of verification is to eliminate defects.

From this point of view, verification is (paradoxically) most useful when it fails; that is, when someone attempting to verify some part of a program finds that the code is, in fact, not correct with respect to its intended function. When this happens, the verifier concludes that something is wrong: there is a mistake either in the code or in the intended function. Then, of course, the mistake is found and corrected. Any bugs found and removed in this way are bugs that do not need to be caught later by testing and debugging, and that cannot survive to cause malfunctions when the program is used.

We have seen how the author of a program can verify each part of the program as it is written. Programmers who do this often discover many defects in their own programs while attempting the verification. Unfortunately, we find in practice that programs that the programmer has verified can still contain defects.

Why? Because programmers are human. We make mistakes in verification just as we do in writing programs. We make unjustified assumptions; we forget the details of how our programming languages work; we hurry through dubious parts of the program's logic that need to be thought out more carefully. Worst of all, we tend to make the same mistakes in reasoning when we verify a program as we did when we wrote it. As a result, we often "verify" programs that are incorrect.

The way to find defects more reliably is with the help of other people. Someone else can look at my work with fresh eyes, and will be less likely to follow exactly the same line of thinking as I did. As a result, that person will often spot defects that I have overlooked.

Good programmers have known this for years. They do not hesitate to ask colleagues to look over their work. In fact, some programmers do this as a matter of routine; they would not think of releasing a piece of code that had not been thoroughly inspected by at least one other person.

In many software organizations, formal code inspections are a key part of the development process. In a code inspection, the code is examined by a group of programmers in an organized meeting. The author of the code is part of the group, but the author's colleagues do much of the work in reading the code, asking questions, and making note of any defects found.

Inspections can also be done on designs, documentation, and other products of the software development process, and can help improve the quality of all of them. Furthermore, inspections help members of the development team become familiar with the code and other products that are inspected, and this is very useful in itself. Software inspections have proved to be quite effective, and are now a well-established part of software engineering practice.

One of the great insights of Harlan Mills and his colleagues, the developers of the Cleanroom method, is that a similar group process might be the most effective way to verify programs. They found that this is indeed the case: verification reviews, conducted in organized meetings as a group process, can detect almost all of the defects in a piece of software.

6.2   Verification Reviews in the Cleanroom Process

In the Cleanroom software development process, verification, not testing and debugging, is the most important weapon against defects. Testing is an important part of the process, as we will see in Chapter 10, but it is done only after verification has been successfully completed. Furthermore, it is done primarily to measure quality, and only secondarily to find defects that escaped detection during verification.

Competent Cleanroom teams find they can detect most or all defects in their verification reviews. In fact, verification reviews are so successful at uncovering defects that they eliminate the need for *unit testing*, or testing of individual routines and modules, by the programmer. Unit testing turns out to be a rather unreliable way of detecting defects anyway, so verification reviews are a better use of a programmer's time than unit testing.

In the usual Cleanroom protocol, a review team verifies a piece of software before it has ever been tested or even executed. As soon as the verification succeeds, the team passes the software on to an independent testing group, which integrates it into the software system being constructed and tests the system as a whole. Thus, the first testing that the software receives is *integration testing*. This means that, typically, Cleanroom programmers do not test their programs at all!

In fact, in the strictest form of the Cleanroom process, a program is verified in a review meeting before it has even been compiled for the first time. This is not the universal rule: some practitioners prefer to try to compile the program first, so that they can find all the syntax errors and remove them before the review. They argue that this gives the reviewers a cleaner product to work with, and that in any case a compiler is better at detecting syntax errors than people are. I would argue, however, that if a program has been carefully written, it will contain few, if any, syntax errors; and that if members of a verification review team inspect a program carefully, they will spot most, if not all, of the syntax errors that it may contain. I like to use the number of syntax errors remaining after the verification review, and detected by the compiler after that, as a rough measure of how carefully the programming and verification were done. In Chapter 11 we will see more about how such statistics can be used to measure the quality of the software development process.

6.3   How Verification Reviews Are Done

In this section I will describe how a program is verified in review meetings, as a group process.

The participants are typically chosen from the team of people that is developing the program. One of the participants is the author of the code being verified. A reasonable number of people is three to eight. If the development team is no larger than this, everyone should attend if possible. Especially, novices to the verification process should be encouraged to attend, even if they do not participate, because this will help to train them for future reviewing assignments.

A time should be scheduled for the review meeting. It is probably best to attempt to verify no more than a few pages of program in one meeting, to limit the amount of work that needs to be discarded or redone if major problems are found in the program, and to keep the meeting reasonably short. This much work can probably be done in about an hour if all goes well, but the participants should be prepared to take more time than this if necessary.

The author of the code should give copies of the code to be verified, complete with intended functions, to all participants in advance. The author should also include any other documentation that the participants will need to understand the intended functions and code. This is so the participants can become familiar with the material in general terms before the meeting; they are not expected to inspect the code in any detail, or attempt to verify it themselves.

The author leads the meeting. After a brief overview of the program (if the other team members need it), the leader directs the team's attention to each part of the program in turn and leads the team through the verification of each part, answering questions and clarifying complicated points if necessary. It is the leader's responsibility to keep the discussions on track and to make sure that every correctness question is answered.

In answering each correctness question, the leader and the other team members use as much mathematical rigor and formalism as is necessary, and no more. Many correctness questions can be answered immediately, "by inspection". For others, the leader may construct trace tables, draw diagrams, or work through steps of the proof. Most proofs are no more formal or detailed than the ones you have seen in earlier chapters of this book, and many are much less so. It is not necessary to belabor obvious points or to prove every point with detailed symbol manipulation right down to the level of mathematical axioms. Furthermore, it is not desirable: it wastes the team's valuable time, and if the verification becomes tedious, the team members may lose interest and their concentration may suffer.

The leader's most important job is to make sure that every member of the reviewing team understands each step of the verification and agrees that it is correct (or points out that it is not). In other forms of software inspection, the leader may ask questions such as "Does anyone see anything wrong?" The problem with this wording is that a team member who is not paying attention, or who doesn't understand the issue, will not respond. In verification reviews, the leader must be careful to phrase the question as "Does everyone agree that this is correct?" This presses each team member to understand each issue and consider it carefully.

The team does not consider a verification condition proved until the slowest person to respond has expressed agreement. It is important to resist the temptation to take short cuts here. The other team members may be tempted to rush ahead, but often the last person to speak is thinking about some issue more carefully and discovers an error that the others have overlooked.

The spirit of a properly conducted review meeting is positive and cooperative. The verification activity itself helps to contribute to this. Even though the purpose of doing the verification is to detect errors, what the team is doing while verifying is trying to prove correctness, not looking for errors. Most parts of the program will contain no errors, and the team will succeed in verifying these parts. Thus, the team is constantly receiving positive reinforcement, so spirits are likely to remain high even when the occasional error is found.

As the team members read the program and verify its correctness, they should also be inspecting the program for other attributes of quality: efficiency, simplicity, clarity, generality, portability, and so on. At any time during the review, any team member can raise questions and make suggestions for improvement of any aspect of the program. Valuable new ideas will often emerge from the team's discussion. The team's goal should always be to produce the best program possible: a program that (for example) can be verified with difficulty, but is more complicated than it needs to be, is not good enough.

Someone in the team should be designated the recorder; this can be the leader, but some teams prefer to assign this job to another member. The recorder notes defects and suggestions for improvement. Where the group agrees that only minor changes are necessary, they can be made immediately, and the review can continue. If major problems are found or if substantial revision appears necessary, the review process is stopped so that the team does not waste time verifying parts of the program that will be changed anyway. The program is sent back to its author for rework. In a later meeting the team will reverify the parts that were changed.

Occasionally the team will find that the verification cannot be completed because intended functions in the program are not adequate. Some critical intended functions may be missing, or the functions may be unclear or ambiguous. Again, if this happens, the review is stopped and the program is sent back to its author for rework. Fortunately, after an author has had some experience with specification and verification, this rarely happens.

Defects are recorded only for the purpose of correcting them. In no way should the recorder's notes be used to evaluate the author's work, as tempting as it may be for managers to use this "free data" for this purpose. This can only change the team's behavior for the worse. Programmers will become defensive and waste time defending themselves in the meetings; they will try to resist any suggestions that their solutions are not the best possible; they will treat their fellow team members as adversaries rather than as friends who are helping them to produce the best work possible.

Besides, the program is not yet a final product, ready to be judged, until all defects have been corrected and it has been successfully verified. What the programmer brings to the review meeting is a draft. It is not a first draft: the programmer should work hard to prepare a product that is as polished and professional as possible. If all goes well in the review, it is perhaps a next-to-last draft. But it is still work in progress, subject to revision and improvement.

The team members must keep in mind that once a program is brought to them for verification, it becomes a collective effort, and each of them shares responsibility for its quality from then on. The whole team, not just the author, must share the blame for any defects that escape detection in the verification review. On the other hand, the whole team should feel that all of them, not just the author, "own" the final product and share in the credit if it is eventually successful.

6.4   Example: Another Routine from the Registrar's Program

This section and the next will present transcripts of what might happen in typical verification review meetings. The transcripts are fictitious, but the routines shown in the examples are adapted from routines in actual application programs. The verification in this section will be quite simple; in the next section we will see what might happen when the verification is a bit harder.

The program in the first example is the registrar's program that we saw in Section 5.4. The code to be verified is another routine from that program.

The team members are Alice, Ben, and Chris; Alice is the author of this routine. Each person has a printed copy of the program listing, with line numbers, as shown in Figure 6.1.

Alice: This shouldn't take too long; the routine is pretty simple. It just encodes a day and a time into an integer in an obvious way.

Ben: Wait a minute. The header says that it returns a `Time_of_week`. Is that actually an integer?

Chris: Let's look at the declaration file to be sure. Yes, here it is.

```
typedef int Time_of_week;
  /* The representation is in minutes from the start of Monday.
     Even if all seven days are represented, the maximum value
     is 7*24*60 - 1 = 10079, which easily fits in a 16-bit
     integer.  We assume that an int is at least that long. */
```

Ben: OK, thanks.

Alice: So, can we verify the top-level sequence of steps? That's the composition of the intended functions on lines 14 and 18.

Chris: The precondition of the function on line 14 is right out of the precondition on the overall function, so we know it's satisfied.

Ben: So d gets the number of days since Monday. Is that what `day_number` gives us?

Alice: We'll check that in a minute. Let's finish verifying the top level first.

```
 1      /*------------------------------------------------------------+
 2      |
 3      |    make_time_of_week(day, time):
 4      |       [ day is in {'M','T','W','R','F','S','U'}
 5      |            and time is a string, representing a time,
 6      |            in the range "000" .. "2359" ->
 7      |                  return an encoding of <day,time> as
 8      |                      minutes from the start of Monday ]
 9      |
10      +------------------------------------------------------------*/
11
12      Time_of_week make_time_of_week(char day, char *time)
13      {
14          /* [ day is in {'M','T','W','R','F','S','U'} ->
15                  d := number of days between day and Monday ] */
16          int d = day_number(day);
17
18          /* [ 0 <= d <= 6 and time is in the range "0" .. "2359"
19                  -> return d*24*60 + (hours part of time)*60
20                          + (minutes part of time) ] */
21          int time_as_int = atoi(time);
22          int hour   = time_as_int / 100;
23          int minute = time_as_int % 100;
24          return
25              d*1440 + hour*60 + minute;
26      }
```

Figure 6.1 A small routine from the registrar's program

Ben: Right, sorry.

Alice: That number is between 0 and 6, so with that and the precondition at the top, the precondition on line 18 is satisfied. So we return the number of days times the number of minutes in a day, plus the number of hours times the number of minutes in an hour, plus the number of minutes.

Ben: That looks right.

Chris: Yes.

Alice: Now let's verify the first step, starting on line 14.

Ben: Now we can look at what day_number does. What function does it compute — is it the one we need?

Alice: It had better be! I just copied its intended function to line 14 here, and edited it to fit in the context.

Chris: Yes, here it is. (They look at another part of the code.)

```
/*-----------------------------------------------------------+
|                                                            |
|     day_number(day):                                       |
|         [ day is in {'M','T','W','R','F','S','U'} ->       |
|             return number of days between day and Monday   |
|         | else -> return -1 ]                              |
|                                                            |
+---------------------------------------------------------*/

int day_number(char day)
```

Alice: I didn't even need to change the argument name, since it's the same in both routines. I did remove the else-case of the conditional, since it doesn't apply here.

Chris: Yes, that matches. Can we consider this verified?

Ben: Sure.

Alice: Good. Now what about the second step? That's line 18 to the end.

Ben: On line 21, atoi converts a string to an integer, right? And then you take off the last two digits, and they are the minutes part! That's clever.

Alice: Well, the real reason I did it that way is that atoi does the messy part for me. And I get the same result whether 9:30 is represented as 930 or 0930. The code turned out to be a lot simpler this way.

Chris: That's always a good thing!

Alice: So let's check that lines 21 through 23 correctly compute hour and minute.

Chris: Do we need to look at the documentation of atoi?

Ben: No, I use it all the time. That's what it does. Lines 21 through 23 look good to me.

Chris: I agree.

Alice: Now, on line 25, do we return the right value?

Ben: Yes.

Alice: (after a pause) Chris?

Chris: I was just multiplying out 24 and 60. Yes, 1440 is right, and the rest is obviously right.

Alice: So we're done! Thanks.

6.5 Example: A Routine from a Test-data Generator

In this session, our team is verifying a routine from a program that generates test data for use in testing other programs, according to a specification taken from the input. Again, the participants are Alice, Ben, and Chris; this time Chris is the author. The program listing is shown in Figure 6.2. Again, the language is C.

Chris: This is the routine that actually makes the random choices as output is being generated.

Alice: I'm not sure I remember exactly what a cumulative-probability list is. Let's get the documentation before we start.

Chris: OK, here it is. (See Figure 6.3.)

Alice: Thanks.

Chris: (after a few moments) Do we all understand the overall intended function now?

Alice: Yes, that helps.

Ben: Yes.

Chris: Good. Now, the body of the routine is just the sequence of the function on lines 14 to 17, which gives a value to the variable `result`, followed by the statement that returns that value, on line 34.

Ben: That looks correct.

Alice: Yes, if there is only one choice in the list, that one must be the result, so the function on line 14 looks a lot like the intended function for the routine.

Chris: In fact, it's really the same thing, when you follow it with the return statement.

Alice: That's right.

Ben: Right.

```
 1          /*-----------------------------------------------------------
 2          |
 3          |    choose(L):
 4          |        [ L is a cumulative-probability list ->
 5          |            return a choice from L, chosen randomly
 6          |            according to probabilities of the choices ]
 7          |
 8          +---------------------------------------------------------*/
 9
10     symbol_list choose(choice_list L)
11     {
12       symbol_list result;
13
14       /* [ only one choice in L -> result := that choice
15          | more than one choice in L ->
16                 result := one of them, chosen at random
17                    according to probabilities of the choices ] */
18       if (L->rest == NULL)
19         result = L->symbols;
20       else
21         {
22           /* [ ran := a uniform random number in [0,1) ] */
23           float ran = rand01();
24
25           /* [ chs := pointer to first node in L
26                       such that prob >= ran ] */
27           choice_list chs = L;
28           while (chs != NULL && chs->prob < ran)
29             chs = chs->next;
30
31           result = chs->symbols;
32         }
33
34       return result;
35     }
```

Figure 6.2 The source listing for the routine "choose"

Chris: Oh, by the way, notice that "L is a cumulative-probability list" is really a precondition of the function on line 14 too. That's how we know that L is nonempty, so that the function is always defined. I really should have written it there explicitly.

Alice: No, I would call that type information, so it should apply everywhere in the routine. I don't think you need to repeat it everywhere.

```
/*------------------------------------------------------------------
 |
 |   data type: choice_list
 |       A choice_list is a linear linked list of choices.
 |       A choice is a list of symbols and a probability
 |           of being chosen.
 |
 |       Provides:
 |
 |           -> symbol_list symbols     -- the list of symbols
 |           -> float prob              -- the probability
 |           -> choice_list next        -- list pointer
 */

     typedef struct choice_list_node {
         symbol_list symbols;
         float prob;
         struct choice_list_node *next;
         } *
     choice_list;

/*
 |
 +---------------------------------------------------------------*/

/*

     Definitions, for use in intended functions:

     A raw-probability list is a nonempty choice-list in which
     the prob field in each node is the probability that that
     node should be chosen. The sum of the probabilities is 1.0,
     within some roundoff error.

     A cumulative-probability list is a nonempty choice-list in
     which the prob field in each node is the cumulative probability
     of that node and its predecessors; in other words, the sum of
     the probabilities to and including that node in the
     corresponding raw-probability list.  As a special case, the
     prob field of the last node is exactly 1.0, to avoid problems
     with roundoff errors.
 */
```

Figure 6.3 Declarations and documentation for the probability lists

Ben: That's OK with me. Besides, we can see that L doesn't change.

Chris: OK, so that sequence is verified, right? (The others nod.) Now let's move on to the function on line 14 and its code. The breakdown of cases is the same in the if-statement as it is in the intended function.

Alice: Right, the expression (L->next == NULL) is the way to test whether L has only one node in it.

Ben: And L->symbols is the field we want in that case? Let me look at the declarations ... yes, that's correct.

Chris: So that takes care of everything but the else-part, right? (The others nod.) So let's look at that.

Alice: It doesn't have an intended function. I assume that you want it to be the same as the assignment on lines 16 and 17.

Chris: Yes, sorry.

Ben: No problem, we can see it.

Alice: OK, so the composition of those three steps should do what lines 16 and 17 say .... I'm having trouble seeing what's happening here.

Ben: Yes, so am I.

Chris: Well, first we take a random number ....

Alice: Yes, but then why does the function on line 25 do what we want?

Chris: The probabilities are cumulative, right? So if ran was greater than the prob field for each previous node but less than or equal for the one we want ... the probability of that is proportional to the raw probability.

Alice: Ah, I think I see.

Ben: Sorry, I'm afraid I still don't.

Chris: That's OK. Here, let me draw a picture.

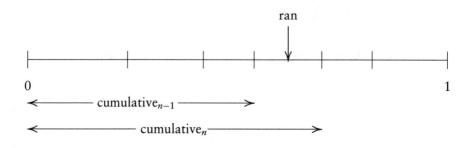

Chris: Here's the interval between 0 and 1 divided up into the raw probabilities, and ran is somewhere in that range. Suppose chs is pointing at node *n* in the list. If we get this far, the cumulative probability for node *n* − 1 is less than ran, right? So the probability that the cumulative probability for node *n* is greater than or equal to ran is proportional to this distance (pointing), which is the raw probability for node *n*.

Ben: And so we select a node with probability equal to the raw probability that we had for it. OK, I see now. Thanks. Yes, it looks right.

Chris: So is the composition good?

Ben: Yes.

Alice: Yes.

Chris: Good. Now let's verify each of those steps. First, the call to rand01.

Ben: Let's look at its documentation to be sure ... yes, it does what the intended function says.

Alice: Right.

Chris: Now the second step, starting on line 25.

Ben: That's an initialized loop. It looks like the intended function on the loop itself is the function on line 25 with chs substituted for L.

Chris: Let me see ... yes, I think so. I really should have written it explicitly.

Alice: That's OK, we can assume that and go ahead. And the loop body can be its own intended function.

Chris: OK. First, termination. It's the usual reason for a list search: chs moves one node down the list at each step, so it eventually reaches the NULL that ends the list, if the loop hasn't terminated before then.

Ben: Do we know that the list ends with a null pointer?

Alice: Yesterday we verified the list constructor routine, which puts it there.

Chris: Besides, the precondition says that it's a cumulative-probability list, which the documentation says is a linear linked list. Doesn't that term imply that the list is null-terminated?

Ben: Yes, of course. Sure, the loop terminates.

Chris: OK then? (Alice nods.) Right, now the false case. When the loop condition is false, does doing nothing do the right thing? Let's see ... oops, I think I see a problem!

Alice: So do I! If chs is NULL, the condition is false, but then chs doesn't point to what the intended function says!

Chris: I guess I just automatically write a test for NULL in situations like this, but it is definitely wrong this time.

Ben: Wait a minute ... will that ever happen? We know that the list is nonempty and that the last node contains 1. Doesn't that mean that chs->prob < ran will become false when chs points to the last node, if it wasn't false for a previous node, and the loop will terminate then? So chs will never become NULL.

Alice: It looks like we can just remove that part of the condition. Then our termination argument isn't valid any more, but what Ben just said is our new termination argument.

Chris: I'm a bit nervous about that — what about roundoff errors?

Alice: If we can trust rand01 to return a value that is strictly less than 1, there's no problem. We don't do anything that could cause rounding on the value we get before we use it in the comparisons.

Chris: Yes, you're right. So let's make the loop header

```
while (chs->prob < ran)
```

Just cross out chs != NULL &&. (They make the change on their copies.) We just talked about termination ... what about the false case now?

Ben: Now it's OK. When the condition is false, chs points to exactly the node that the intended function specifies.

Alice: Right.

Chris: Good! Does the true case work?

Alice: Yes. If the condition is true, the first node is not the one we want. So we set chs to chs->next and then do the intended function on the loop. It finds the node we want in the list which starts at chs->next, which is equivalent to searching the whole list because the first node is not the one we want. It's the usual pattern of code for a list search.

Chris: Does anyone want to see a trace table?

Ben: No, I can follow the argument without that. It's correct.

Alice: I agree. So we're done!

Ben: One more thing . . . I wonder if this will be efficient enough. After all, it's a linear search, and this will be a frequent operation.

Alice: We could substitute a more efficient algorithm, but that would probably mean changing the data structure. We could probably do it with some kind of a balanced tree instead of a linked list . . . .

Chris: I'm not sure it's necessary. I think that the lists will usually be pretty short in our application.

Ben: Let's not worry about this unless we find that we need to. We can always measure the performance of this routine once we can run the program.

Chris: I'll plan to do that. And I'll make a note of the issue, in the main documentation and in a comment in the code here.

Alice: If you make a change, you'll bring the changed part back for reverification, won't you?

Chris: Of course!

6.6   Discussion of the Examples

As I said, the transcripts in the previous two sections are fictional. However, they are typical of verification reviews that I have seen my students and my colleagues perform.

For formality and rigor, the verification in these examples is definitely toward the informal end of the scale. Many inspections would be somewhat more rigorous than these, making more use of trace tables and written proof steps. However, even when the verification is very informal, the inspection protocol described in Section 6.3 must still be followed, and all correctness questions must be answered for every part of the code.

Alice, Ben and Chris (as I have tried to portray them) are experienced programmers and have worked together for several years. They have been specifying and verifying as a team, using the methods of this book, for several months. They have a good feeling for how much time they need to spend on each step of a proof and how formal they need to be. A team whose members are less experienced or have not worked together very long might want to spend more time on their verifications and be a bit more rigorous and careful.

In the first example (Section 6.4), one of the first things that the team did was to look at the declaration of an important data type, to make sure that they all remembered the relevant details. They did something similar at the beginning of the second example (Section 6.5), when they looked at the declarations and definitions in Figure 6.3. It is very important that all team members understand the meaning of the terms and concepts that they will be talking about, and the best way to do this is often to look at the actual code and documentation.

When the team members were verifying the top-level sequence in the routine from the registrar's program, they should have been looking only at the intended functions on lines 14–15 and 18–20, and calculating (perhaps in their heads) the composition of these two functions. Ben wanted to jump ahead and verify that line 16 really computed the first intended function. Even experienced verifiers can have trouble keeping their attention focused on one small part of the code at a time. Alice was right in immediately bringing Ben back to the topic at hand.

In verifying line 16 against its intended function, the team actually found and read the definition of day_number, rather than rely on their memories of how it was defined. This was exactly what they should have done. Many errors occur in the interfaces between routines, especially in the number, types, and meanings of the arguments. These details should be checked carefully for every statement containing a call.

By the way, a good way to help reduce such errors is to copy the intended function from the routine being called to the place where the call occurs, perhaps by using the cut-and-paste features of a text editor. After editing to change argument names to the actual arguments, and perhaps to fit the returned value into the context of the statement that performs the call, this becomes the function computed by that statement. This is what Alice has done here.

Alice has done the same kind of cutting and pasting from the precondition of the routine, on lines 4–6, to the precondition on line 14 and part of the precondition on line 18. This has simplified the team members' job: they can see at a glance that some parts of the intended functions are identical, rather than waste time trying to see whether they are mathematically equivalent. As a general rule, where parts of intended functions mean the same thing, it helps to express them in exactly the same way.

As another aside, notice that the team members read and understood the mathematical set notation on line 4 without hesitation or comment. They did the same with the notation for integer intervals on line 6, the notation for ordered pairs on line 7, and the notation for real intervals on line 22 of the second example. Programmers should understand these elementary concepts of mathematics, of course, and they should use the corresponding mathematical notation in intended functions wherever appropriate. Furthermore, the whole team should make sure that it agrees on the mathematical notation that it intends to use throughout the project.

Alice, Ben, and Chris verified these two routines rather quickly. Was it because the code was artificially simple? Not at all. The code was indeed rather simple, straightforward, and clearly written — perhaps much more so than most code written in the real world — but only because our authors worked very hard to write it that way. If they had not, the verification would have been much more difficult.

Exercises

1. In a group with two or more other people, verify one or more of the programs that you wrote for Exercise 5.1. Your instructor may assign other programs to write and verify.

2. Find a program or routine that you have previously written without intended functions and without having verification in mind. (Choose one that uses only the control constructs for which we have defined the verification conditions in previous chapters.) Insert the necessary intended functions, then try to verify the program. If possible, do it with the same group that you used in Exercise 1. Was the verification harder to do this time?

Notes

The value of having other people inspect your code is discussed in [Wein71], Chapter 4. Some programmers resist this idea, fearing that their reputations and their egos will be damaged if errors in their work are discovered. Such programmers should read what Weinberg has to say about "egoless programming."

Fagan's methods for group inspection of designs and code [Faga76], [Faga86] were first introduced at IBM and have been widely adopted, with variations, in other organizations.

According to some estimates and studies, unit testing typically detects only about 20% to 25% of the defects present in code ([Jone86a] p. 179, [Dyer92] p. 22), whereas verification reviews can detect about 90% ([Mills87c] p. 20, [Dyer92] p. 10). The corresponding number for formal code inspections is about 57% to 60% ([Jone86a] p. 179, [Jone91] p. 175).

Here is what Mills has to say about syntax errors, from [Mill88a], p. 204:

> Our concern with correct syntax is to identify an attitude of precision that will carry over with good effect into the problem of program logic. In fact, this emphasis on syntax is based on the reverse experience that when programmers get program logic correct from the start, the attitude of precision carries back into the coding, and they begin to get program syntax right from the start, with no special effort.

> With the advent of compilers and other debugging aids, it has been easy to adopt an attitude of "let the compiler do it" in finding errors of syntax. But in the long run this is a devastating attitude because it fosters ignorance and carelessness that slides over into program logic that the compiler cannot uncover.

If your programming is a vocation rather than an avocation, there is no reason for you to take errors of syntax lightly in writing a program. Syntax errors are errors of either ignorance or carelessness. If they are errors of ignorance, you need to do more homework on the syntax of your programming languages. If they are errors of carelessness, you need to learn how to concentrate and take what you are doing more seriously.

For recommendations concerning the length of a review meeeting and the amount of material to be verified, [Dyer92], p. 101, gives numbers that are similar to mine.

In a more conventional software development process, components of a software system undergo several stages of testing, including both unit testing and integration testing. For descriptions of the different stages of testing, see a software engineering textbook such as [Pfle87] or [Scha90].

One study of a large NASA programming project found that 39% of all errors were in the interfaces between modules ([Basi84] p. 48).

7

Definite Iteration

7.1 Definite Iteration Over Sequences

This chapter will present special techniques for verifying definite iterations: more particularly, loops that iterate over all elements of a sequence, set, or other collection of values. In Chapter 4 we saw techniques for verifying while-loops, which are the most general kind of iteration. If we chose, we could handle definite iterations as if they were instances of the general case. We will see, however, that by using techniques specifically designed for definite iteration, we can often simplify our task.

We will begin by discussing definite iterations over elements of a string, list, integer interval, or some other sequence of data values. Later in this chapter we will consider iteration over elements of a set, table, tree, or other data structure.

A great many of the data structures that we use in our programs can be viewed as sequences of smaller data objects. Strings, for example, are sequences of characters. We might also view an input stream as a sequence of characters; or, depending on the programming language or operating system we are using, we might view it as a sequence of lines, each of which is a sequence of characters. The "lists" that many programming languages provide are sequences of smaller data objects, and so, conceptually, is the data held by the linked lists that we often construct when our programming language does not already provide lists as a data-structuring primitive.

Consider the problem of performing some operation on every element of some such data structure. Let us represent the operation that selects the first element of a sequence S as $first(S)$, the operation that selects the remaining elements as $rest(S)$, and the operation that tests S for emptiness as *empty(S)*. Then we could iterate over S, performing the operation p on each element of it, using a while-loop of the following kind:

```
T := S
while not empty(T) do
    x := first(T)
    p(x)
    T := rest(T)
end
```

Notice that we need to use the temporary variable T, to avoid destroying S as we iterate over it.

Patterns of code of this kind are extremely common in programs of all kinds, whenever the programming language does not directly support definite iteration over elements of a sequential data structure. Represented more abstractly, however, what we really mean to say is simply this:

```
for each x in S
    p(x)
end
```

and it would be convenient if the programming language would let us say this directly.

Some programming languages have definite iteration constructs of exactly this kind. In the Python language, for example, the statement

```
for x in L:
    p(x)
```

performs operation p on every element of L, where L is a list (as in LISP). (In Python, indentation is used to indicate the extent of a control construct such as for; there are no explicit delimiters such as begin ... end or { ... }.) Strings are considered lists of characters, so the for operation can also be used to iterate over the characters of a string. For example, since the function ord returns the numerical encoding of a character, the following piece of program would print the lowercase letters with their encodings:

```
letters = "abcdefghijklmnopqrstuvwxyz"
for x in letters:
    print x, ord(x)
```

Icon is another language that supports definite iteration over sequences. In Icon, some expressions are *generators*, which means that they can generate sequences of values one at a time. For example, the expression !S, where S is a sequence data structure, generates the element of S in this way. There is a statement type of the form

```
every variable := generator do...
```

that iterates over the values generated by the generator. Here is the "lettercount" program of Section 5.2 as it might be written in Icon:

```
procedure main()
   letters := 0
   digits := 0
   others := 0

   every c := !! &input do
      if isletter(c) then
         letters := letters + 1
      else if isdigit(c) then
         digits := digits + 1
      else
         others := others + 1

   write(letters || " " || digits || " " || others)
end
```

The syntax `every c := !! &input()` means "for every character c in the input stream". In Icon, the input stream is a sequence of lines, each of which is a sequence of characters. The operator `!` generates the elements of a sequence. Generators may be applied to the results produced by other generators, so that `every c := !! &input() do...` is actually equivalent to the nested iteration

```
every line := ! &input do
   every c := ! line do
      ...
```

However, in this case it is easiest to view `!!` as a single operator that generates characters from the input stream. (In Icon, the functions `isletter` and `isdigit` are not predefined, as they are in C, but would be provided by the programmer.)

Now, how do we verify a definite iteration? As with any other control construct, we begin by writing an intended function for it. Here is the iteration from our character-encoding example, annotated with an intended function:

```
[ output := for each character in letters, a line containing
                  that character and its encoding ]
for x in letters:
   print x, ord(x)
```

The intended function is phrased quite informally, but its meaning is clear.

In this example the code may seem to match its intended function obviously, by inspection. But what would we need to do to carry out the verification in detail? We will need verification conditions for definite iterations. These, and examples of how to use them, will be the subject of the next two sections of this chapter.

7.2   Sequence Variables

In many kinds of programs, the most common definite iterations are those that iterate over the elements of a state variable of the program: a linked list, input stream, string variable, or something of this kind. Fortunately, the verification conditions are particularly simple for such iterations.

Let us consider the general form of a definite iteration over the contents of a sequence variable, with its intended function:

$$[\, f(S) \,]$$
```
for each x in S
    p(x)
end
```

Here S is a variable. The intended function f will be, in some way, a function of the elements contained in S; we have explicitly written it as $f(S)$ to show that it is a function of those elements. For simplicity, let us assume that the incidental variable x is local to the for-statement, according to the rules of our programming language, so that the intended function does not need to state that x may be set to anything. We also assume that, if the programming language allows p to change S, this does not affect the sequence of values iterated over, as if the for-loop made a local copy of the value of S before beginning the iteration.

To formulate the appropriate verification conditions, we first observe that when S is empty the loop does nothing. Thus, obviously, the loop is correct with respect to its intended function only if doing nothing is what f specifies in that case.

Second, we observe that, assuming that S is nonempty, executing the loop for all elements of S is equivalent to performing the operation p on the first element of S, then executing the loop for the remaining elements. Again, that had better be what f specifies in that case.

Therefore, in terms of the abstract operations *first*, *rest*, and *empty*, we can formulate the verification conditions as follows. The loop is correct with respect to intended function f if, for every state in the domain of f, these two conditions hold:

1. In a state in which *empty(S)* is true, the identity function I is correct with respect to intended function $f(S)$; and
2. In a state in which *empty(S)* is false, the sequence of $p(first(S))$ followed by $f(rest(S))$ is correct with respect to $f(S)$.

Notice that there are only two verification conditions, rather than the three that we have for while-loops. The reason is that the question of termination does not arise. We will assume that all of our sequences are finite, and therefore that definite iterations always terminate.

Here is an outline of a proof that these verification conditions are valid. It is an induction argument on the number of elements of S yet to be iterated over. Assume that, for a given iteration, the conditions hold; we will show that the iteration is correct.

Consider the program's data state after some number (zero or more) of times around the loop, after starting the loop in some state in the domain of f. Let R be the state variable that contains the part of S not yet iterated over. It contains some suffix of S (a subsequence from some element of S to the end, or the empty sequence when the end of S is reached). Notice that the verification conditions (the first if R is empty, the second otherwise) imply that this state is also in the domain of f. This means that we could have started the loop in this state, with $S = R$, and the loop would have terminated in a state satisfying the intended function f.

The basis case of the induction argument is covered by condition 1: R is empty, so the loop does nothing, and this is what the intended function specifies.

For the inductive case, let n be the length of R. Assume that the iteration is correct for states in the domain of f in which the length of R is $n - 1$. We execute the loop body, resulting in a state in which p has been executed on $first(R)$. In this state, by the hypothesis, we can replace the remaining computation performed by the loop by $f(rest(R))$. And since verification condition 2 holds, this sequence of $p(first(R))$ followed by $f(rest(R))$ is correct with respect to $f(R)$; therefore, so is the entire computation performed by the loop.

Notice that this proof depends on the fact that the intermediate states are also in the domain of f. In particular, for a given sequence value s for S, the corresponding states in which S contains any suffix of s must be in the domain of f. However, we are currently discussing only the case in which S is a variable. We assume that, if S can hold any given sequence value, it can also hold all the suffixes of that value; this is certainly true for almost all sequence data types commonly found in programs. Thus, where there are no other constraints on S and the other program variables, as expressed in preconditions to f, the intermediate states containing suffixes of S and any values for the other program variables will also be in the domain of f. Where there are such constraints, the verification conditions will hold only if they are satisfied, so we will conclude that the iteration is correct only if they are.

As we have done in previous chapters, we can rephrase our verification conditions as more informal correctness questions:

1. When S is empty, does doing nothing do f?
2. When S is nonempty, does doing p to $first(S)$, followed by doing f to $rest(S)$, do f to S?

Here is our character-encoding example again:

[*output* := for each character in *letters*, a line containing
that character and its encoding]

```
for x in letters
    print x, ord(x)
```

Let us apply the correctness questions to this iteration. First, when *letters* is empty, doing nothing clearly does what the intended function specifies. Second, when *letters* is nonempty, we print a line containing the first character in *letters* and its encoding, which, if x is that letter, is what the statement `print x, ord(x)` does. Then we do what the intended function specifies for the remaining characters in *letters*. The result is to do what the intended function specifies for all characters in *letters*. Therefore, we conclude that this loop is correct.

In cases that are as simple as this, we often can take a short cut in the verification. We can replace our two correctness questions by the following:

Does doing *p* to each element of *S* in order do *f*?

Let us call this the *short-form* correctness question for definite iterations, and our original two correctness questions the *long-form*.

In our example, *f* is phrased so that it is easy to see that the answer to the short-form correctness question is yes. When we can see the answer at a glance, as in this case, we can use the short-form question and be done. When the answer is not immediately obvious, we should do the proof in more detail by considering the empty and nonempty cases separately, using the two long-form correctness questions or verification conditions. Proceeding in this way is consistent with the philosophy of verification that we saw in Chapter 6. When a part of a program is obviously correct, we should say so immediately and go on; we do the proofs in detail only in more complicated cases.

Either of these ways is simpler than the alternative, which would be to rewrite the definite iteration in terms of a while-loop, then to verify the code in that form. In the example above, the rewritten code would look something like this:

[*output, temp, x* :=
        for each character in *letters*, a line containing
            that character and its encoding,
        anything, anything]

```
temp := letters
while not empty(temp) do
    x := first(temp)
    print x, ord(x)
    temp := rest(temp)
end
```

Verifying this is left as an exercise.

7.3   Other Sequence Expressions

Now let us consider the situation in which E is an expression, but not necessarily a variable. Let us consider definite iterations of the form

```
[ f(E) ]
for each x in E
      p(x)
end
```

Here, E may be any expression whose value is a sequence.

For many such expressions, we can apply the verification conditions or correctness questions of the previous section of this chapter, with no changes. We can do so when we can see that all intermediate states of the iteration will be in the domain of its intended function. In particular, this will be the case only if, for any state in the domain of f in which E has a particular value, there are states in the domain of f in which E has all suffixes of that value.

Consider, for example, the following simple example:

```
[ line is nonempty → t := t || all but first character of line ]
for each x in rest(line)
       t := t || x
    end
```

Here, *line* and *t* are string variables. For simplicity, we assume that the operator $\|$ is used both for string concatenation and to append a single character to a string.

We note that, since *line* can have any value but the empty string in the domain of the intended function, *rest(line)* can have any string as a value. In particular, for any given value of *rest(line)*, all of its suffixes can also be values of *rest(line)* (for values of *line* in other states in the domain). This means that all intermediate states of the iteration are in the domain of the intended function, since it has no precondition constraining the other state variables of the program. Therefore, we can verify this iteration using the correctness questions:

1. When *rest(line)* is empty, does doing nothing do [$t := t \| rest(line)$]?
2. When *rest(line)* is nonempty, does the sequence

$$[t := t \| first(rest(line))]$$
$$[t := t \| rest(rest(line))]$$

do [$t := t \| rest(line)$]?

The answer to both questions is clearly yes.

We need to use somewhat different methods only when it is possible that the intermediate states of the iteration are not in the domain of its intended function.

When this happens, we may find that we are unable to prove the iteration correct using the verification conditions of Section 7.2, even though the iteration may actually be correct. Even worse, we may use invalid reasoning to conclude that an iteration is correct even when it is actually not.

Let us take as an example an extreme case, in which E is a constant. Consider this loop:

> [*between* := *between* + the number of times a vowel
>   occurs between two consonants in *text*]
> ```
> for v in "aeiou" do
> ```
>   [*between* := *between* + the number of times v
>   occurs between two consonants in *text*]

How do our correctness questions apply to this example? It is probably simple enough that we can see its correctness immediately, using the short-form correctness question. This is especially easy if we rewrite the loop's intended function in the following equivalent form:

> [*between* := *between* + the number of times a character in   `"aeiou"`
>   occurs between two consonants in *text*]

But what if we wanted to use the long-form correctness questions instead? We cannot apply them directly, because they don't quite make sense when applied to iteration over a constant sequence.

For one thing, consider the empty-sequence case. We cannot ask whether this loop computes its intended function when `"aeiou"` is empty, because it obviously isn't! Also, if we tried to apply the second verification condition, we would find that the intended function contains no variable S for which we could substitute the expression *rest*(S).

The problem here is that the domain of the loop's intended function is too small to allow us to perform the verification. According to that intended function, the loop is to iterate over the specific sequence `"aeiou"`. But what about the intermediate states of the iteration, in which the sequence remaining to be iterated over is a suffix of `"aeiou"`?

In a situation like this, we can verify the loop as if it contained a variable in place of the constant. To do so, we can take an equivalent sequence of code in which the value to be iterated over is a variable rather than a constant, and verify that code. That code would, of course, need to contain an initialization of the variable to the value of the constant. In the case of our example, the result might look like this:

> [*between* := *between* + the number of times a vowel
>   occurs between two consonants in *text*]
> ```
> T := "aeiou"
> ```
>
> [*between* := *between* + the number of times a character in *T*
>   occurs between two consonants in *text*]
> ```
> for v in T do
> ```
> [*between* := *between* + the number of times *v*
>   occurs between two consonants in *text*]

Notice that we have inserted a new intended function for the rewritten for-loop, below the initialization. This is necessary, because we will need to verify the for-loop (with respect to this intended function) alone, separate from the initialization that we have inserted. In some ways, this is like finding an intended function for an uninitialized while-loop.

Fortunately, in the case of a definite iteration, we can usually see rather easily how the intended function for the initialized loop depends on the particular sequence to be iterated over. When this is the case, we can obtain the intended function that we need by rephrasing the intended function using the name of our new variable instead. That is what we have done in the example.

There is a quick test that will detect most situations in which we need to perform this transformation, before we even attempt the verification. We can ask whether the empty sequence is a possible value of E, the expression denoting the sequence to be iterated over, and whether E can have this value for some state in the domain of the intended function for the loop. If not, all of the intermediate states cannot be in the domain of the intended function, since the empty sequence is a suffix of any possible value of E. We can see in a moment that the iteration in our example fails this test: the empty string is not a possible value of `"aeiou"`.

Simply introducing a variable, as we did in this example, will be sufficient to allow us to complete the verification in most cases. However, in some cases we may need to add a precondition to the intended function for the uninitialized for-loop, according to properties of the constant sequence that we are assuming to hold in the loop body. Suppose, for example, that the computation in the loop body above depended for some reason on the fact that v was a vowel and not any arbitrary character. Then the intended function on the loop body would have contained a precondition:

$$[v \text{ is a vowel} \rightarrow \ldots]$$

This would be a clue that the intended function for the loop should also contain a precondition:

$$[T \text{ contains only vowels} \rightarrow \ldots]$$

It would have been redundant to include this precondition with the original loop:

```
[ "aeiou" contains only vowels → ... ]
for v in "aeiou" do
```

However, the precondition will be necessary for the verification of the code as rewritten.

But let us look at this example again. We already know what value T has when we begin the iteration: the value "aeiou". Why could we not put this precondition on the loop?

$$[\, T = \text{ "aeiou"} \to \ldots \,]$$

This is even stronger, and should be a sufficient precondition to satisfy the requirements of the body of the loop if the loop is correct. But we cannot use this as a precondition because, as we have seen, the intended function for the loop must also be defined for the intermediate states reached each time around the loop. This is the precondition that we really want:

$$[\, T \text{ is a suffix of } \text{ "aeiou"} \to \ldots \,]$$

That is, T must be "aeiou", "eiou", "iou", "ou", "u", or the empty string.

The general case is this: Let us assume that we can write the intended function for the definite iteration in the form $f(E)$; that is, we can isolate the part that refers to E, the expression that denotes the sequence to be iterated over, in such a way that we can substitute something for it. Then the definite iteration has the form

```
[ f(E) ]
for x in E
    p(x)
end
```

Then, when we rewrite this by introducing a variable, we can also insert a precondition on the intended function for the uninitialized loop, as follows:

```
[ f(E) ]
    T := E

[ T is a suffix of the sequence denoted by E → f(T) ]
for x in T
    p(x)
end
```

As a matter of fact, if we can write the intended function in this form, we can take a short cut and subsume the precondition into our correctness questions. We would simply verify iterations of this form

```
[ f(T) ]
for x in T
    p(x)
end
```

using the following variation of the correctness questions:

1a. When *T* is empty, does doing nothing do *f*?

2a. When *T* is any nonempty suffix of the sequence denoted by *E*, does doing *p* to *first*(*T*), followed by doing *f* to *rest*(*T*), do *f* to *T*?

Returning to our vowel-counting example, we would apply these questions to

> [*between* := *between* + the number of times a character in *T*
> occurs between two consonants in *text*]
> ```
> for v in T do
> ```
> [*between* := *between* + the number of times *v*
> occurs between two consonants in *text*]

with *E* = "aeiou". The answer to the first question is trivially yes, because when *T* is empty the value of "the number of times a character in *T* occurs between two consonants in text" is 0, and it is not hard to see that the answer to the second question is also yes.

7.4 Ranges of Integers

There is one kind of sequence that is so common it deserves special mention: the arithmetic progression, as in the do-statement of FORTRAN or the for-statement of Pascal. Here is an example in Pascal:

```
for i := 1 to n do ...
```

This means the same as the following iteration over a constant list of numbers (although it cannot be written in this way in Pascal):

```
for each i in [ 1, ..., n ] do ...
```

As we have seen, we can verify this as if it had been written as follows:

```
T := [ 1, ..., n ]
for each i in T do ...
```

However, there is another way that is equally valid and usually easier. Suppose we were to rewrite the iteration as follows:

```
m := 1
for i := m to n do ...
```

Now the sequence that we are iterating over is the range of integers from *m* to *n*; call it *T*. Then *first*(*T*) is *m*, *rest*(*T*) is the range from *m* + 1 to *n*, and *empty*(*T*) is equivalent to the expression *m* > *n*.

For purposes of verification, the definition of these three functions is the only representation of a sequence that we need, since our verification conditions are expressed in terms of them. Let us proceed by using this representation, rather than using the sequence directly. We will provide an intended function for this for-loop, in terms of the variable m that we have introduced, and apply the long-form correctness questions or the verification conditions as expressed in terms of m.

Let us see how this works in the following example:

$$[\ sum := \textstyle\sum_{j=1}^{n} a[j]\ ]$$
```
begin
    sum := 0
```
$$[\ sum := sum + \textstyle\sum_{j=1}^{n} a[j]\ ]$$
```
    for i := 1 to n do
        sum := sum + a[i]
    end
end
```

If we felt it necessary to verify the for-loop in detail using the long-form correctness questions, we would proceed as follows. First, we would rewrite that part of the program as

$$[\ sum := sum + \textstyle\sum_{j=1}^{n} a[j]\ ]$$
```
begin
    m := 1
```
$$[\ sum := sum + \textstyle\sum_{j=m}^{n} a[j]\ ]$$
```
    for i := m to n do
        sum := sum + a[i]
    end
end
```

And now the correctness questions for the for-loop are

1. When $m > n$, does doing nothing compute

$$[\ sum := sum + \sum_{j=m}^{n} a[j]\ ]\ ?$$

Yes, because the range of the summation is empty.

2. When $m \leq n$, does doing

```
        sum := sum + a[m]
```

followed by

$$[\ sum := sum + \sum_{j=m+1}^{n} a[j]\ ]$$

compute

$$[\; sum := sum + \sum_{j=m}^{n} a[j]\;]\;?$$

Again, clearly it does.

This is another iteration that is simple enough that we would probably prefer to verify it using the short-form correctness question for definite iterations. The purpose of the example is to show that verifying it in more detail, using the long-form correctness questions, is reasonably straightforward as well.

Of course, there are cases in which the lower bound is not a constant such as 1, but a variable. In this case we would need no rewriting to make the lower bound a variable. Notice that it makes no difference whether the upper bound is a variable or not! (However, we assume that the upper bound cannot be changed within the loop, as is the case in most programming languages that support loop statements of this kind.) Thus, for an iteration of the form

```
[ f(m) ]
for i := m to E do
    p(i)
end
```

for any expression E, the correctness questions are

1. When $m > E$, does doing nothing do $f(m)$?
2. When $m \le E$, does doing $p(m)$, followed by doing $f(m+1)$, do $f(m)$?

7.5   Other Data Structures

What about iteration over structures other than sequences? There are many data structures used in program design that are not really sequences. Sets, for example, contain elements that are not sequentially ordered. Trees and directed graphs are examples of other structures that define relationships, but not a linear ordering, on their elements.

In programs that contain such data structures, a common operation is to iterate over all the elements contained in a structure, performing some computation on each. Often, it is easiest to program and verify such iterations in very much the same way as we do for iterations over sequences.

In some programming languages, there are statements for iterating over sets in the same way as sequences. Icon is one such language. In Icon, the syntax for iterating over elements of a set is the same as for iterating over elements of a sequence. Here is an example:

```
[ s := s  ∪  t ]
every x := ! t do
    [ s := s  ∪  {x} ]
    insert(s, x)
```

(Actually, an Icon programmer would be unlikely to write such an iteration, since Icon provides a built-in operation that does the same thing.)

To verify such a definite iteration over a set, we might adapt our verification conditions for iteration over a sequence so that they apply to sets. Let us assume for the moment that the definition of our programming language does not specify the order in which an iteration generates elements of a set (which is the case for Icon). Then here are the appropriate verification conditions:

1. In a state in which $empty(S)$ is true, the identity function I is correct with respect to intended function $f(S)$.
2. In a state in which $empty(S)$ is false, let e be an arbitrary element of S; then the sequence of $p(e)$ followed by $f(S - \{e\})$ is correct with respect to $f(S)$.

In our example, when t is empty it is clear that doing nothing does $[\, s := s \cup t \,]$; and when t is nonempty, the sequence

$$[s := s \cup \{x\}]$$
$$[s := s \cup (t - \{x\})]$$

computes

$$[s := s \cup \{x\} \cup (t - \{x\})$$
$$\equiv s \cup t]$$

as required.

As a matter of fact, it is not really necessary to introduce new verification conditions for sets. We could reason, not in terms of the elements of the set, but in terms of the sequence of set elements that is generated by the iteration. Then we would use the verification conditions for sequences.

Using verification conditions that talk about the set directly is probably simpler in most cases. However, if the definition of the programming language defines the order in which elements are iterated over (alphabetically for sets of strings, for example), we might need to make use of that fact in our proofs. In this case, we would need to do our verifications explicitly in terms of sequences of generated elements, rather than sets of elements.

If our programming language has statements for definite iteration over other data structures, like the iterations that we have seen for sequences and sets, we would use similar methods to verify such iterations. In each case, we would either adapt our verification conditions to the particular kind of structure that we are reasoning about, or else refer to the sequence of values generated by the iteration and use the verification methods that we already have for sequences.

There is one other important way that definite iterations can be written in the

Icon language (and a few other programming languages, such as CLU). The programmer can write a procedure that generates elements of a sequence dynamically, and a definite-iteration statement can iterate over these elements as the procedure generates them. Generator procedures can be used to produce other sequences of values: the words in a sentence, the factors of a number, and so on. Also, Icon programmers frequently use generator procedures to implement definite iteration over elements of data structures of all kinds: the leaves of a tree, the nodes of a directed graph, and so on. In each case, the values produced by the generator procedure form a sequence, so these iterations are verified just as we have done for sequences that are data structures in a program.

Here is a simple example: The following procedure builds a list of all the fields on a line (a command line, for example), where a field is any sequence of non-blank characters and fields are separated by sequences of blanks. The generator procedure *fields* generates these fields, as strings, and the loop is executed once for each field generated. (In Icon, the square brackets produce a list, and ||| is the list-concatenation operator.)

```
[ return a list of the fields in line ]
procedure fieldlist(line)
    [ result := a list of the fields in line ]
    result := []
    every f := fields(line) do result := result ||| [f]
    return result
end
```

The verification of the every-statement would be done by using *fields(line)* as the sequence being iterated over, reasoning about *first(fields(line))*, *rest(fields(line))*, and so on.

By the way, here is how the procedure *fields* might be defined:

```
procedure fields(str)
    str := str || " "
    while str  == "" do
        {
            [ str contains at least one blank →
                    f := characters of str up to the first blank ]
            f := uptoblank(str)

            suspend f

            [ str contains at least one blank →
                    str := str with its first field
                               and the following blanks removed ]
            str := removefield(str)
        }
end
```

When the every-statement begins executing, *fields* is called. When the suspend-statement is reached, the value of *f* is generated. Execution of *fields* is suspended and control returns to the every-statement, which executes the loop body once with that value of *f*. Then control returns to *fields*, which picks up where it left off in the middle of its while-statement, possibly to generate more values. When the while-loop in *fields* terminates, the sequence of generated values is ended and the execution of the every-statement terminates.

Of course, if we program a definite iteration in this way, we must also verify that the generator procedure does indeed generate the sequence of values that we require. We will see how to do this in the next section of this chapter.

7.6   The Iteration Mechanisms

So far, we have considered only definite iteration mechanisms that are built into our programming languages. What can we do in lower-level languages such as C, which do not have built-in mechanisms for iterating over sequences and other structures? In such languages, the programmer must implement a definite iteration over a sequence of values by coding the iteration mechanism in terms of the primitives that the programmng language does provide.

But then the programmer has one more obligation: to verify that the iteration mechanism does indeed iterate over the desired sequence of values.

For example, let us return to the character-encoding example from Section 7.1. We saw that the loop in that example could be written this way in Python:

```
[ output :=  for each character in letters, a line containing
                    that character and its encoding ]
for x in letters:
    print x, ord(x)
```

But here is how it would be written in C:

```
char *p;

[ output :=  for each character *p in letters, a line containing
                    *p and its encoding ]
for (p = letters; *p != '\0'; p++)
    printf("%c %u\n", *p, *p)
```

According to the language definition, the syntax

```
for (init; test; next)
    statement
```

is equivalent to

```
init;
while (test)
    {
        statement
        next
    }
```

In C, strings are terminated with the null character '\0'. Thus, the pointer variable *p* is initialized to point to the first character of *letters*, then incremented every time around the loop so that it points to the next character, until finally it points to the terminating null character and the loop terminates. (The format string "%c %u\n" prints a line containing a character and an unsigned integer; no explicit conversion from character to integer is needed.)

In this particular example, the iteration mechanism is in the header of the for-statement:

```
for (p = letters; *p != '\0'; p++)
```

This is such a stereotyped sequence of code for iterating through the characters of a string that any experienced C programmer can see that it is correct. We would not need to verify in detail that it iterates over the desired sequence of characters; we would say that it is correct by inspection.

Very often, iterations like this also contain code within the loop to access values within the data structure that we are iterating over. In this example, that code is the dereferencing operator * in the expression *p. It is a good idea to express the intended function for the loop in terms of this accessing syntax, to make it very clear which values are being iterated over. We have done this in the example.

As another matter of notation, it is sometimes helpful to write an explicit specification for the iteration mechanism that we are trying to implement, apart from the specification of the loop as a whole. Here is how we might write this example to include such a specification:

```
        [ output := for each character *p in letters,
                        a line containing *p and its encoding ]
    for (p = letters; *p != '\0'; p++)
                            [ for each character *p in letters... ]
        [ output := a line containing *p and its encoding ]
        printf("%c %u\n", *p, *p)
```

Even though [for each character *p in *letters* ...] is not really an intended function, it is reasonable to use our square-bracket notation here too. But, to indicate that it is something slightly different, we can place it to the right of the for-statement header rather than above it, and use the ellipsis (...) as well.

As another example, let us return to an example from Section 7.4:

$$[\; sum := sum + \sum_{j=1}^{n} a[j] \;]$$
```
for i := 1 to n do
    sum := sum + a[i]
end
```

In Section 7.4 we verified this as an iteration over the sequence of integers from 1 to n. But it makes just as much sense, and is more straightforward in some ways, to view it as an iteration over the sequence of values in the array a, with the for-loop as the iteration mechanism:

$$[\; sum := sum + \sum_{j=1}^{n} a[j] \;]$$
```
for i := 1 to n do      [ for each element a[i] in array a... ]
    sum := sum + a[i]
end
```

This is another example in which the iteration mechanism is so obviously correct that we would probably not bother to verify it in detail.

If we did want to verify an iteration mechanism, we could do it informally by verifying that its parts correspond to the functions *first*, *rest*, and *empty* that we use in our verification conditions. This would prove that these verification conditions are valid when applied to this particular iteration mechanism.

How we do this would depend heavily on the programming language we are using and the syntax and semantics of the iteration constructs of that language. A common situation, however, is that we can express the meaning of the iteration mechanism in terms of a while-loop of this form:

```
init;
while (test)
    {
        body of the loop
        next
    }
```

As we have seen, that is exactly the meaning of the C construct

```
for (init; test; next)
    body of the loop
```

and many loop structures in other languages fall into the same pattern.

Then, suppose we want to prove that a loop of this kind iterates over the elements of a structure S. Let *access* be the code in the body of the loop that accesses the values we are iterating over. Here are the conditions that we would need to verify:

1. The operation *init* has the effect of setting up a sequence v which contains the elements of S that are to be iterated over. It does this by giving values to one or more incidental variables that are used by *access* and *test*, and modified only by *next*.

2. *access* is equivalent to *first(v)*.
3. *next* is equivalent to $v := rest(v)$.
4. The negation of *test* is equivalent to *empty(v)*.

Consider our character-encoding example:

```
char *p;
for (p = letters; *p != '\0'; p++)
    printf("%c %u\n", *p, *p)
```

Here is how we would verify that this code iterates over the characters of `letters`:

1. v is the pointer p, which points to the same string that `letters` does.
2. *access(v)* is the expression `*p`, whose value is the first character of the string pointed to by p.
3. p++ increments p so that it points to the string of all but the first character of the string that it previously pointed to.
4. The test `*p != '\0'` is false when the string pointed to by p is empty, since `'\0'` is the string-terminator character in C.

As another example, let us look again at the loop

```
for i := 1 to n do
    sum := sum + a[i]
end
```

We want to verify that this code iterates over the elements of the array a. We start by defining what the for-statement means in this particular programming language. Let us assume that it is equivalent to this sequence of code, which matches the pattern for which we have established verification conditions:

```
i := 1
while i <= n do
    sum := sum + a[i];
    i := i + 1
end
```

Then we can simply argue as follows:

1. v is the sequence of elements from `a[i]` to `a[n]`.
2. *access(v)* is `a[i]`, which is the first element of that sequence.
3. i++ has the effect of removing the first element from that sequence.
4. `i <= n` is false when that sequence is empty.

In more complicated situations, we might wish to verify the iteration mechanism more formally and in a bit more detail. We might do it as follows: separate it from the computation within the loop, rewrite it as an equivalent while-loop, add intended functions that assert that the sequence of values that it produces is the sequence that we desire, then verify that this is so. Here is how we might do this with the character-encoding example:

```
[ sequence of values := the characters of letters ]
{
    [ sequence of values = empty ]

    p = letters;

    while (*p != '\0')
    {
        [ sequence of values := sequence of values || *p ]

        p++;
    }
}
```

Then we would proceed as if "sequence of values" were a state variable, performing the verification as we normally do with code containing while-loops. To do so, we might need to insert some additional intended functions, perhaps like this:

```
[ sequence of values := the characters of letters ]
{
    [ sequence of values = empty ]
    p = letters;

    [ sequence of values :=  sequence of values || the characters of
                                    the string pointed to by p ]
    while (*p != '\0')
    {
        [ sequence of values := sequence of values || *p ]

        [ the string pointed to by p :=
            rest(the string pointed to by p) ]
        p++;
    }
}
```

We would verify a generator procedure, like those of Icon, in a similar way. Let us return to the example from the previous section:

```
procedure fields(str)
   str := str || " "
   while str  == "" do
      {
```
       [*str* contains at least one blank →
            f := characters of *str* up to the first blank]
```
         f := uptoblank(str)

         suspend f
```
       [*str* contains at least one blank →
            str := *str* with its first field and
                  the following blanks removed]
```
         str := removefield(str)
      }
   end
```

This is already written in terms of a while-loop, so no rewriting of the code is required. We would insert intended functions that specify the sequence of values generated by the procedure, as shown below.

[generated values := the blank-separated fields in *str*]
```
procedure fields(str)
```
   [generated values := empty]
```
   str := str || " "
```
[generated values := generated values followed by
                   the blank-separated fields in *str*]
```
   while str  == "" do
      {
```
       [*str* contains at least one blank →
            f := characters of *str* up to the first blank]
```
         f := uptoblank(str)
```
       [generated values := generated values followed by *f*]
```
         suspend f
```
       [*str* contains at least one blank →
            str := *str* with its first field and
                 the following blanks removed]
```
         str := removefield(str)
      }
   end
```

Then we would verify this, treating "generated values" as if it were a state variable.

Is all of this too complicated? It may seem that when we write a definite iteration in place of a while-loop we have doubled our work, since we need to verify both the loop and the iteration mechanism. However, in practice, many iteration mechanisms are so simple that they are obviously correct, like some of the examples that we have seen here.

Also, notice that, even when we need to verify an iteration mechanism, we can do it once and then use it in many loops in a program. Thus we have separated out part of the work that we would have had to do if we had written and verified many while-loops that iterated over a kind of structure in the same way, and done that work only once.

In either case, we usually find that using definite iteration, when it really corresponds to the computation that we need to do, gives us a net savings in complexity of the program and a net savings in the amount of work we need to do in verifying the program.

7.7   Sets and Sequences in Program Design

Now that you have straightforward methods for verifying definite iterations, you will find it advantageous to use definite iteration, rather than while-loops, for many of the loops in your programs. In fact, if you start watching for opportunities to do so, you are likely to find that a surprising number of loops can easily be expressed as definite iterations.

You are also likely to find that data structures that you can view as sequences or sets are very common in your programs. Most programs contain structures that are collections of data items, and a great many of these collections are conceptually just sequences (when the data items have some significant ordering) or sets (when the order of the items is not important).

Many experienced programmers approach the design of a program by describing its input, output, and internal data objects in the vocabulary of discrete mathematics: sets, sequences, functions, relations, and so on. This is a useful habit for us to cultivate. It can help to clarify our thinking about design problems; in fact, solutions often become obvious. And we inherit a well-understood vocabulary to use for writing our specifications and for documenting our programs and discussing them with other programmers.

Then, once we have designed our program in discrete-mathematical terms, we are likely to find, in particular, that many of the loops in the program are really definite iterations over all elements of some set or sequence. And now we are likely to find them very easy to write and verify.

For example, suppose that we need a text-processing program that will read two documents and find all of the names that are in both documents. Some programmers might approach the problem like this:

First I'll read the first document and store all the names I find in a list. Then I'll read the second document and, every time I find a name, search the list for it. But I don't want to include the same word more than once, so I'll need a second list of the words that I've already found. I'll search that one before I search the list of words from the first document.

However, a programmer who is accustomed to thinking in terms of discrete-mathematical structures might immediately think of a different approach:

The words in a document are a set. I'll read each document and build up the set of names in each, using a set-insertion algorithm. Then I can get the words common to both documents by using set intersection.

Either approach will work, but the second seems conceptually simpler, and it will probably be much more straightforward to specify, code, and verify. Also, the programmer has probably implemented data structures and algorithms for similar sets many times before, and so will be likely to do it correctly this time. In fact, the programmer may well have code from another project that can be reused or adapted.

The principle here is to think first in your problem domain (the words that occur in both documents); then in terms of discrete-mathematical structures and operations (sets, insertion, and union); and in programming terms (linked lists or some other data structures, and operations on them) only when you are about to start coding.

Here is another example. We have seen the following pattern of C code for iterating over all characters in the input stream:

```
c = getchar();
while (c != EOF)
{
    some computation using c
    c = getchar();
}
```

But we know that we are trying to implement a definite iteration over a sequence, the sequence of characters in the input. Why not make the definite iteration more explicit in the code, and write it like this:

```
for (c = getchar(); c != EOF; c = getchar())
            [ for each character c in stdin ... ]
{
    some computation using c
}
```

This for-loop obviously iterates over all characters of the input; it is hardly worthwhile bothering to prove this in detail. Now this is explicitly a definite iteration over the sequence of characters in the input, and we can verify it that way.

As a matter of fact, many C programmers would write this pattern of code as

```
while ((c = getchar()) != EOF)
{
        some computation using c
}
```

and think of it as a definite iteration equivalent to

[for each character *c* in *stdin* ...]
{
        some computation using *c*
}

since this is such a common and stereotyped piece of code for performing that iteration. This is a perfectly legitimate thing to do. Until now, we have avoided expressions like

```
(c = getchar()) != EOF
```

because of the side effect embedded within the test. But if, in our verification, we can treat the whole loop header as a single component that implements an iteration mechanism, we can avoid the complications that arise in reasoning about such expressions in isolation.

Then consider, for example, the following code from the example of Section 5.2:

[(*c* ‖ *stdin*) := *stdin*]
```
c = getchar();
```

[*letters*, *digits*, *others*, (*c* ‖ *stdin*) :=
        letters + number of letters in (*c* ‖ *stdin*),
        digits + number of digits in (*c* ‖ *stdin*),
        others + number of other characters in (*c* ‖ *stdin*),
        empty]
```
while (c != EOF)        /* while (c || stdin) is nonempty */
```
        [*c* is a letter → *letters* := *letters* + 1
        | *c* is a digit → *digits* := *digits* + 1
        | *else*   → *others* := *others* + 1;
        in any case, (*c* ‖ *stdin*) := *stdin*]
```
    {
        if (isletter(c))
            letters++;
        else if (isdigit(c))
            digits++;
        else
            others++;
```

        [(*c* ‖ *stdin*) := *stdin*]
```
        c = getchar();
    }
```

Now we can rewrite it in the following form, as most C programmers probably would have written it in the first place:

[*letters*, *digits*, *others*, *stdin* :=
     letters + number of letters in *stdin*,
     digits + number of digits in *stdin*,
     others + number of other characters in *stdin*,
     empty]

```
while ((c = getchar()) != EOF)    [ for each character c in stdin ... ]
```
     [*c* is a letter → *letters* := *letters* + 1
     | *c* is a digit → *digits* := *digits* + 1
     | *else*   → *others* := *others* + 1]
```
     if (isletter(c))
         letters++;
     else if (isdigit(c))
         digits++;
     else
         others++;
```

We can now verify this using our methods for definite iteration. This will probably be much easier than the verification that we did in Section 5.2.

It does not really matter much whether we code the loop header as

```
while ((c = getchar()) != EOF)
```

or as

```
for (c = getchar(); c != EOF; c = getchar())
```

My own preference, when coding in C, is to use for-statements for all definite iterations and while-statements for all other loops, to emphasize the distinction. However, the important thing is that we recognize that we are performing definite iteration over elements of a sequence, and that we design and verify the program in these terms.

Exercises

1. Complete the example at the end of Section 7.2 by verifying the following:

[*output*, *temp*, *x* :=
     for each character in *letters*, a line containing
         that character and its encoding,
     anything, anything]
```
temp := letters
```

```
while not empty(temp) do
    x := first(temp)
    print x, ord(x)
    temp := rest(temp)
end
```

Your first step will be to write an intended function for the while-loop.

2. Consider this pattern of iteration (from Section 7.3) again:

[*between* := *between* + the number of times a character in "aeiou"
                 occurs between two consonants in *text*]
```
for v in "aeiou" do
    p(v)
```

Suppose that you tried to verify this using the following (invalid) reasoning:

The iteration is correct if the following verification conditions hold:
1. In a state in which "aeiou" is empty, the identity function *I* is correct with respect to the intended function. Well, there is no such state, so there is nothing to prove: this condition is trivially satisfied.
2. In a state in which "aeiou" is nonempty, the sequence of $p("a")$ followed by

[*between* :=
         between + the number of times a character in "eiou"
                 occurs between two consonants in *text*]
is correct with respect to the intended function.

What might $p(v)$ be, such that the second of these conditions holds but the iteration is incorrect anyway?

3. (for C programmers) Verify that the C code

```
while ((c = getchar()) != EOF)
```

does indeed do

[for each character *c* in *stdin* ...]

(The point of this exercise is for you to see exactly what it is that you need to prove. You should find the proof itself very easy by now.)

4. Look at some of the programming exercises that you have done in previous chapters. Can any of them be rewritten using definite iteration instead of while-loops? Do so, and verify them again using the methods of this chapter. How do the new versions compare with the old versions?

    Your instructor may give you additional programming assignments.

Notes

The methods presented in this chapter are based on [Stav95].

In a study of a number of diverse application programs produced at several organizations in my town [Stav93], I found that definite iteration over data structures (mostly over sets and sequences) accounted for a large percentage of the total number of loops in each program (ranging from 27% to 60%, with a median of 58%).

A reference manual for the Python language is [vanR97]. Good references for the CLU language are [Lisk77] and [Lisk86]. In particular, Chapter 6 of the latter book extensively covers generator procedures, which are called *iterators* in CLU.

8

Data Abstraction and Object-oriented Programs

8.1   Data Abstraction and Encapsulation

Data abstraction is one of the most important concepts in program design. It is one of our most powerful tools for keeping the complexity of our programs under control. Together with a few other key ideas, it forms the basis for object-oriented programming. How to specify and verify the parts of programs that create data abstractions and objects will be the subject of this chapter.

Occasionally the data types that are provided by our programming languages (for example, integers, pointers, and arrays) are just the kinds of entities that we write programs to manipulate, but this is rare. More often, we are really writing programs to perform calculations about mathematical entities (for example, sets or differential equations), or about things that are connected to the real world in some way (for example, mailing lists or price trends). Sometimes, especially in object-oriented programming, the objects in our programs are meant to correspond to real entities in the world outside the computer (for example, employees or airliners) and their attributes (for example, salaries or air speeds).

The idea of data abstraction is that we write our programs, as much as possible, in terms of these abstract entities and corresponding operations on them. For example, recall the program that we used as an example of design in Section 7.7: to read two documents and find the names that occur in both of them. The design that does this using sets of names and set intersection provides a good example of data abstraction.

We would use "set of names" as an abstract data type in the program. The operations on sets of names would be insertion of an element and intersection. We can specify these as follows (using C syntax for the routine headers):

$[\, s := s \;\cup\; \{nn\}\,]$
```
void insert(Nameset s, Name nn)
```

$[\, return \; s \;\cap\; t\,]$
```
Nameset intersection(Nameset s, Nameset t)
```

The specifications for these operations, as well as the interfaces to the operations as expressed in the function headers, are entirely in the vocabulary of names and sets of names, rather than, for example, strings and linked lists containing strings. Notice that we are treating the type "Name" as another abstract data type; the program will contain operations that operate on names as well. The program might also define "Document" as yet another abstract data type.

Of course, in an actual program we must implement each abstract entity as a data object or data type made out of lower-level entities. The lowest-level objects will be constructed out of the data types of our programming language. Then the implementation of each operation (the bodies of the routines) will contain code that accesses or manipulates the implementation of the data. No other parts of the program should do this.

Some programming languages, like Modula and CLU, provide syntactic constructs for grouping declarations of abstract types, their implementations, and operations on them together as modules in a program. They also provide scope rules to enforce access restrictions so that only operations in the module can access the data objects in the implementation. All this is often called *data encapsulation*. But even in languages that do not provide support for data encapsulation, like C, it is a good idea for us to do our own encapsulation by grouping together the declarations and operations for each significant data object or type, perhaps in a separate source file for each (if the language allows this), and by refraining from accessing this data except through the operations.

Returning to our document-processing program, we will need to choose an implementation for sets of names. We might do this as a separate design step, after we have designed the top-level algorithm for the program. For simplicity of the example, let us choose an implementation in which a set is just an unordered linked list of the elements in the set. (Of course, this implementation might not be efficient enough in practice; we might often want to choose a more sophisticated data structure so that the implementations of the operations can use more efficient algorithms.)

Besides the actual programming-language declarations that we would write to create this implementation, it is a good idea to include a description of the implementation in the program's documentation, as we do with the definition of specification functions. It often doesn't need to be phrased any more formally than this:

Implementation:
A name set is represented by an unordered linked list of names.

Then, when we write the implementation of each operation, we will need an intended function for the body of the routine. The obvious way to obtain one is by translating the intended function for the operation, which is written in terms of the abstract entity, into the vocabulary of the implementation. Then, to verify this routine, we first verify that the translated intended function (the "inner" intended function) really says the same thing as the abstract intended function (the "outer" intended function), and then verify the body of the routine with respect to the inner intended function just as we would verify any other code.

Here is how we would do this for the `insert` operation on name sets, assuming that we are using the list implementation:

```
[ s := s ∪ {nn} ]
void insert(Nameset s, Name nn)
{
        [ nn is in the list s → I
        | else → s := [nn] ∥ s ]

        . . .

}
```

Inside the routine, we use the wording "*nn* is in the list *s*" to emphasize that we are viewing *s* as a list and not a set there.

To do what the intended function specifies, we would probably use a list-search algorithm followed by a list-insertion algorithm:

```
[ s := s ∪ {nn} ]
void insert(Nameset s, Name nn)
{
        [ nn is in the list s → I
        | else → s := [nn] ∥ s ]
        {
            int found;

            [ found := whether nn is in the list s ]

            if (! found)
                [ s := [nn] ∥ s ]
        }
}
```

As a matter of fact, there is nothing wrong with using one operation on an abstract object in the implementation of another operation. Suppose, for example, that we also had an operation to test a name for membership in a set:

```
[ nn ∈ s → return 1
| nn ∉ s → return 0 ]
int member(nn, s)
```

Then we could use this operation in the implementation of insert:

```
[ s := s ∪ {nn} ]
void insert(Nameset s, Name nn)
{
    [ nn ∈ s (as a set) → I
    | else → s (as a list) := [nn] ‖ s ]
    if (member(nn, s))
        ;                  /* do nothing */
    else
        ...
}
```

Here we are using both the abstract view and the implementation view of *s* inside the routine body. This is not a problem, as long as we are careful to use the appropriate notation and terminology in each place. If there might be any confusion as to which view we are taking in each place, we should make this explicit, as we have done here.

8.2   The Abstraction Function

We have been describing the representation relationship rather informally. However, just as in the rest of our verifications, sometimes we may need to proceed a bit more carefully and rigorously. In such cases we will need a somewhat more mathematical way to describe our representations.

We can express more rigorously the relationship between an abstract object and its implementation by defining an *abstraction function*. This is a function from states of the data structure in the implementation to states of the abstract object that it represents. We might also call this the *meaning function*, because it gives the meaning of the implementation in abstract terms. Let us call this function *meaning*. Then here is how we would define the representation of the name-set that we have been using as an example:

Representation:
meaning(L) ≡ the set of the elements of the list L

Here is an example of how three different lists would be mapped to the corresponding sets by this abstraction function:

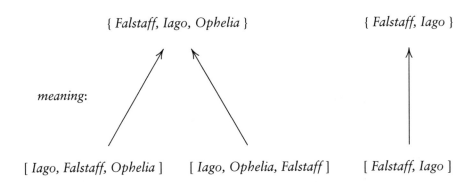

The diagram has been drawn so that the arrows point upward, because we often speak of the abstract objects as being at a "higher level" than their implementations.

You might think that it would be more straightforward to have a function going in the other direction: a "representation function" from the abstract object to its representation. However, notice that in this example this won't work, because there may be many lists that represent the same set (with the elements in different orders in the lists). This means that a relation in this direction would not be a function. It is actually a rather common situation that more than one state of a data structure may correspond to a single state of the abstract object that the data structure represents.

On the other hand, the abstraction function always is (or should be) a proper, single-valued function, because a given state of a data structure in the implementation should always represent the same state of the corresponding abstract object. Otherwise there is an ambiguity over what the data structure represents.

Using the abstraction function, we can derive the meaning of phrases and expressions containing references to the implementation. For example, "x is in the list L," at the level of the implementation, has the meaning "x is in the set of the elements of the list L," which is equivalent, in the terminology of the abstraction, to "x is a member of the set L."

Then we can use the abstraction function to compare more formally our two different representations of the intended function for an operation: the outer one expressed in abstract terms, and the inner one expressed in terms of the implementation. Here is one way that we might proceed: We will take the inner intended function and apply the abstraction function to each occurrence of an expression that refers to the implementation of the abstract object. Then we will manipulate and simplify those expressions until the function is expressed in the vocabulary of the abstraction. Finally, we will compare the result with the outer intended function.

Let us try this with our namelist-insertion example:

```
[ s := s  ∪  {nn} ]
void insert(Nameset s, Name nn)
{
        [ nn is in the list s → I
        | else → s := [nn] ‖ s ]
}
```

First we apply the abstraction function throughout the inner intended function:

$$[\ meaning(nn \text{ is in the list } s) → I$$
$$| \ else → meaning(s) := meaning([nn] ‖ s)]$$

Then we substitute the meaning of each expression wherever *meaning* occurs:

[*nn* is in the set of elements of the list s → I
| *else* → the set of elements of the list s :=
                    the set of elements of ([*nn*] ‖ s)]

Simplifying, we obtain:

[*nn* ∈ the set of elements of the list s → I
| *else* → the set of elements of the list s :=
                    {*nn*} ∪ the set of elements of the list s]

Now the function refers to lists, the data structure of the implementation, only in the phrase "the set of elements of the list s," which is the definition of *meaning(s)*. Everything else is in the vocabulary of sets. We now substitute *meaning* back into the function in place of its definition:

[*nn* ∈ *meaning(s)* → I
| *else* → *meaning(s)* := {*nn*} ∪ *meaning(s)*]

In each of these versions of the intended function, s still means the list s, but now we move to the abstract view of s as a set, and rewrite the function as

[*nn* ∈ s → I
| *else* → s := {*nn*} ∪ s]

which is equivalent to the outer intended function

[s := s ∪ {*nn*}]

Strictly speaking, all we really need is that the inner intended function be correct with respect to the outer one. However, if we obtained the inner function in the first place by translating the outer function into the vocabulary of the implementation, we would expect the two functions to be equivalent, as is the case here.

In each of these transformations, it is important to distinguish whether we are viewing s as a set or as a list. Perhaps it is unfortunate that we are using the same name in both cases. Some programming languages, such as CLU, have notation that makes the distinction unambiguous. But in languages like C, there is no such notation, so we need to be sure that we always know which view we are taking in each place that the object is mentioned.

8.3   Data Invariants

You may have noticed that our definition of the implementation of name sets did not say that the list that represents one of these sets may not contain duplicate elements. As a matter of fact, our abstraction function makes sense even so, because the set of elements in a list contains no duplicates even if the list does. But we may prefer to tighten up our implementation and require that our lists contain no duplicates.

This is an example of a *data invariant*: a constraint on a data object, or among several data objects, that restricts the values that the object or objects can take, and that is always satisfied. In particular, the data objects that implement abstract data objects or data types frequently have invariants on them. In this context, the invariants are sometimes called *implementation invariants* or *representation invariants*.

In our example, we might have good reasons for wanting the invariant. If nothing else, if the lists contain no duplicates they will be as short as possible, and this in turn may make operations on them more efficient. It also turns out that we can often make our algorithms simpler by depending on an invariant. For example, suppose we wanted to provide an operation to delete a name from a name set. We could use an algorithm that simply searches for the first instance of a name and deletes it, rather than an algorithm that continues to search for any other instances that may exist.

We could make the invariant part of the definition of an implementation, like this:

Implementation:
A name set is represented by an unordered linked list of names containing no duplicates.

However, in some ways it is better to state it separately:

Implementation:
A name set is represented by an unordered linked list of names.

Invariant:
The list contains no duplicate elements.

One reason for the separation is that the invariant is a somewhat different sort of thing from the definition of the implementation. In most programming languages, we create an implementation with declarations. But the invariant is the part of the type information that cannot be expressed with declarations.

As a matter of fact, since invariants are not enforced by the compiler, we must verify that they do indeed hold. Stating an invariant separately emphasizes it and makes it clear what it is that we need to verify.

Specifically, for each invariant, our obligation is to show that:

1. Every object initially satisfies the invariant when first created. That is, each initialization or constructor operation for the object leaves the object in a state that satisfies the invariant.
2. Every other operation on the object preserves the invariant. That is, the operation leaves the object in a state that satisfies the invariant, assuming that the object satisfied the invariant before the operation.

Together, these two conditions imply that the invariant will always hold, at least between operations on the object. It may happen that the invariant is temporarily violated during the execution of an operation body. For example, if an operation needs to reorder two elements in a linked list, it may need to update two pointers, and it may be that the invariant does not hold after the first pointer is updated but before the second pointer is updated. However, since the intermediate steps in the execution of an operation body are not visible outside the operation, it appears to the rest of the program as if the invariant always holds.

In our document-processing program, for example, we are likely to want to start with empty sets for the names in each document, then insert names as we find them in the documents. Then we would want a constructor function that would create an empty name-set. Obviously, an empty set satisfies our invariant that there be no duplicate elements.

We must also verify that the operation `insert` preserves the invariant. Fortunately, it does, because the implementation of the operation does not add the new element to the list if it is already in the list. Therefore, if the list contained no duplicates before the insertion, it contains no duplicates after the insertion. It is often useful to put commentary in the intended functions or code of the implementation to help verifiers see why an invariant is preserved, perhaps like this:

```
[ s := s  ∪  nn ]
void insert(Nameset s, Name nn)
{
        [ nn is in the list s → I  (preserving the invariant)
        | else → s := [nn] || s ]

        . . .

}
```

We would have similar obligations for every other operation on name sets. For example, when we have implemented the operation `intersection`, we would need to prove that the name set it creates satisfies the invariant.

An implementation may have more than one invariant. Here is another example, from an actual C program. The header file that describes the abstract type and declares its implementation is shown in Figure 8.1.

```
/*================================================================
#
#   Bigstring: a string that can grow to any size.
#
#   Provides:
#
#   typedef Bigstring
#   Bigstring bigstringEmpty()                    -- an empty string
#   void bigstringMakeEmpty(Bigstring b)          -- reset b to empty
#   void bigstringAppend(Bigstring b, char c)     -- append c to b
#   char *bigstringToString(Bigstring b)          -- contents of b
#
#================================================================*/


/*-----------------------------------------------------------------
|   Implementation:  A dynamically allocated array of chars.  Its
|   size is initially BIGSTRINGSIZE.  When full, it is reallocated
|   to twice the previous size.  This is an expensive operation,
|   should be infrequent, especially because the size thus grows
|   exponentially.  The string represented is the sequence of
|   characters in text[0 .. length-1].
*/
    typedef struct bigstringstruct {
            char* text;                -- char array, to be allocated
            long unsigned length;      -- no. of chars currently used
            long unsigned allocated_length;
                          -- no. of chars in allocated size of text
            } *Bigstring;

/*  DATA STRUCTURE INVARIANTS:
|       must be established by bigstringEmpty()
|       and preserved by all other operations.
|   "ALLOC":  0 < allocated_length and
|             allocated_length = allocated size of text in chars
|   "LENGTH": 0 <= length <= allocated_length
|
+----------------------------------------------------------------*/

BIGSTRING bigstringInitialize();
void      bigstringMakeEmpty(BIGSTRING b);
void      bigstringAppend(BIGSTRING b, char c);
char *    bigstringToString(BIGSTRING b);
```

Figure 8.1 The abstract type "Bigstring"

The block comment at the top states the types and operations that are provided for use by the rest of the program. However, C does not provide constructs to hide the internal data structure from the rest of the program, so it is the programmer's responsibility to refrain from accessing it except through the operations.

Notice also the naming convention for operations, in which the first part of the name is the name of the abstract data type to which the operation belongs. With this convention, a program can have (for example) both the MakeEmpty operation for Bigstrings and a MakeEmpty operation for some other type. Such a device would not be necessary in typical object-oriented languages, or in other languages that support the use of the same name for routines that operate on objects of different types.

The abstract type "Bigstring" has two invariants: a constraint on allo-cated_length, and a constraint on length which depends on the value of allocated_length. The programmer has given names to these invariants so that they can be referred to individually, as in the following implementation of one of the operations:

```
/*-------------------------------------------------+
 |                                                 |
 |    bigstringAppend(Bigstring b, char c):        |
 |         [ b := b || c ]                         |
 |                                                 |
 +-------------------------------------------------*/
void
bigstringAppend(Bigstring b, char c)
{
  /* [ length == allocated_length  ->
          allocated_length, allocated size of text :=
              2*allocated_length, 2*(allocated size of text)
       else  ->  I  ] */
  if (b->length == b->allocated_length)
    {
      b->allocated_length *= 2;

      /* [ b->text := b->text reallocated to
                        allocated_length chars ] */
      b->text =
        (char *) realloc(b->text,
                         b->allocated_length * (sizeof(char)));
                         /* preserves "ALLOC" */
    }

  /* [ length < allocated_length  ->  append c to b ] */
  b->text[b->length] = c;
  b->length++;              /* preserves "LENGTH" */
}
```

The statement containing the call to the library routine `realloc` does indeed reallocate `b->text` to a size of `allocated_length` characters, preserving its previous contents. Once we know this, the verification of this routine is straightforward.

Here is how we would do the verification. By constructing conditional trace tables or simply by inspection, we would calculate the function computed by the routine body in the case in which *b* is initially full and in the case in which it is not. In the first case, we obtain:

[*contents*, allocated size of *text*, *length*, *allocated_length* =
    contents ‖ *c*, 2 * (allocated size of *text*), *length*, 2 * *allocated_length*]

Here *contents* refers to the characters of *text* at indices 0 through *length* − 1. Notice that the allocated size of *text* is also a state variable.

From the value of *contents*, it is clear that the routine computes its intended function. We must also show that both invariants are preserved. Specifically, what we must show is that

0 < 2 * *allocated_length* and
    2 * *allocated_length* = 2 * allocated size of *text* in chars and
0 <= *length* + 1 <= 2 * *allocated_length*

assuming that

0 < *allocated_length* and
    allocated_length = allocated size of *text* in chars and
0 <= *length* <= *allocated_length*

and it is not hard to see that this is true. The second case, in which *length* < *allocated_length* initially, is trivial.

Notice that the invariant "ALLOC" does not hold between the steps in the body of the if-statement, after `b->allocated_length` has been multiplied by 2 but before `b->text` has been reallocated. But the reallocation establishes it again, so that it is true at the end of the `bigstringAppend` operation, as required.

The idea of data invariants is not limited to the components of a data abstraction. It can be applied to any state variable or combination of state variables of a program. Furthermore, an invariant may hold throughout the program, or only in certain designated parts of it. Then the fact that an invariant holds can be used in other proofs. Essentially, the invariant is a lemma that we prove separately and can then use to prove other facts.

Let us return to an example from Section 7.5:

```
procedure fields(str)
    str := str || " "
    while str  == "" do
       {
```

                  [*str* contains at least one blank $\rightarrow$
                        f := characters of *str* up to the first blank]

```
         f  := uptoblank(str)

         suspend f
```

                  [*str* contains at least one blank $\rightarrow$
                      str := *str* with its first field
                              and the following blanks removed]

```
         str := removefield(str)
       }
    end
```

Here we have the invariant that *str* contains at least one blank, unless it is empty. This invariant is established by the statement `str  := str || " "` and holds throughout the procedure after that. If we state the invariant explicitly, we can simplify the intended functions in the loop body somewhat:

```
procedure fields(str)
    str := str || " "
    # INVARIANT: after this, str is either empty
    #                    or contains at least one blank

    while str  == "" do
       {
```

                  [*f* := characters of *str* up to the first blank]

```
         f  := uptoblank(str)

         suspend f
```

                  [*str* :=*str* with its first field and
                            the following blanks removed]

```
         str := removefield(str)
       }
    end
```

If you look back at the "lettercount" example of Section 5.2, you will see that throughout that program we used *c* as a one-character buffer to hold successive characters read from *stdin*. We didn't say so at the time, but we were really relying on the invariant that *c* = *EOF* if and only if *stdin* is empty. This is established by the first c = `getchar()` ; operation; since doing that same operation again is the only way that *c* or *stdin* is modified after that, the invariant continues to hold. This fact is so obvious to C programmers that they tend to rely on it without realizing that they are doing so, in code like this. But it really is an invariant, and to be completely proper we should state it as such and verify that it holds.

8.4   Object-oriented Programs

Object-oriented programming combines data abstraction with a few other programming language concepts, particularly inheritance, and encourages a style of program development in which objects in the program model objects in the world outside the computer. These additional subjects are outside the scope of this book.

However, you will be happy to know that, once you know how to specify and verify programs containing data abstractions, you know almost everything you need to know to be able to specify and verify object-oriented programs. There are a few details of object-oriented programming languages that we will need to watch out for, but not many.

For example, Figure 8.2 shows the abstract data type "Bigstring" as it would appear in C++. Unlike the C version in Figure 8.1, this C++ class declaration hides the internal fields of the data structure. Only the routines included in the "public" section are accessible in the rest of the program. (In C++, / / makes the rest of the line a comment.)

Figure 8.3, on page 163, shows how the implementation of two of the operations would look in C++. The notation `Bigstring::` identifies these operations as belonging to the class `Bigstring`.

Both of these operations have an implicit first argument: the object to which the operation is applied. For example, to append the character `'!'` to the object `sentence`, we would apply the `append` operation to `sentence`, passing the parameter `'!'`. The syntax of the statement that does this would be

```
sentence.append('!');
```

The operation `Bigstring::Bigstring()` is the constructor operation for the class; it is called whenever an instance of this class is declared, to initialize it. When that happens, the instance being declared is the implicit first argument.

Within the operations, references to components such as *text* (called *data members* in C++) refer to those components of the implicit argument. The word *this* refers to that object as a whole; even though this notation is not used in the code in this example, we have used it in the intended functions. (The word *self* is also commonly used for this purpose in object-oriented programming.)

Once we understand these details of the programming language, the verification of these operations is just as it would be for routines in C or any other ordinary language.

```
class Bigstring {

   // Implementation:
   //     A dynamically allocated array of chars. Its
   //     size is initially BIGSTRINGSIZE.  When full,
   //     it is reallocated to twice the previous size.
   //     This is an expensive operation, but should be
   //     infrequent, especially because the size thus
   //     grows exponentially.  The string represented is
   //     the sequence of characters in text[0 .. length-1].

   char* text;               // char array, to be allocated
   long unsigned length;     // no. of chars in text currently used
   long unsigned allocated_length;
                             // no. of chars in allocated size of text
   // DATA STRUCTURE INVARIANTS:
   //     must be established by bigstringInitialize()
   //     and preserved by all other operations.
   // "ALLOC":  0 < allocated_length and
   //              allocated_length = allocated size of text in chars
   // "LENGTH": 0 <= length <= allocated_length

#define BIGSTRINGSIZE 1024

public:

        Bigstring();       // constructor: initialize to empty
   void makeEmpty();       // reset to empty
   void append(char c);    // append c to end
   char *toString();       // return contents

};
```

Figure 8.2 The abstract type "Bigstring" in C++

Apart from such details, in many object-oriented languages we must also be sure
that, when we refer to a component (sometimes called a *member*) or operation
(sometimes called a *method*) of an object or class, we are referring to the one that
we think that we are. This is especially necessary in languages without strong
typing at compile time, and is complicated by inheritance (deriving classes from
other classes) and overloading (using the same name for more than one thing).

Here is an example in the Python language, which provides objects and classes
but not strong typing. It is from a program that compares various attributes of files:
size, data and time of last modification, and so on. The files may be either local
(on the same machine on which the program is running) or remote (on a different

```
    //---------------------------------------------------------
    //
    //  Bigstring():
    //          [ BIGSTRINGSIZE > 0  -> initialize to empty ]
    //
    //---------------------------------------------------------
Bigstring::Bigstring()
{
  // [ BIGSTRINGSIZE > 0  ->
  //       initialize with allocated size = BIGSTRINGSIZE chars ]
  allocated_length = BIGSTRINGSIZE;
  text = (char *) malloc(BIGSTRINGSIZE * (sizeof (char)));
                                  // establishes "ALLOC"
  // [ set to empty ]
  length = 0;                     // establishes "LENGTH"
}

    //---------------------------------------------------------
    //
    //  append(char c):
    //          [ this := this || c ]
    //
    //---------------------------------------------------------
void Bigstring::append(char c)
{
  // [ this is full  ->  this := this reallocated twice as large
  //    else  ->  I ]
  if (length == allocated_length)
    {
      allocated_length *= 2;

      // [ reallocate b->text to allocated_length chars ]
      text = (char *) realloc(text,
                          allocated_length * (sizeof (char)));
                      // preserves "ALLOC"
    }

  // [ length < allocated_length  ->  append c ]
  text[length] = c;
  length++;                     // preserves "LENGTH"
}
```

Figure 8.3 Operations of the class `Bigstring`

machine). In either case, a file is identified by a path, which in the case of a remote file includes a machine name.

There is a class `File` which represents files in general, and classes `Local-File` and `RemoteFile` which inherit from `File`. The relevant parts of the class definitions are shown in Figure 8.4.

When the program creates a file object, it does so by calling the constructor of either `LocalFile` or `RemoteFile`, as determined by the nature of the path to the file. (The constructor is the operation `__init__` in each class.)

```
if path1.isLocal():
    f1 = LocalFile(path1)
else:
    f1 = RemoteFile(path1)
```

We do not know which class `f1` is an instance of as we are verifying the program, since the decision is made at run time. This means that, whenever the program refers to an attribute or operation of `f1`, we must verify that the attribute or operation does indeed exist. Furthermore, we must verify that what it contains or computes satisfies what is required of it in the place where it is used.

One way of doing this is by asserting in a precondition that `f1` is an instance of the appropriate class, as in the following statement. We need the precondition that `f1` is a remote file to know that `f1` has attributes *localname* and *machinename*.

```
[   f1 is a RemoteFile →
        statinfo :=
              status info tuple about f1 from remote machine ]
    statinfo = inquireStatus(f1.machinename, f1.localname)
```

Another way is to ensure that, no matter which class `f1` is an instance of, that class contains the attribute or operation that we require, as in the following statement:

```
[ output := a readable description of f1 ]
print f1.description()
```

We don't know which kind of file `f1` is but, if it is either a *LocalFile* or a *RemoteFile*, it has a `description` operation that computes what is required. Of course, if there is any possibility that it may be of a different class entirely, we would need a precondition here too.

Another example of this situation would be a call of `f1`'s `size` operation. Even though the operation is implemented entirely differently for the two kinds of files, it computes the same function in either case. Thus, the code that obtained a file's size and did some computation with it would not need to distinguish between local files and remote files in doing so.

```
class File:
    def __init__(self, path):
        self.path = path
        [ path contains a machine name →
                hostname, localpart :=
                        that machine name, the remaining file name
         | else → hostname, localpart := empty, path ]
        ...             # and setting of other attributes

    ...             # and other operations


class LocalFile(File):
    def __init__(self, path):
        File.__init__(self, path)
        self.name = self.path.localpart

    [ return a readable description of self ]
    def description(self):
        return self.name

    [ return the size of self in bytes ]
    def size(self):
        # done using a library routine
        ...

    ...             # and other operations


class RemoteFile(File):
    def __init__(self, path):
        File.__init__(self, path)
        self.machinename = self.path.hostname
        self.localname = self.path.localpart

    [ return a readable description of self ]
    def description(self):
        return self.localname + " on machine "
                                + self.machinename

    [ return the size of self in bytes ]
    def size(self):
        # done by sending a query to self.machinename
        ...

    ...             # and other operations
```

Figure 8.4 Python classes for files

Also, where there is inheritance or overloading, we must take extra care to trace the definition of attributes and operations to the class that actually defines them, as we verify parts of a program that reference them. For example, suppose our program contained a reference to fl.path, and suppose that we knew that fl was a *LocalFile* at that place in the program. We would look first at the definition of the class *LocalFile*, but the attribute *path* is not defined there. We would need to look in the definition of *File*, the parent class, to verify that this attribute exists (and perhaps to find out what it represents). In a more complex program, we might need to do this sort of thing in many places, and trace back through many long chains of inheritance.

Situations like these are common in object-oriented programs, although (as usual) the details vary with the programming language. The important thing is that we watch out for such situations, and check, as we verify, that the parts of the program that we are looking at are well defined and refer to what we think they do.

Exercises

At this point you should do some programming exercises. What problems are appropriate will depend very much on your proficiency at data abstraction and object-oriented programming, and on the programming languages that you use and how well they support these concepts. You might try taking some old programs of yours that contain data abstractions or objects, adding intended functions, and verifying them. You may find that you need to rewrite the code to make the verification feasible; feel free to do so. Your instructor may assign additional exercises.

Notes

Data abstraction and encapsulation, as well as inheritance and overloading, are covered in many textbooks on programming language principles, such as [Prat96] (Chapters 5 and 8) and [Sebe93] (Chapters 10 and 15 and section 8.7).

Data encapsulation is a particular kind of "information hiding", in which each module hides a different design decision [Parn72]. This is similar to the idea, promoted in Section 5.5, of trying to confine complexity to small parts of a program. Like structured programming, data encapsulation has become a standard programming technique.

Meaning functions and data invariants were both introduced in [Hoar72]. These concepts also appear in [Lisk86], Chapter 4, which is a thorough treatment of data abstraction and its embodiment in the CLU programming language.

Among the many publications on object-oriented programming, I would recommend two classics: [Meye88] for an introduction, and [Gamm95] for many useful design suggestions.

For a treatment of object-oriented programming using box structures, see [Hevn93].

The standard reference for the C++ programming language is [Stro94].

9

Recursion and Functional Languages

9.1   Recursive Routines

In previous chapters we have seen examples of the specification and verification of routines (often called *procedures*, *subroutines*, and *functions*) in various programming languages. You may have noticed that none of them has been recursive. As it happens, when we allow routines to be recursive, not very much needs to be done differently. However there are a few special considerations that we will need to be aware of. They will be the subject of this chapter. We will also see how verification can be done for programs written in functional languages; this is a related topic, since routines in functional languages are often recursive.

A recursive routine is one that can call itself. That is, its declaration contains at least one call to the routine being declared. As you know, this is not a problem and does not lead to a circular definition, assuming that the recursive call is executed conditionally and that every sequence of recursive calls always terminates in a call in which the recursion is not done. If so, when the routine is called from another routine, it can be executed just like any other routine, according to the execution rules of the programming language. Similarly, in verifying a recursive routine, we must verify that the recursion terminates; that will be the subject of the next section of this chapter. Otherwise, the verification is very much like the verification of any other routine.

The declaration of a recursive routine, like the declaration of any other routine, will have an intended function written in terms of the routine's parameters. To determine the function computed by a recursive call within this declaration, we take the intended function for the routine and substitute the parameters that appear in the call for the corresponding parameters in that function, just as we would do for the call to any other routine. We can then use the result in verifying the body of the routine against the routine's intended function.

For example, suppose that a C program contains linked lists of the following form:

```
typedef struct Nameliststruct {
    char *name;
    struct Nameliststruct *next;
    } *Namelist;
```

This defines a type called `Namelist`. A `Namelist` is a pointer to a structure containing two fields: `name`, which is a string, and `next`, which is a pointer to another structure of the same kind. A `Namelist` may be the distinguished pointer value `NULL`, which represents an empty list, and a `next` field can be `NULL`, which represents the end of the list.

We can think of the `next` pointer as being the head of another linked list of the same kind as `Namelist`. A `Namelist`, then, is either empty or contains a name and another `Namelist`, which in turn contains all names but the first.

The fact that this data structure contains a smaller instance of the same kind of structure suggests that it can be processed recursively. Here is a typical recursive routine that operates on lists of this type:

```
[ list is nonempty →
        print the names in list, separated by commas ]
printNamelist(Namelist list)
{
    printf("%s", list->name);

    if (list->next != NULL)
    {
        printf(",");

        [ list->next is nonempty →
                print the names in list->next,
                    separated by commas ]
        printNamelist(list->next);
    }
}
```

This can be verified informally as follows. First, we verify the outermost sequence of statements. The first statement prints the first name in the list. Then, if the condition in the if-statement is true, there is more than one name in the list, so the inner sequence of statements prints a comma, then the remaining names separated by commas; all this has the effect of printing all the names separated by commas. If the condition is false, there is only one name in the list, so we have already printed all the names in the list and no commas are needed. Finally, we verify that the recursive call satisfies its intended function; this is done by substituting the parameter `list->next` for `list` in the intended function for the routine, which then becomes identical to the intended function on the call.

For practice, let us see how we could verify the outermost sequence a bit more formally using trace tables. To prepare for this, we would rewrite the intended functions in the form of conditional concurrent assignments, and perhaps insert other intended functions, as follows:

```
[ list is nonempty →
        output := output ‖ the names in list,
                            separated by commas ]
printNamelist(Namelist list)
{
        [ list contains one name → output := output ‖ that name
        | true → output := output ‖ the first name in list ‖ "," ‖
                            the names in list->next,
                            separated by commas ]

        [ output := output ‖ the first name in list ]
        printf("%s", list->name);

        if (list->next != NULL)
        {
            printf(",");

            [ list->next is nonempty →
                    output := output ‖ the names in list->next,
                                    separated by commas ]
            printNamelist(list->next);
        }
}
```

First we check that the intended function just inside the braces is the same as the intended function above the routine heading. We see that they say the same thing, although they are expressed differently: the intended function inside the braces is broken into two cases, corresponding to the cases in the code below.

Then we construct two conditional trace tables, one for each case of the if-statement. The one for the false case is trivial, and the one for the true case would show us that *output* gets *output* ‖ the first name in *list*

and then

output ‖ the first name in *list* ‖ " , "

and finally

output ‖ the first name in *list* ‖ " , " ‖
the names in *list->next*, separated by commas

which is exactly as required. We then verify (by inspection) that the first call to printf does indeed print the first name in *list*, and we verify the recursive call to printNamelist by substitution as before.

Let us return to our definition of a Namelist as either being empty or containing a name and another Namelist. This is a recursive definition, just as a routine defined in terms of itself is recursive. We can make good use of the similarity between these two kinds or recursive definitions, as we shall see.

A properly written recursive definition is broken down into cases. There will be at least one case that contains a recursive reference to the thing being defined; this is called a *recursive case*. There will also be at least one case that contains no such recursive reference; this is called a *basis case* (or *base case*). For a Namelist, for example, an empty list is the basis case, and a list containing a name and another list is the recursive case. Recursive definitions without basis cases are occasionally used to define (for example) nonterminating computations or infinite data structures, but we will not consider such things here.

We can often use the recursive definition of a data structure as a guide in designing a recursive routine that operates on the structure. We begin by breaking down the routine's intended function into cases, to match the cases in the data structure's definition. For each case in the data structure's definition, we write down what the routine should compute. We can then assemble the cases into a conditional concurrent assignment, and use it as the specification for the body of the routine.

For example, suppose that we need a routine to take all of the names in a Namelist and insert them into a symbol table. This would be easy to do with an iterative routine but, for the sake of the example, let us write a recursive routine. The first step is to figure out what needs to be done in the two cases of a Namelist — an empty list and a nonempty list. When we have done this and written a corresponding specification in conditional form, we will have something like the following:

```
[ symtab := symtab  with the names in list inserted ]
insertNamelist(Symboltable symtab, Namelist list)
{
```
    [*list* is empty → *I*
    | *list* is nonempty → *symtab := symtab* with *list->name*
                  and the names in *list->next* inserted]
```
}
```

From this, it is not hard to complete the routine to obtain the following:

```
[ symtab := symtab  with the names in list inserted ]
insertNamelist(Symboltable symtab, Namelist list)
{
```
    [*list* is empty → *I*
    | *list* is nonempty → *symtab := symtab* with *list->name*
                and the names in *list->next* inserted]
```
    if (list != NULL)
    {
```
        [*symtab := symtab* with *list->name* inserted]
```
        insertSymbol(symtab, list->name);
```
        [*symtab := symtab* with the names in *list->next* inserted]
```
        insertNamelist(symtab, list->next);
    }
}
```

Things are not always quite as simple and obvious as this, of course. For example, if we tried to develop our previous example `printNamelist` in this way, we might end up with something like the following:

```
[ output := output || the names in list, separated by commas ]
printNamelist(Namelist list)
{
```
    [*list* is empty → *I*
    | *list* contains one name → *output := output* || that name
    | *true* → *output := output* || the first name in *list* || "," ||
                the names in *list->next*, separated by commas]
```
    if (list != NULL)
    {
```
        [*output := output* || the first name in *list*]
```
        printf("%s", list->name);
```

```
                    if (list->next != NULL)
                    {
                        printf(",");
```

[*list->next* is nonempty →
  output := *output* ‖ the names in *list->next*,
  separated by commas]
```
                        printNamelist(list->next);
                    }
                }
            }
```

The case of an empty list is a basis case, as in `insertNamelist`. However, we would discover that the case in which *list* contains only one name must be another special case, because in this case we do not want to print a comma. Thus, there are two basis cases in the routine that we obtain.

There is nothing wrong with this solution, except that it causes some redundant computation. If the routine is called with a list of one or more elements, the sequence of recursive calls will always reach the one-element basis case before it reaches the no-element basis case, so the test for an empty list is redundant. If we can accept a routine that can be used only on nonempty lists, we can eliminate this test and use the slightly simpler and more efficient version that we first developed.

9.2   Termination

For the function computed by a recursive routine to be defined in a given state, the recursion must terminate when started in that state. As part of the verification that a recursive routine is correct with respect to a given intended function, we must prove that the recursion terminates for every state in the domain of that function. That is, every sequence of recursive calls ends in an execution of a basis case in the definition of the routine.

Fortunately, this is easy for most recursive routines that you will encounter in practice. The usual termination argument is very much like a termination argument for an iteration: some value becomes smaller on each call, and when it becomes small enough, a basis case is reached and the recursion terminates. Most often, the value is a parameter to the routine, and each recursive call takes that value, computes a smaller value from it, and passes that smaller value as the parameter of the next recursive call.

For example, consider the routine `printNamelist` from the previous section. That routine has the parameter `list`, and the routine's body contains the call `printNamelist(list->next)`. Thus, each recursive call passes a list that has one element fewer than on the previous call. When the list is reduced to one element, no recursive call is done. Therefore, we conclude that the recursion terminates.

Another common situation is that the parameter is a value that becomes numerically smaller, as in the following Pascal implementation of the familiar recursive factorial algorithm:

```
[ n ≥ 0 → return n! ]
function factorial(n: integer): integer;
begin
    if n = 0 then
        factorial := 1
    else
        factorial := n * factorial(n-1)
end;
```

Here it is easy to see that, for any argument in the domain of the intended function, the argument decreases with each recursive call until it reaches 0.

In some cases the value that becomes smaller is not a parameter to the recursive routine, but a state variable that is global to it. For example, the routine might consume part of the program's input before it calls itself recursively. Or, as with while-loops, we can sometimes identify a value that is not a state variable, but that decreases as a function of some state variables until it reaches a limit.

Termination arguments are not always this easy to find. In fact, they can be arbitrarily hard, just as with while-loops, as we can deduce from the fact (which is not hard to prove) that every while-loop can be converted into a recursion that computes the same function. Thus, in the general case, termination of recursion is undecidable just as termination of iteration is (assuming no bound on storage, as usual). Here is a version of the $3n + 1$ algorithm from Section 4.2, written as a recursive routine in C syntax:

```
int Collatz(int n)
{
    if (n <= 1)
        return n;
    else
        if (n % 2 == 0)
            return Collatz(n/2);
        else
            return Collatz(3n + 1);
}
```

Just as for the corresponding iterative algorithm, there is no obvious termination argument. Fortunately, termination problems as hard as this are rather rare except in contrived situations. By far the most common recursive routines are those that operate on a data structure by recursion on a part of the same structure. In such cases, and in most other cases of recursion, the termination arguments are easy.

9.3   Mutual Recursion

Things are not quite so simple when routines are mutually recursive. In particular, proving termination is harder. Rather than reasoning about each routine separately, we must reason about all of the routines involved in the mutual recursion together.

A typical example of mutual recursion is in parsing of programming languages, using the method called *recursive descent*. There is one routine to parse each kind of construct in the language, and these routines call other such routines to parse their parts.

As a much-simplified example, suppose that, in the language being parsed, an expression is defined as being one or more terms separated by + or − operators; a term is defined as being one or more factors separated by * or / operators; and a factor is defined as being a constant, a variable name, or an expression enclosed in parentheses. An outline of the corresponding parsing routines might be as follows:

```
expression():
    term();
    while next input symbol is "+" or "−"
            consume that symbol;
            term();

term():
    factor();
    while next input symbol is "*" or "/"
            consume that symbol;
            factor();

factor():
    if next input symbol is "("
            consume that symbol;
            expression();
            if next input symbol is ")"
                consume that symbol
            else
                report a syntax error
    else if next input symbol is a constant
            or variable name then
        consume that symbol
    else
        report a syntax error
```

The three routines `expression`, `term`, and `factor` are mutually recursive because they can call each other in the following circular pattern:

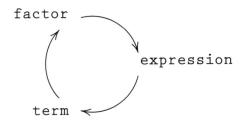

Unfortunately, we cannot prove termination of any one of these routines by reasoning about it in isolation; we must consider the three together. When would this mutual recursion be infinite; that is, cause an infinite execution? Only if the routines could call each other in this circular pattern forever. This would mean that execution would keep returning to expression (for example) infinitely often.

We can prove that the mutual recursion does terminate if we can identify a value that becomes smaller until it reaches a limit, as we did with ordinary recursion. However, it is not necessary for each routine to make the value smaller. We need only show that, along the cycle of calls from some routine back to itself, this value becomes smaller, and that this cycle is broken when it reaches some limit.

In this case, we can consider the input stream: specifically, the number of left parentheses currently at the beginning of the input stream. We see that expression always begins by calling term, and term always begins by calling factor; nothing has changed in the input yet. However, factor calls expression, completing the cycle of recursion, only when the next symbol in the input is a left parenthesis; and, before doing this, it consumes the left parenthesis. Therefore, the number of left parentheses at the beginning of the input decreases by 1 each time around the cycle of calls, and must eventually become 0, in which case the call to expression is not done again. Thus, the mutual recursion must always terminate.

In the general case, what we must do is construct a directed graph, with a vertex for each routine and a directed edge from each routine to each other routine that it calls. If this graph contains any cycles, we have mutual recursion. We need to provide a termination argument for each such cycle, or one or more termination arguments that cover all the cycles. In a recursive descent parser for a complete programming language, for example, there will probably be many cycles of calls. For each of them, the termination argument is usually that some input is consumed.

This situation is unfortunate. Until now, we have been able to do all of our verification by looking at only one isolated part of a program at a time. To prove termination of mutual recursion, we may need to reason about many routines at once. Furthermore, it is easy to overlook mutual recursion altogether, and so to neglect to verify termination; we need to be especially careful about this.

All this cannot be helped. Mutual recursion is a useful programming technique, but the termination aspect of it can be rather complex and hard to understand, and we must take special care when we reason about it.

9.4   Functional Languages

Functional programming languages, such as those in the LISP and ML families, are in some ways very different from the usual "procedural" programming languages such as Pascal, C, Icon, and so on. Instead of statements that are executed to cause changes in state variables, programs are made of expressions that are evaluated. These expressions usually contain calls to functions, often recursive functions, that are called for the values that they return but not to produce side effects. (Many functional languages also have procedural aspects, but we will consider only "pure" functional languages, or "pure" subsets of "impure" functional languages, here.)

Until now, our view of computation has been based on state variables whose values change as the program runs. Does this mean that we cannot use the methods that we have been learning to specify and verify programs in functional languages? Not quite. We can still write specifications for expressions and functions in terms of the values that they should have, and we can use substitution, reasoning by cases, and so on to verify that they do.

We will need something other than intended functions to use for our specifications, though. What we want is something that we can attach to an expression or function definition to specify the value that the expression or function should have. Let us call this construct an *intended value*.

Syntactically, an intended value is like an intended function, but with an expression or phrase that denotes a value where an intended function would have a concurrent assignment or sentence that specifies a state change. Just like an intended function, an intended value can be conditional, so we can define it by cases or limit the states in which it is defined. We will write intended values enclosed in square brackets and place them above the program components that they specify, just as we do with intended functions in procedural programs.

Here is an example in Scheme, a dialect of LISP. It is a function that is familiar to most beginning students of functional languages: it appends (concatenates) two lists. Above the function definition is its intended value. This is the value that the function is to return, expressed in terms of the function's arguments.

```
[ the elements of L followed by the elements of M ]
(define (append L M)
   (if (null L)
       M
       (cons (car L) (append (cdr L) M))
   ))
```

In Scheme, an expression of the form $(f\ a_1\ a_2\ \ldots\ a_n)$, where f is an operator or a function name, is an application of f to the arguments $a_1\ a_2\ \ldots\ a_n$. (if c e_1 e_2) is a conditional expression that has the value e_1 if condition c is true and e_2 if it is false. (null L), where L is a list, tests whether L is empty. (car L) is the first element of the list *L* and (cdr *L*) is the rest of the list; (cons *A L*) is the list formed from the element *A* followed by the elements of the list *L*.

Like Icon (see Section 5.3), Scheme is a language that lacks type declarations, so it is a good idea to specify the types of its arguments in a precondition and to state the type of the result. Thus the following is better than the version above:

```
[ L and M are lists →
        a list of the elements of L followed by the elements of M ]
(define (append L M)
    (if (null L)
        M
        (cons (car L) (append (cdr L) M))
    ))
```

To annotate the function for verification, we would add additional intended values at appropriate intermediate places. A good place to start would be to give the body of the function an intended value that is broken down by cases according to the structure of a list, as we saw how to do in Section 9.1. As in the example insertNamelist in that section, we give one case for an empty list and another for a nonempty list. We would probably want to provide an intended value for the recursive call as well. The result might be as follows:

```
[ L and M are lists →
        a list of the elements of L followed by the elements of M ]
(define (append L M)
    [ L is empty → the elements of M
    | else → the first element of L, followed by the rest of L,
            followed by the elements of M ]
    (if (null L)
        M
        (cons (car L)
                [ the elements of (cdr L)
                        followed by the elements of M ]
                (append (cdr L) M))
    ))
```

To verify the function, we would first check that the conditional intended value for the function body is the same as the intended value for the function as a whole, in all states that satisfy the precondition of the function. (We would interpret that precondition as type information that applies throughout the function definition.) Then, we would verify the if-expression against the conditional intended value, doing this by cases as we do with if-statements. For the non-null case, this involves checking that "the first element of *L*, followed by the rest of *L*, followed by the elements of *M*" means the same thing as "(car *L*) followed by (the elements of (cdr *L*) followed by the elements of *M*)."

Here is another example in Scheme. It is a function for computing the median value from an ordered list of numbers. The precise meaning of "ordered" is defined elsewhere but, as it happens, whether the numbers are in increasing or decreasing order, or whether duplicates are allowed, is irrelevant.

```
[ L is a nonempty ordered list of numbers →
       median value of elements of L ]
(define (median L) ...
```

Let us develop the function starting from this specification.

There is more than one way to define what we mean by the median element of an ordered list. The median element is meant to be the "middle" element, and this makes sense if there are an odd number of elements, but what if there is an even number? In that case, the "middle" of the list falls between two elements. One possible definition says that the median is found by averaging the two middle elements, and that is the definition that we will use here.

We anticipate that we will need to use the length of the list in more than one place, so we use a let-expression to give the local name len to this value. (A Scheme let-expression consists of the word let, a set of bindings of values to names, and an expression; the bindings apply throughout the latter expression.) We then write the intended value for the rest of the function definition, breaking it down by cases using a conditional, as follows:

```
[ L is a nonempty ordered list of numbers →
       median value of elements of L ]
(define (median L)
    (let ((len (length L)))
         [ len is even → mean of two middle elements of L
         | len is odd → middle element of L ]
    ))
```

Refining the inner intended value using a Scheme if-expression, and using another let-expression to define another intermediate value, we obtain

```
[ L is a nonempty ordered list of numbers →
       median value of elements of L ]
(define (median L)
    (let ((len (length L)))

         [ len is even → mean of two middle elements of L
         | len is odd → middle element of L ]
         (if (divides? 2 len)
             (let ((mid (/ len 2)))
                  [ mean of $L_{mid}$ and $L_{mid+1}$ ]  )
             [ $L_{(len+1)/2}$ ]
    )))
```

and finally

```
[ L is a nonempty ordered list of numbers →
      median value of elements of L ]
(define (median L)
     (let ((len (length L)))
```

```
          [ len is even → mean of two middle elements of L
          | len is odd → middle element of L ]
          (if (divides? 2 len)
               (let ((mid (/ len 2)))
```

```
                    [ mean of Lmid and Lmid+1 ]
                    (/ (+ (nth mid L)
                             (nth (+ mid 1) L))
                         2))
```

```
               [ L(len+1)/2 ]
               (nth (/ (+ len 1) 2) L)
     )))
```

In Scheme, when let-expressions are nested, each level adds more bindings to those that existed at the previous level. If we wished, we could keep track of the values bound to all the names using a trace table. Where there are conditional expressions, we would use conditional trace tables. For example, the table corresponding to the true case of the if-expression would look like this:

expression	condition	len	mid
(let ((len (length L)))		(length L)	
(if (divides? 2 len)	(divides? 2 (length L))		
(let ((mid (/ len 2)))			(/ (length L) 2)

Some other functional languages look, on the surface, quite different from languages in the LISP family, but the principles of specifying and verifying are not much different in these languages. One such language is ML. As a matter of fact, things are often a bit easier in ML, because in that language functions that operate on data structures can often be written directly in terms of the cases in the definition of the structure. The ML interpreter or compiler uses pattern matching to determine which case applies. For example, here is the ML equivalent of the Scheme append function shown in Section 9.1. (In ML, [] is the empty list, and the :: operator is the equivalent of the Scheme cons function.

> [*append L M* = the elements of *L* followed
>   by the elements of *M*]
> ```
> fun append [] M = M
>   | append (a::rest) M = a :: (append rest M);
> ```

In function declarations that use pattern matching, like this one, the arguments to the function are not always explicitly named. So that we can refer to the arguments in the specification, we can vary our notation slightly and write the specification in the form

$$[f\, a_1\, a_2\, \ldots\, a_n\, =\, expr\,]$$

Here is a more interesting example in ML. It is a function that produces a list of all possible bit strings of length n, where n is an argument. The bit strings are represented as lists containing the numbers 0 and 1.

> [*bitstrings* *n* = a list of all possible lists of length *n* over { 0,1 }]
> ```
> fun bitstrings 0 = [[]]
>   | bitstrings n =
>       let val lowbits =
> ```
>   [a list of all possible lists of length *n* − 1 over { 0,1 }]
> ```
>           bitstrings (n-1)
>       in
>           append
> ```
>   [a list of all possible lists of length *n*
>   over { 0,1 } that start with 0]
> ```
>           (distribute 0 lowbits)
> ```
>
>   [a list of all possible lists of length *n*
>   over { 0,1 } that start with 1]
> ```
>           (distribute 1 lowbits)
>       end;
> ```

To verify this, we need to see the specification for distribute:

> [*LL* is a list of lists →
>   *distribute a LL* =
>   *LL* with *a* inserted at the
>   beginning of each of its elements]

With this and the intended values that annotate the intermediate steps in bit-strings, it should not be too hard to verify that function.

Here is the complete definition of distribute:

```
[ LL is a list of lists →
     distribute a LL =
          LL with a inserted at the
          beginning of each of its elements ]
fun distribute a [] = []
  | distribute a (L::rest) =
          (a::L) :: (distribute a rest);
```

Finally, the idea of intended values can often be usefully applied to ordinary procedural languages as well as to functional languages. Even in procedural languages, many programs contain routines that are written very much in a functional style. Such a routine is a function that does nothing more than return the value of an expression. Very often, the routine shares many characteristics with the routines that we have seen in functional languages: definition by cases, recursion, and application to recursively defined data structures.

When a routine has this form, intended values are a natural way to specify the routine and intermediate expressions within the body of the routine. An example is the following function, written in C, which computes the maximum depth of a tree. This is defined, for our purposes, as the length of the longest path from the root to a leaf. (Other declarations are omitted; you may assume that names have their obvious meanings.)

```
[ maximum depth of tree t ]
int treeMaxDepth(tree t)
{
    if (isleaf(t))
        return 0;
    else
        return 1 + max(

                          [ maximum depth of left subtree of t ]
                          treeMaxDepth(t->left),

                          [ maximum depth of right subtree of t ]
                          treeMaxDepth(t->right));
}
```

Of course, we could have written an intended function, rather than an intended value, as a specification for this routine:

[return the maximum depth of tree *t*]

But intended values are still useful for annotating intermediate expressions, especially when they are parts of long and complicated expressions or statements.

It is usually not hard to distinguish intended functions from intended values when reading a program, by their meanings or because intended functions contain distinguishing symbols such as := or "return". However, if both intended functions and intended values are used in a particular section of a program, it may help to distinguish them by a difference in notation. Two possibilities are to write intended values as

$$[\ (expression)\ ]$$

or

$$[\ =\ expression\ ]$$

and to write intended functions in the usual way. But in most parts of programs in functional languages, there will be no confusion because there will be no intended functions, only intended values.

Exercises

1. Write and verify recursive routines to perform each of the following operations on lists of names, like those of Section 9.1. Each routine takes a list as argument. If your preferred language is not C, or if your instructor requires you to use a different language, begin by defining the closest possible equivalent to the data type `Namelist` in the language that you use.

   a. Return the sum of the lengths of all the names.

   b. Return the longest name.

   c. Return the list, reversed.

   d. Print the list as `printNamelist` does, except that adjacent names are separated by a comma and a space; however, the last two names are separated by the word *and* with spaces around it.

2. Expand the outline of a recursive descent parser in Section 9.3 into a calculator program, which evaluates expressions whose operands are integer constants. Verify the program.

3. Verify the function `bitstrings` in Section 9.4.

4. In a functional language such as LISP, Scheme, or ML, write and verify each of the following functions. In each case, a set is a list containing no duplicate elements. (Be sure to verify that the lists that you produce are indeed sets!)

   a. The cardinality (number of elements) of a set.

   b. The intersection of two sets.

   c. A set of the subsets of a given set, including the set itself and the empty set.

Notes

The standard textbook for the Scheme language is [Abel85]. A good introduction to ML is [Paul91].

Scheme and a few other languages support infinite recursively defined data structures, which are manipulated using a kind of delayed evaluation that creates only the elements that are actually needed in a computation ([Abel85], Sections 3.4.4 and 3.4.5).

Recursive descent is mentioned at least briefly in most compiler-writing textbooks. For example, several simple examples of actual C code for recursive-descent parsers are presented in [Aho86], Chapter 2, and [Fisc91], Section 2.4. The method is presented in some detail in [Wait93], Chapter 5.

The idea of an "intended value" is original (as far as I know) and appears here for the first time.

Chapter 6 of [Paul91] presents methods for proving properties of ML functions, including proving that a function has a given value. The methods are similar to those presented here, although they do not use intended values for subexpressions within a function definition. That chapter also introduces the reader to some of the complications that arise in reasoning about recursive routines and recursively defined data structures more formally than we have done in this chapter.

10

Testing

10.1   The Role of Testing

Once we have verified a program in a verification review, do we have a zero-defect program? Maybe, but maybe not. We must always remember that we are capable of making mistakes as verifiers, just as we are as programmers. Verifying as a group process helps to reduce the number of mistakes that slip by undetected, but we can't assume that there will be none.

This means that we cannot put our programs into service immediately after we verify them. Just as with more traditional processes for developing programs, we must perform thorough and systematic testing on them.

However, testing plays a somewhat different role in Cleanroom-style development from its role in more traditional development. You will remember that our philosophy from the beginning has been that we are *not* going to rely on testing and debugging to give us a high-quality product. If we have done our development well up to this point, we already have a high-quality product. That is why we have put so much effort into careful development, including specifying and verifying every part of the program.

As we test our programs, we are likely to find a few bugs and, of course, we will fix them. This will raise the quality of our product, as measured by low defect content, even higher. We would be foolish to pass up this last opportunity to find and fix defects before releasing our product to its users.

But testing will serve an even more important purpose for us: as a check on the quality of our development process. If we find too many bugs in testing, it is a sign that we are not doing our development well enough. Especially, it means that we are not doing our verification well enough, because verification should be catching almost all of the bugs.

How many bugs are too many? This depends on circumstances. For one thing, it depends on what is normal for a particular person or organization. Experience is an important factor: we might expect beginners to achieve a bug level that is only moderately low, but an experienced team with a history of near-zero-defect work should come close to this performance every time.

A commonly used measure of bug content is bugs per thousand lines of code, not counting blank lines, and not counting documentation lines that contain only comments, intended functions, definitions of specification functions, and so on. *We should expect that the number of bugs per thousand lines will be less than 10* after verification, and after compilation and correcting of syntax errors, but before any testing. Even a relative beginner, who has learned how to specify and verify and who has had some verification review experience, should be able to do as well as this.

You will recall from Chapter 1 that the average defect density measured in the seventeen real-world projects cited there was 2.3 per thousand lines. In an organization in which this is a normal number, a bug density or 4 or 5 per thousand lines might not be considered good enough. In fact, some organizations have a policy of rejecting any program, or large component of a program, in which a bug density higher than some such threshold is found during testing. The large number of bugs is taken as evidence that the development was not done carefully enough and that the code is likely to be of unacceptable quality overall. No attempt is made to salvage such code by debugging it; instead, the code is sent back to the developers to be rewritten and reverified, then it is tested again as if it were a completely new product.

We should be sure to take action if the bug density in testing is higher than we want, regardless of whether part of this action is to send the code back for a complete rewrite. Most importantly, we should take a careful look at our development process, particularly the way in which we are writing intended functions and conducting verification reviews. Perhaps we need to conduct the reviews more slowly and carefully. Perhaps we need to be more rigorous, using trace tables or proofs by cases more frequently, or tracing through steps in more detail than we have been doing, rather than calling parts of our programs "correct by inspection" so often. In our intended functions, perhaps we need to write out preconditions explicitly more often, instead of leaving them as implicit preconditions, or perhaps we need to use more precise language or notation.

You will also recall from Chapter 1 that our testing is done on complete programs. In a large organization, this testing is usually done by an independent group; the developers turn the programs over to this group after verification has been completed successfully. If we don't have an independent testing group available to us, we can turn our development team into a testing team and do the job ourselves.

The developers do not unit-test their code in small pieces as they complete them. As you know, we rely on verification reviews instead of unit testing to remove enough of the defects in our code that we can test the whole program effectively. One reason that we do not do unit testing is that we do not need it to bring our code to this level of quality.

Now we can see another reason: unit testing would interfere with our use of testing for quality control. Private unit testing by the developer is uncontrolled and highly variable. Some programmers test their work very thoroughly and systematically, and others run a few cursory tests and consider their work done. Besides, programmers vary greatly in their skill in devising test data, and also in their skill in debugging. In fact, debugging is a notoriously error-prone process, and changes made during debugging often introduce new bugs. For all of these reasons, allowing any amount of unit testing after verification would introduce so much uncontrolled variation that it would destroy our ability to measure the effectiveness of our development process by counting the defects that we find in testing.

In fact, we should avoid any kind of private testing, whether it is unit testing or some other kind. We want to make sure that all defects are counted uniformly and objectively so that we get an accurate measure of quality. The best way to do this is to do our testing in the open, under the eyes of people other than the developer.

A third reason to avoid unit testing, and perhaps the most important, is so that we will not be tempted to rely on it at the expense of doing a thorough and careful job in verification reviews. If we know that our code will be run for the first time under the eyes of other people, even if those people are our colleagues on the development team, we will want to be as sure as possible that the code is defect-free before we turn it over for testing.

This does not mean that we must never use the computer at all during development. Obviously, most of us will use a text editor or similar tool to prepare our programs. Experimentation using the computer is often appropriate too. For example, we might want to experiment with an algorithm, timing it to see if it will be fast enough. We might want to build prototypes of user interfaces to see if they will be convenient to use. Especially, we might want to experiment with other software that our programs will operate with, if the interfaces that the other software provide are not well documented (a common situation, unfortunately). But we must resist the temptation to test our actual code.

10.2   Usage-based Testing

When Harlan Mills and his colleagues were studying data from reports of failures of IBM software products, he found that the failure rates due to different defects was far from uniform. On the contrary, some defects caused far more failures than others did. The most frequently encountered 1.4% of the defects accounted for 53.7% of the failures reported by users, whereas the least frequently encountered 61.6% of the defects accounted for only 2.9% of the failures. These figures were much the same for each of the nine products in the study.

Mills and his colleagues reasoned, then, that if our goal is to minimize the dissatisfaction of users by minimizing the number of failures that they encounter, we would do far better by finding and fixing the defects that the users will encounter most frequently than by finding and fixing any arbitrary defects.

An appropriate measure of quality in this context is *mean time to failure*, or MTTF. This is the length of time, on average, that a copy of the program will run without its user observing a malfunction. MTTF can be measured in seconds, hours, or weeks, for example; or, if the software does not run continuously, then runs, input lines, or keystrokes might be more appropriate units. Mills and his colleagues calculated, based on the IBM data, that finding one defect with the same probability that it would be the first defect encountered by a user, and fixing that defect, would improve a program's MTTF much more than finding and fixing an arbitrarily chosen defect: in fact, 21 times as much!

All of this suggests, then, that we should test our programs by running them in the same ways that our users will run them, if our goal is to keep our users happy by minimizing the failures that they encounter. To do this, we test the programs with input data that is representative of the input that the users will give the program in actual use. Let us call this kind of testing *usage-based testing*.

This is quite different from *structural testing*, for example, in which we choose test data based on the structure of the code that we are testing. Typical structural testing strategies aim at complete or maximal *coverage* of the code: for example, executing each statement at least once, taking each branch of a conditional at least once, or executing each path through each sequence of conditionals. Testing based on coverage is an effective strategy for finding the most bugs with the fewest tests — in fact, it typically does this better than usage-based testing does. But, since it finds bugs in an order that may or may not be related to the order in which they would be encountered by users, it is likely to be much less effective at increasing MTTF.

Where do we get the input data to do usage-based testing? If we have a sufficiently large body of actual input data from users, we can test our programs with that. We might have such data when a program is a re-implementation or enhancement of an existing program, for example.

Otherwise, we need to generate the input data. We will need to estimate, as accurately as possible, how our program will typically be used, and to generate data that reflects this. We might be able to extrapolate from the information we have about past usage of similar programs, or we may be able to survey the program's future users to find out how they think they will use it. Sometimes we may not be in a very good position to make an accurate estimate, but any guess is likely to be better than none at all.

A good place to start is the program's specification or user's manual, to see what inputs the program is designed to handle, but this gives us only a start. Besides knowing what inputs are legitimate, we need to know, or guess at, the relative frequencies of the different legitimate inputs, and to generate data consistent with these frequencies. Also, we should generate at least some input that is *not* legitimate, since users often make mistakes and give erroneous input to programs. The program's specification may or may not say what should happen in this case, but the program should do something that we would consider reasonable.

10.3   Test-data Generators

Generating the data for testing can be tedious, but, in the case of usage-based testing, we can automate much of the work by using *test-data generators*. These are programs that generate data randomly, based on a specification of the form of the data and its parts, and the possible values that can occur in the data.

Furthermore, with a good test-data generator, this specification can include information about the relative frequencies of different data values. This will allow us to adjust these frequencies according to our estimates of how often the different values will occur in actual use, so that the data generated, over a sequence of runs, will resemble the data that would be given to the program over a sequence of runs in actual use. This is necessary if we are to perform really accurate usage-based testing.

With many test-data generators, the specification takes the form of a *context-free grammar*, much like the BNF grammars that are used to define the syntax of programming languages. A context-free grammar is a set of *productions*, each of which defines the structure of some part of the data. The name of that part appears on the left-hand side of the production, and is called a *nonterminal symbol*. A production contains one or more right-hand sides, which are the various forms that the part named by the left-hand side can take. A right-hand side may contain actual strings of characters, which are called *terminal symbols*, or other nonterminal symbols that define smaller parts of the output through other productions, or both.

An example of part of such a specification is shown in Figure 10.1. It represents the data transmitted from one mail handler to another in a system for transmitting

```
session:  ok_session                    [0.95]
          | out_of_order_session
          | garbage_session ;

ok_session:  no_ops helo no_ops messages no_ops quit [0.95]
             | no_ops quit
             | no_ops helo no_ops quit ;

out_of_order_session:
            /* may generate an ok_session too,
               but with low probability! */
        any_command
      | any_command out_of_order_session ;

any_command:  helo | mail | rcpt | data | rset | no_op | quit ;

messages:  incomplete_message  [0.1]
              /* if "QUIT" comes prematurely */
           | message                 [0.6]
           | message no_ops messages ;

message:  completed_message         [0.9]
          | rset no_ops message
          | incomplete_message no_ops rset no_ops message ;

completed_message:  mail no_ops rcpts no_ops data ;

incomplete_message:  mail
                     | mail no_ops rcpts ;

helo: "HELO " domain crlf ;
quit: "QUIT" crlf ;
rset:  "RSET" crlf ;
mail:  "MAIL FROM:" path crlf ;

rcpts:  rcpt
        | rcpt no_ops rcpts ;
rcpt:  "RCPT TO:" path crlf ;

data:  "DATA" crlf body ;

no_ops:                    [0.9]
        | no_op no_ops ;
no_op:  "NO_OP" crlf ;
```

Figure 10.1 Part of an input to a test-data generator

electronic mail. (As it happens, this specification was taken from an actual development project and was used to test an actual program.) In the notation used here, a production appears as a left-hand side, a colon, one or more right-hand sides separated by vertical bars, and a semicolon as a terminator. The first production is assumed to define the structure of the data as a whole. Comments are as in the C language.

The right-hand sides of a production can be annotated with numbers in square brackets, which are probabilities for choosing that right-hand side when data is generated using the production. Where no probability is given for right-hand sides, they have equal probabilities, and of course the probabilities for all choices must sum to 1. The first three lines, for example, say that when generating the data corresponding to a `session`, an `ok_session` should be generated with probability 0.95, an `out_of_order_session` should be generated with probability 0.025, and a `garbage_session` should be generated with probability 0.025.

The test-data generator will generate data from this specification with the following algorithm, which keeps a sequence of pending symbols: terminal symbols (strings) which have not yet been emitted, and nonterminal symbols which have not yet been expanded using a production.

> initialize *pending-symbols* with the left-hand side
>   of the first production
> **while** *pending-symbols* is nonempty
>   remove the first symbol from *pending-symbols*
>   **if** that symbol is a terminal symbol
>   emit it
>   **else**
>   find the production with that symbol as left-hand side
>   choose one of the production's right-hand sides at random
>   according to their probabilities
>   insert the symbols of that right-hand side at the beginning
>   of *pending-symbols*

For some other test-data generators, the specification of the data is in the form of a finite-state *Markov chain*. This is like a finite-state machine, but with probabilities on the transitions from one state to another. Instead of state transitions being determined by input symbols, transitions are chosen randomly according to these probabilities.

An example is shown at the top of Figure 10.2. The states represent the modes of a simple text editor. Characters that the test-data generator will produce (in other Markov chains, these might be strings) are associated with the transitions. When a transition is taken, the corresponding character is emitted. (For simplicity, classes of characters such as "digit" and "text character" are grouped together so that we do not have to draw a separate transition for each character.)

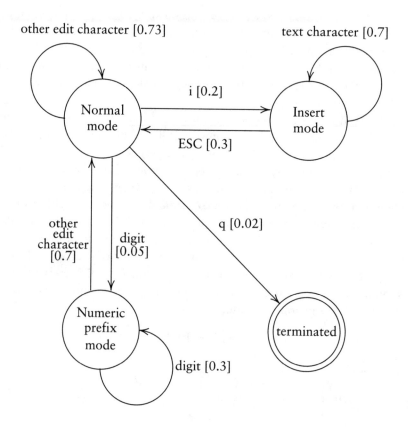

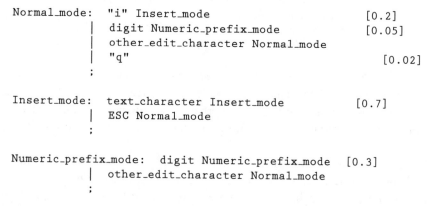

Figure 10.2 A Markov chain and an equivalent grammar

As a matter of fact, we can use such a specification with the kind of test-data generator described earlier, by writing a grammar that is equivalent to the Markov chain. One way of doing this is to use a nonterminal symbol for each state of the Markov chain, and terminal symbols for the symbols associated with the transitions. Then right-hand sides of productions correspond to transitions, and contain some number of terminal symbols followed by the nonterminal symbol corresponding to the new state, unless the new state is the "terminated" state, in which case the right-hand side simply ends.

At the bottom of Figure 10.2 is a grammar corresponding to the Markov chain at the top of the figure. In this grammar, nonterminal symbols are also used for classes of characters; this shortens the specification, but it still represents a finite-state system. (The productions that define these classes are not shown.)

When should this test-data specification be written? If possible, in parallel with the development of the program. There is no reason that either activity needs to precede the other, and doing them in parallel is the fastest way to get things done. If there is a separate testing team, that team can be writing the data specification while waiting for the development team to deliver the program. In fact, it can even generate the test data, and in many cases determine what the correct results of each test should be, in advance of the testing.

As we begin testing using our randomly generated data, we are likely to detect a bug on the very first run, and perhaps a few more not long after that. This is normal, and should not discourage us. It turns out that almost all of these bugs are simple oversights, like typographical errors, forgetting to initialize a variable, or forgetting to open a file before writing to it. We will usually be able to find and fix them with little effort. They will seldom be subtle algorithm flaws that are hard to track down and hard to correct; it turns out that bugs like this are the kinds that verification reviews are particularly effective at detecting.

As we find and fix bugs one at a time, we should find that the number of tests that we need to run to find the next bug increases rapidly. This is a sign that the original bug density was low and that we are finding almost all of the bugs that were present. If we continue to find bugs frequently, it is an indication that there are probably many more still to be found.

But it is only the random nature of our testing that makes this reasoning valid. It is not valid at all with *directed testing*, in which the test data is deliberately chose by the tester, to maximize coverage of the code, or to probe boundary conditions and special cases, or for some other such purpose. Suppose Alice does directed testing and finds lots of bugs: was the code particularly buggy, or is Alice a particularly clever tester? Or suppose Ben tests using data that he devises, and finds very few bugs: was the code of very high quality, or has Ben failed to do his job properly?

There is no way to tell. It is the random nature of our testing that turns testing into a kind of statistical experiment and lets us draw valid conclusions about program quality from the results.

It happens that there are more powerful conclusions that can be drawn from testing that is random but usage-based: we can use the results to predict the reliability (in terms of MTTF) of the program in actual use. In fact, we can measure the time to failure due to the bugs that we find in testing, fix those bugs, then use all the data that we have collected to estimate the MTTF due to any bugs that we may not have found! Such estimates are often used in the Cleanroom process to certify programs to a specific level of reliability, in terms of MTTF. This topic is beyond the scope of this book, because I haven't assumed that my readers have any particular knowledge of statistics, but those of you with some familiarity with statistics might wish to consult the references cited in the Notes section at the end of this chapter.

10.4   Other Forms of Testing

Random testing based on expected usage is not necessarily the only kind of testing that we should do. As we have seen, fixing the bugs that we find in this way is a particularly good way to decrease the frequency of failure of our programs in actual use. If the only consequence of failure is to annoy our users, this may be all we want. But usually this is not our only concern. If a program is safety-critical, like a program that controls a nuclear reactor, a failure that occurs very infrequently may still have disastrous consequences. Or perhaps a program must run unattended for long periods of time on a computer in a remote location, and a failure of any kind would cause loss of valuable data or be costly to correct. Consider, for example, a program that takes data from a seismograph in the middle of a desert, or from an oil well deep in the Arctic tundra. Even in less extreme situations, an infrequently encountered defect in a program is likely to cost someone some money or cause inconvenience that is more than just annoying. In fact, this is probably true of most real-world programs.

Therefore, we will usually wish to perform other kinds of tests, besides tests based on normal usage. In particular, we may run tests using randomly generated data of other kinds: extreme values, for example, or unusual data that we suspect might cause a program to fail. For particularly critical applications, we may need to do a large amount of testing of this kind, perhaps using a number of different data specifications to generate different classes of unusual data.

In fact, we might even want to supplement our random testing with directed testing, in which we choose each test case individually. If nothing else, we should certainly test special cases and boundary conditions in the input values, to make sure that the program handles them correctly. Doing a great deal more than this can be costly and time-consuming, but may well be appropriate when we really need to remove every defect that we possibly can, and can afford to spend extra time and effort to find any rarely encountered bugs that may still remain.

All of the usual testing strategies are candidates, including coverage-based testing. If necessary, we can even break our programs into pieces and do unit testing on the pieces! We had good reasons for avoiding unit testing during development, but it can do no harm now, and it may be very helpful. In fact, if we attempt to do coverage testing, we may find that unit testing is the only reasonable way to get the coverage that we want.

Of course, after we detect a bug with any of our tests, we will want to run the test again after the offending part of the program has been repaired, to make sure that the bug has really been removed. This is another kind of directed testing.

However, we must do these additional kinds of tests only after we have performed our usual random testing based on normal usage. Or, at the very least, we must refrain from fixing any bugs that we find using unusual or deliberately devised test data until after we have performed testing using randomly generated data based on normal usage. Otherwise, any conclusions regarding quality that we might draw from the results of the usage-based testing would be invalidated.

Exercises

1. Construct a test-data generator of the kind described in Section 10.3. If possible, specify and verify it as you would any other program. Use it in your testing, where appropriate, from now on.

2. Take one or more programs that you have verified but never executed. Perform usage-based testing on each one, until you fail to find any more bugs after many tests, or until you conclude that the program had too many bugs to start with. What bug density did you find in each program? Did these results meet your expectations?

3. Take one or more of the programs that you tested for Exercise 2. Try as hard as you can to find as many more bugs as you can in each one, using whatever kinds of testing you like. What were your results?

4. Suppose that, by accident, you happen to be looking over the code of a program that you have verified but not tested, and you discover a bug. What should you do about it?

Notes

The IBM failure data is presented and discussed in [Curr86] and [Cobb90].

A staff member at Hewlett-Packard, reporting on HP's experiences with Cleanroom methods, writes ([Head94] p. 41):

> When IBM was asked about the criteria for judging a module worthy of being discarded, they stated that the basic criterion is that if testing reveals more than five defects per thousand lines of code, the module is discarded. . . . Our experience is that any half-serious attempt to implement cleanroom [sic] will easily achieve this. We achieved a defect density of one defect per thousand lines of code the first time we did a cleanroom project. It would appear that this "discard the offending module" policy is primarily intended to be a strong attention getter to achieve commitment to the process. It is seldom necessary to invoke it.

Most software engineering textbooks cover various kinds of testing, usually including unit testing, structural testing, and coverage-based testing. There are a number of books devoted entirely to testing; [Beiz90] is a particularly complete treatment of directed testing.

Context-free grammars and finite-state machines are covered in detail in textbooks such as [Hopc79]. The test-data generator described in Section 10.3 uses specifications that are similar to those used by the YACC parser generator [Levi92]. A more elaborate test data generator is described in [Mill95]. For additional advice on constructing grammars or Markov chains for generating test data, see [Walt95].

For those who wish to investigate statistical inference and reliability certification based on testing, [Poor93] is a good place to start, followed perhaps by [Tram94]. Some relevant implications of statistical properties of Markov chains are presented in [Whit94].

Research continues on both random and directed testing; much of this work is being done outside of the Cleanroom community. See, for example, papers in conference proceedings such as [Youn98]. One such paper [Mitc98] presents some evidence that it is possible to combine the two kinds of testing so that statistical inference is still valid.

11

Incremental Development

11.1   Developing a Program in Increments

The previous chapters have presented methods for constructing, verifying, and testing programs. By now you should have had some practice in applying these methods to small programs, so that you see how the methods work in practice and how they fit together.

But what happens when programming projects get bigger? Will we perform the steps in the same order, first writing the whole program as it will be delivered, then verifying all of its parts, and only then testing it for the first time?

Not at all. Instead, our strategy will be to use a process of *incremental development*. The job will be broken up into *increments*, in which we construct, verify, and test a part of the program in each increment. This will give us more control over the process, and more visibility into it, so that we can observe progress and judge how well we are doing all through the process.

In incremental development, we build the program top-down, starting with a main program and perhaps a few supporting parts, and gradually adding other parts. The first increment is usually a very minimal program, much smaller than the final product will be. In fact, it may be little more than a minimal user interface, perhaps with a small amount of code that does real computation underneath. Much of the code that will eventually do the real work is missing. Where necessary, simple stubs are inserted to take the place of missing code, just enough to let the increment be compiled and run. Then this increment is verified just as any other program would be, in review meetings, and when it is successfully verified it is tested just as any other program would be.

Each increment after the first is built by writing more parts of the program and integrating them into the previous increment. New code is inserted, much of it replacing stubs. All of the new code and all code that is changed is verified. Then the increment is tested again, testing the new and changed code and its interaction with the old code. This means that integration and integration testing are done incrementally too, instead of being done in the "big bang" fashion that is common in traditional software development.

More and more functionality is added to the program in each increment, until the final increment does everything that the program is required to do. That increment is the completed product.

Every increment is a real, executable program. It is not a prototype or a rough draft: every part of it except for the stub code will be present in the final, delivered product. Therefore, every part of it, except perhaps for the stub code, must be developed carefully using our usual Cleanroom-based methods, including specification and verification.

Furthermore, every increment can be run using real data. This may be a subset of the data that the final increment will accept, possibly a limited number of kinds of data or limited ranges of values, but it is real data in the same form that the final program will accept.

This also means that we can test each increment, right from the first one, using a test-data generator and a data specification that corresponds to the subset of data that the increment can accept. Then we can augment and refine this specification for each new increment, corresponding to the new functionality in that increment. Thus development of our tests becomes an incremental process as well.

How big should an increment be? That depends on how big the final program will be, but also on other factors such as the size of the development team and the size of the programs that it has built before. A program that will be only a few thousand lines long, with a development team of only a few people, might be built in increments that are only a few hundred lines long, if it is built incrementally at all. In a bigger project with a bigger development team, the increments might be thousands of lines long, perhaps even ten thousand or more.

As an example of how we might define our increments, suppose we are building a screen-based editor for hypertext documents. Our first increment might implement only the commands for reading a file, moving a cursor around the screen, inserting and deleting characters, and writing to a file. It is a good idea to make the first increment quite small, but still substantial enough that a user or tester can enter real input and see real results.

The second increment might introduce the ability to work with more than one file at once and to insert links between files. Later increments might implement additional editing commands, such as searching for a given string, replacing one string with another, and cutting and pasting; and additional kinds of links, such as links to graphical images or executable code.

Some increments of a program can serve as versions that are released to users. In our editor example, the second increment might be a good candidate for this. Probably not all increments will be worth releasing to users; in most cases the first, minimal increment, and possibly several other intermediate increments, will be seen only by the programmers, verifiers, and testers. But it is a very good idea to let users try out early versions of the program. The users will often give you useful suggestions for further development, and may spot problems or misconceptions in time for the developers to address them. It is never pleasant to have to make adjustments during development in this way, but waiting until the program is complete, or delivering an unsatisfactory product, is worse.

Furthermore, since each increment is a complete program, even an early increment contains a working user interface, or a substantial part of one. This means that, even if the increment does not contain enough functionality to allow the user to do useful work with it, it can be demonstrated to users as a prototype. This is another good way to get useful opinions and suggestions from the users.

11.2 Planning and Carrying Out the Process

The development of a program must be based on a specification, of course. The development team may be responsible, at least in part, for producing this specification. If so, this is usually done through a process of consultation with users and other concerned persons to determine requirements in general terms, and then refining these requirements, with further consultation as needed, into a detailed specification. Or the specification may simply be imposed from outside the development team. However the specification is obtained, it should specify the behavior of the whole program in its final form, even if the development is to be done incrementally.

The next step is to plan the increments. To do this, the specification is broken down into the individual capabilities that it prescribes. The easiest way to do this is often on the basis of inputs: different commands, different classes of data values, different patterns that might be significant in input sequences, typical values versus special cases, and so on. Then these capabilities are grouped and ordered into those that will be supported by the successive increments.

There are many considerations that we might take into account in doing this. Here are a few: Each increment, including the first, must allow all of the capabilities supported by that release to be exercised in testing, and in such a way that the results can be observed. Thus, for example, if command type A produces an effect that can be observed only by executing command type B, it would make sense to implement A and B in the same increment, but not to implement A in an earlier increment than B. Basic features should usually be implemented first so that more advanced features can be built on them. And, of course, it will probably be easiest to implement related features in the same increment.

Our plan should also identify which increments will be versions that will be released to users. Each released version should provide a reasonably complete and coherent set of capabilities, so which versions we decide to release may affect the way we group features into increments.

After we have completed our increment plan, we proceed to construct increment 1. If we have a separate testing team, it can be designing the tests for increment 1 while the developers are constructing it.

When increment 1 is completely constructed and verified, it enters testing. If we have a separate testing team, the development team can start on increment 2 while increment 1 is being tested. When the testers finish their work, they can proceed to design the tests for increment 2. Assuming that all goes well in testing, and no major modifications or complete rewriting of increment 1 is necessary, increment 3 is begun while increment 2 is being tested, and so on.

This smooth progression of increments through the pipeline of development and testing activities can be slowed down a bit as testers find defects that need to be fixed. If they find defects in increment n, they will report them to the developers, who will fix them in increment $n + 1$ as they work on it. (The testers should make note of the tests that found these defects and run them again on increment $n + 1$, to be sure that the defects were fixed, but only after conducting their usual usage-based tests on increment $n + 1$.) Of course, if major reworking of an increment is found to be necessary, the testers may be left with nothing to do while the developers do the reworking, except to design the tests for future increments. But major reworking should seldom be necessary once the developers become competent in Cleanroom-style methods.

Requests or demands for changes often come from users as well, after they have used an early release of a program or have seen it demonstrated. Luckily, incremental development gives us an opportunity to defend the project and its schedule against this common occurrence. Suppose increment 2 becomes Release One, and a user tries it and suggests adding a feature that was not in the original specification. Instead of saying, "Sorry, we can't do that; the requirements were frozen eight months ago," or, "Yes, we could go back and put that in, but it will delay completion by six weeks," we may now be in a position to say, "That's a good idea; we'll put it in increment 5, and you'll be able to try it in Release Two." Since the developers are still working on increment 4 (or possibly even increment 3), minor changes or additions to the specification can be accommodated without disrupting work in progress, so they will often add little extra cost or schedule time to the project as a whole.

11.3   Example: Rehearsal Scheduling

Alice, Ben, and Chris have just started their next project. They are speaking with Doug, the music director of the college. He and other people from the college and the town will be presenting a musical comedy in a month, and rehearsals and other preparations are under way.

Doug always finds that it is a very complicated and time-consuming job to schedule and coordinate all of the rehearsals, meetings, and other activities that are part of the preparation for an amateur theatrical production. He thinks that software could help him to do the job, and he is discussing his requirements with Alice, Ben, and Chris.

There are a number of tracks of activity that must be scheduled: rehearsal of the stage action, rehearsal of musical numbers, set design and construction, meetings of the directors and the vocal and dance coaches, and so on. Some tracks are subdivided: for example, rehearsals of the stage action are divided into blocking, lines and acting, and acting with music (for purposes of timing; either with a piano or with the pit orchestra). Each track should be scheduled for a certain number of hours per week. Of course, these numbers may change as opening night approaches, and extra rehearsals of particular scenes or musical numbers are usually necessary. Each track will have a starting date, some intermediate deadlines, and a final deadline, and there may be constraints relating these dates among different tracks.

Each person involved in the production has a different schedule of available times during the week and, of course, exceptions in some weeks. A person may be involved in more than one track (the music director, for example, or a chorus member who also helps to build sets). Rehearsals of some scenes and musical numbers require the presence of only a few of the actors or musicians. In fact, rehearsals of some scenes can proceed if a few of the actors playing minor parts cannot come, as long as all of the lead actors are present.

Locations for each activity must also be scheduled. There are a variety of spaces available: the stage, the scene shop, rehearsal rooms, and other meeting rooms. Not all spaces are suitable for all activities: for example, rehearsals of vocal numbers must be done in a rehearsal room that has a piano, and dress rehearsals must be done on the stage. Of course, each activity requires a space that is large enough. Different spaces are available only at certain times of the week, and most of them will already be booked for other purposes at certain times on certain days. Some spaces cannot be used at the same time as others: for example, the scene shop is adjacent to the stage and cannot be used when there is another performance in progress, and some of the rehearsal rooms cannot be used for any loud activity at such a time because the sound insulation in the building is inadequate.

All in all, a rather complicated scheduling problem.

Doug would like to be able to view or print a master schedule, the schedule for each track, and the schedule for each person. Of course, he needs to be able to change any of the data and produce a new schedule that reflects the changes. In fact, he would really like to be able to see the schedule as it was, but with any new conflicts highlighted. Then perhaps the schedule and the data could be tweaked interactively until the conflicts are removed.

He would also like help in keeping track of progress. For example, he would like to be able to display a list of all the scenes or musical numbers, differentiated (perhaps by displaying in different colors) according to how many times they have been rehearsed. He wants to be able to store and view histories of rehearsals and meetings: for each one, what was accomplished and who was present. When an extra rehearsal or meeting is called, he would like to be able to get information on how to contact the people involved, and to keep track of which of them have been notified of the extra event and have confirmed that they can come.

Alice, Ben, and Chris take their notes from this meeting and make a list of the major capabilities that are required, arranged in what they think might be a plausible order to implement them:

1. Scheduling of people for a single track, given the normal weekly schedule of each person.
2. Exceptions to those weekly schedules.
3. Dividing of tracks into blocks of time (for rehearsals of different scenes, for example), taking into account the need for only certain people to be present at some times, and producing individual schedules for people accordingly.
4. Multiple tracks, taking into account people who are involved in more than one track.
5. Deadlines, and ordering of deadlines among tracks.
6. Scheduling of rooms.
7. Scheduling of extra meetings and rehearsals.
8. Interactive resolution of conflicts that arise after a schedule has been prepared.
9. Histories of the rehearsals and other events.
10. Contact information, and recording notification and confirmations for the extra events.

They meet with Doug again to discuss this list. They point out that scheduling of people seems to be the most important theme. Scheduling of rooms is a somewhat separate issue, and this could be omitted if there is not enough time or money to do everything, or deferred until everything to do with people is implemented. Similarly, histories of the rehearsals seems to be a somewhat separate issue. Information on who has been contacted for special rehearsals seems even more of a separate issue, and could easily be deferred or omitted. There seems to be no great need to store information on how to contact people as part of the proposed program at all; this information doesn't really interact with any of the other features, and could just as easily be kept in a completely separate data file, or on paper.

Doug agrees with all of these observations, and agrees that storing the information on how to contact people is not necessary. He also requests that the scheduling of rooms be moved farther down in the ordering of capabilities, after "histories of the rehearsals" and before "recording notifications and confirmations for the extra events."

After further discussion, it appears that relationships among some of the capabilities on the list may affect how they are grouped into increments. For one thing, the recording of notifications and confirmations for the extra events seems to belong naturally with the scheduling of those events; in fact, the scheduling of an event might not be considered final until all confirmations have been received. For another, the processing of deadlines interacts with the processing of histories, since a deadline might be something like "all scenes in Act One have been rehearsed at least twice."

They eventually decide on the following tentative plan for the increments:

Increment 1: scheduling of people for a single track, given the normal weekly schedule of each person.

Increment 2: exceptions to those weekly schedules.

Increment 3: dividing of tracks into blocks of time, multiple tracks, and individual schedules for people.

Increment 4: scheduling of extra events, including recording notifications and confirmations, and interactive resolution of conflicts.

Increment 5: histories of the rehearsals, deadlines, and ordering of deadlines among tracks.

Increment 6: room scheduling.

The first increment will be minimal, which is good strategy, and will be seen only by our developers. The second increment will probably contain only a relatively small amount of new code, but Doug would like to see it demonstrated so that he has a chance to express his opinions and suggestions very early in the development. The third increment will be released to Doug for his use; he says that he can actually do useful work with the capabilities that it will provide. Each increment after that will also be given to Doug, because each one will give him significantly more help.

Alice, Ben, and Chris now go away and write specifications for the program as a whole and for the individual increments. These specifications make heavy use of specification functions, of course. They also make heavy use of mathematical notation and operations: sets of time periods, sets of people, unions and intersections of these sets, and so on.

Our team members return to Doug, and they all review these specifications, with the others interpreting the mathematics for Doug in some places. After a few minor corrections, the specifications are pronounced complete, and the development of the first increment begins.

Some time later, Doug is watching a demonstration of increment 2.

Alice: Would you like to see what happens when you start from scratch, with no data entered yet?

Doug: Sure.

He sees a screen with menu items labeled "overall," "tracks," and "people."

Chris: In later increments there will be more choices on the menu, of course.

Ben: Normally you'd see the name of the show at the top of the screen, but that hasn't been entered yet. And at the bottom you'd see a summary of today's activities, if we had a schedule already worked out.

Doug: Good. Can I try something?

Ben: Sure, go ahead.

Doug selects the menu item "tracks" and sees another screen titled "define a new track" and some spaces to fill in data.

Doug: I wasn't expecting to see this screen yet!

Ben: When there is at least one track already defined, you would first go to a screen that would let you select one of the existing tracks for editing, or you could choose to come to this screen instead.

Doug: I think I'd prefer to go to that screen first in any case, even if all I see is a message saying "No tracks defined yet" and a link to this screen. Then it would always work the same way, and I think it would be less confusing.

Alice: I see your point. (to Chris) That would be an easy change to make, wouldn't it?

Chris: Yes, of course. I'll make a note of it. And I'll edit the change into the specifications and show all of you the changes.

Alice: So that's the way it will work starting with increment 3. That's the version that we'll be giving you to work with on your own.

Doug: Right. Thanks!

Later:

Ben: The times that everyone is free that week are shown here. Now you can select the times that you need from those. This counter will always show you how many more hours you still need to select.

Doug: What if I could click on some time that is *not* marked as available, and see a list of the people who have conflicts at that time? Then I could phone those people to see whether they could possibly come after all.

Alice: That's a good idea. (to her colleagues) Can we put that in increment 3?

Chris: We could, but I think it would make more sense to put it in increment 4. It seems to fit under the heading of "interactive resolution of conflicts."

Doug: Yes, that makes sense. And I can wait for it until then.

Alice: Good, that sounds like a good plan. I'll have to look at the specifications for increment 4 to see how we can fit it in, but it should be straightforward. I'll bring the revised increment 4 specification to our next meeting so that we can inspect the changes.

Doug: Thanks!

And the demonstration continues.

Exercises

1. Prepare a plan for the incremental development of one or more programs for which you have specifications or user's manuals, as if you were going to carry out the developments. Good candidates might be moderate-sized utility programs with which you are familiar, such as a word-processing program, a spreadsheet program, or a simple relational database manager.
2. If time permits in your course or your work schedule, carry out an actual development project in a group with at least two other people. Try to pick a project that you can complete in perhaps a thousand lines of code, not counting documentation lines containing only comments, specifications, and so on; your instructor can assign a project or help you in choosing one. Plan and construct at least two increments, verifying and testing each one.

Notes

Incremental development has been growing in popularity in the software world. It is now treated in most textbooks on software engineering.

However, different people and organizations have quite different ideas about the way in which incremental development should be done, some of them radically different from our way. For example, Frederick Brooks advocates a process of "growing" a program by designing, coding, and testing it in small increments, perhaps even one subroutine at a time. He is quite enthusiastic about this approach ([Broo87] p. 18):

> Nothing in the past decade has so radically changed my own practice, or its effectiveness. . . . The morale effects are startling. Enthusiasm jumps when there is a running system, even a simple one. Efforts redouble when the first picture from a new graphics software system appears on the screen, even if it is only a rectangle. One always has, at every stage in the process, a working system. I find that teams can *grow* much more complex systems than they can *build*.

Boehm's "spiral model" is another approach to incremental development [Boeh88]. The spiral model can be viewed as applying incremental development to the whole development process, from the initial concept of the software on through implementation.

Here are some opinions from Cleanroom experts on the appropriate size of the increments in a large project:

- "... seldom more than 10,000 lines of third-generation code" ([Cobb90] p. 49.)
- "Typical increments are 5 to 15 KLOC [thousands of lines of code]; with experience and confidence, such increments can be expected to greatly increase in size." ([Mill88c] p. 55.)
- "... a 100 KLOC system might be developed in five increments averaging 20 KLOC each..." ([Ling94] p. 51.)

12

Where Do We Go From Here?

12.1   Other Parts of the Cleanroom Process

What now? Where do we go from here? Some of you might be ready to go beyond what has been presented in this book, so this final chapter will introduce several related topics that you might wish to investigate. Finally, we will pause to sum up what we have accomplished and to speculate on what further developments in the field might be useful.

First, there are a few parts of the standard Cleanroom process — as defined by its inventors and used in many of the large-scale industrial projects that have been conducted using Cleanroom methods — that have not been presented in this book. We will introduce them here; readers who would like to investigate them may consult the references cited in the Notes sections of this and previous chapters.

One of these parts is the use of *box structures* as a notation for specifying and designing programs and parts of programs. Box structures can be nested, and they can be refined in a stepwise manner. In fact, box structures come in three forms, each more detailed than the previous, and there is a standard way of refining box structures from one form to the next.

The first form, which serves as a specification, is a *black box*. As in other common uses of the term "black box," nothing inside the black box is visible from outside the box. The box accepts stimuli, and produces a response for each stimulus. However, in general, the response depends not only on the most recent stimulus, but on previous stimuli. Thus the box is a function that maps sequences of stimuli, or *stimulus histories*, to responses.

The next step is to refine the black box into a *state box*. A state box has an internal state, and the behavior of a state box is defined to be a function that takes a stimulus and a current state, and produces a response and a new state.

The state may be expressed in terms of one or more data components. In fact, the construction of a state box corresponding to a black box is a kind of design step, in which the significant design decision is the choice of data components that, together with a stimulus, are sufficient to determine the correct response.

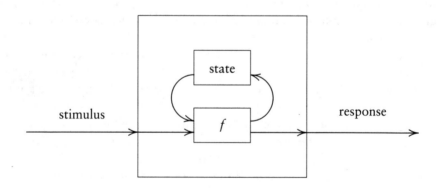

Finally, the state box is further refined into a *clear box*.[1] The internal mechanism of a clear box is visible; specifically, a clear box is defined in terms of the

---

[1]   No, not a "white box"! The term "white box" used as the opposite of "black box," as in "white-box testing," is one of the more brainless bits of jargon in our field. A white box is just as opaque as a black box. "Clear box" is the term that Harlan Mills used; Mills, as usual, got it right.

algorithm that produces the new state and the response from the stimulus and the previous state. The algorithm is typically expressed in a notation that resembles a programming language or pseudocode; the individual steps, unless they are very simple, are smaller black boxes.

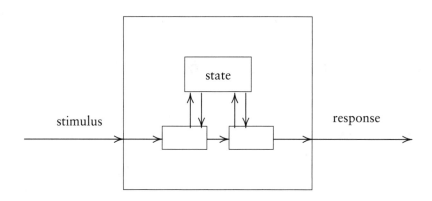

Then, of course, the smaller black boxes are refined and developed in the same way as the first one.

Each step of the refinement, from black box to state box to clear box, is verified in a review meeting, like the review meetings that we have been using, to make sure that the change in representation has preserved the behavior of the previous representation.

As we have seen, we can do functional specification, stepwise refinement, and verification without using box structures, and get very good results that way. But box structures provide useful structuring and refinement techniques, and give an extra measure of structure and discipline to the development process. Some programmers may benefit from this, especially if their ability to produce clean designs and code using other methods is not all that it should be. And the strategy of beginning with a function from complete stimulus histories to responses, then designing state components that capture information from the stimulus histories, and finally designing an algorithmic mechanism that implements the function, is a useful addition to any programmer's repertoire of design techniques.

Also a part of the standard Cleanroom process is the statistical certification of the quality of the software, using the results of testing, as referred to at the end of Section 10.3.

Finally, in a real-world project of any size, there are meetings to review many of the products of the development process besides the program itself. The program's overall requirements and specifications should be reviewed thoroughly, of course, but other products that should be reviewed include increment plans, designs, test plans and specification of test data, and documentation. Most of these reviews are like conventional inspections rather than verification reviews of the kind that we perform on programs, although verification reviews can even be performed on designs if they are expressed in a suitable way. As mentioned in Section 6.1, reviews and inspections such as these are not used only in the Cleanroom process, but are common even in more traditional software engineering processes.

12.2   Other Formal Methods

Another fruitful area for further study is the wider field of *formal methods* — that is, mathematical methods — in software development. The Cleanroom approach is only one of many.

Even among people who develop, promote, and work with formal methods, there does not seem to be complete agreement about the meaning of the term. However, almost all would agree that it includes one or more of the following activities:

- Specifying software using a mathematical notation, in some cases a notation that is unique to the method.
- Deriving, by mathematical methods, properties of a specification, such as inconsistencies in it or logical consequences of it.
- Deriving, by mathematical transformation or by using formal rules for re-finement, code from a specification; or an intermediate form (perhaps called a *design*) from a specification, or code from designs, or both.
- Verifying, by mathematical proof, that code or design meets its specification. This can be done in one or more of the following ways:
    - o Oral argument.
    - o Written proofs.
    - o Automated theorem proving.

And, in some cases, all of these activities are based on the following:

- A particular mathematical definition of the meaning and behavior of programs, sometimes using specialized mathematical constructs.

The Cleanroom-based methods that we have been studying are formal methods by this definition, since we use specification and we use verification by oral argument and (where necessary) written proofs. However, as you have seen, we often do so using rather informal notations and arguments. And our methods are based on the definition of a program as a function from states to states, although this is a rather simple formalism and at times we depart from it somewhat when we write intended functions less formally. Thus you might call our methods *informal use of formal methods* or *semi-formal methods*.

Much of the work that has been done with formal methods has concentrated on specifications. Often, specifications are written, sometimes very formally and in great detail, and used to guide the rest of the development process, but formal derivation and verification are not attempted. Many people consider these latter aspects of formal methods too difficult, given the current state of the art, and not as useful as getting a solid specification in any case. This seems to have been the most common opinion in Britain and Europe in particular. Anthony Hall, in the paper "Seven Myths of Formal Methods," refutes the myth that the essence of formal methods is proof of program correctness:

> In the US, a lot of the work in formal methods has concentrated on program verification. This has made formal methods seem very hard and not very relevant to real life. However, you can achieve a lot without any formal proofs at all. . . .
>
> The fact is that formal methods are all about specifications.

Some of the most influential and widely used formal methods, especially in Britain and Europe, have been

- The Vienna Development Method, or VDM. It is based on the familiar structures of discrete mathematics: sets, sequences, maps, and so on. Operations are specified using preconditions and postconditions.
- The Z (pronounced "zed") specification language. It also is based on discrete mathematics, and much of its notation is similar to that of VDM, but Z provides unique constructs for structuring the specification of a system and for composing a system from smaller parts.
- CCS and CSP. These are both used with concurrent systems, and both define the behavior of a system primarily in terms of the traces, or sequences of events, that the system produces. A typical event is the transmission of a signal or message from one process to another, and so CCS and CSP are particularly suited to describing synchronization and communication among processes.

From the 1980s on, formal methods have been used on a growing number of industrial projects, and there have been a number of success stories. One was the use of Z at IBM's Hursley Park laboratory in England. In collaboration with the developers of Z at Oxford University, IBM used Z to specify and design substantial parts of a new release of CICS, a large transaction-processing system. Members of the project team write:

> The primary aims of this use of formal methods were to improve the quality of the product, as seen by the customer, and to reduce development costs. This was

to be achieved by reducing the overall number of errors in the product, and by identifying the remaining errors as early as possible in the development cycle. . . .

The release consisted of 268,000 lines of new and modified code (together with over 500,000 lines of unchanged code). Of the new and modified code, approximately 37,000 lines were produced from Z specifications and designs, and a further 11,000 lines were partially specified in Z. Some 2000 pages of formal specifications were produced.

The team used Z only to record specifications; it did not attempt to do formal derivation or verification of code. Each specification was thoroughly inspected in review meetings and revised until it was judged to be satisfactory.

The errors detected throughout the development process were counted for the code developed with and without the use of Z. The code developed using Z had a higher rate of errors detected in the earliest design stage, but a lower rate after that, as IBM had hoped.

IBM has also calculated that there is a reduction in the total development cost of the release. Based on the reduction of programmer days spent fixing problems, they estimated that there was a 9% reduction, as compared to developing the 37,000 lines without Z specifications.

There also seems to have been a reduction in the number of errors reported by customers on the new release . . . in the first 8 months after the release was made available, the code which was specified in Z seems to have approximately $2\frac{1}{2}$ times fewer problems than the code which was not specified in Z . . . There is also evidence to show that the severity of the problems for code specified in Z is much lower than for other problems.

Some of these are qualitative judgments and estimates, and detailed data was never published. However, IBM judged the project to be a success, and it received the Queen's Award for Technological Achievement in 1992.

Dan Craigen, Susan Gerhart, and Ted Ralston conducted a survey of twelve industrial projects in Europe and North America that used formal methods. Most of the work on these projects was done in the late 1980s, although some projects were started in the early 1980s and some continued into the early 1990s. The CICS project at IBM was among the projects surveyed; some others were in the fields of data communications, medical instrumentation, railway signalling, and nuclear reactor safety.

The survey found that

Formal methods are maturing, slowly but steadily.

and that

. . . formal methods, while still immature in certain important respects, are beginning to be used seriously and successfully by industry . . .

According to the survey, the projects did not all experience the same degree of success by all measures. The quality of the product was improved in almost all cases, and client satisfaction was improved in many. Only a few projects experienced improvements in time to market or cost of the process. However, the overall effect of the use of formal methods was generally positive:

> Overall, formal methods, as shown in our survey, enjoy a moderately high degree of relative advantage over other methods. This conclusion is supported by the evidence of clear technical superiority of formal methods in use on high assurance and safety-critical systems, coupled with a demonstrated ability to achieve intellectual control of legacy systems or technologies which are new and unfamiliar. This positive finding is attenuated by the lack of a clear demonstrable business superiority over other methods (e.g. object-oriented design) in terms of cost, quality, and time to market. Hence, formal methods do not compellingly pass the economic profitability test.

However, formal methods continue to be used on substantial projects in the real world, and on some of them the benefits have been economic as well as technical. One recent example, a system called CDIS, was an air traffic control system for the airports in the London area, and was developed by Praxis. According to Anthony Hall,

> We used formal methods in the specification, design, and verification of CDIS, making it one of the largest applications of formal methods attempted thus far. Because of the system's size and complexity, we used several formal methods to develop its sequential and concurrent aspects, in some cases combining formal with more conventional techniques. We also used different notations at different project stages, both for technical reasons, such as when one notation gave us better modularity, and nontechnical reasons, such as to suit a particular team's expertise.

The notations used were VDM; CCS and CSP for parts of the system; and several less-formal notations, such as entity-relationship diagrams, dataflow diagrams, and state-transition diagrams.

In a later discussion of the project, Hall writes:

> This is a safety-critical system, but there was no regulatory pressure to use formal methods for that reason. However, we wanted to make sure that we understood the requirements accurately and decided to use formal methods at the early stages of the life cycle to help us do that. We therefore wrote a formal specification of the whole system as the basis for our development. There are about 150 user-level operations in CDIS (the final system is about 200,000 lines of code), so the specification is a large document (about 1,000 pages). This in turn means that we are making fairly "shallow" use of formality — we did not attempt any proofs of consistency or of particular properties. Nevertheless, we found the specification enormously useful in pinning down just what it was that we were going to build.

The system specification was not the only way we used formality on CDIS. We also wrote a similar specification of the main design-level modules, again at a shallow level. In one particular part of the design we used formality in a much deeper way, writing detailed process specifications and attempting to prove them correct. The fact that some proofs failed demonstrated that our design was in fact incorrect, and as it turned out, incorrect in a way that might well have escaped detection in our tests. Fault metrics for CDIS confirmed our hope that it would be of higher quality than systems built using conventional methods. They also showed an unusual distribution in that, unlike many other systems, very few of the faults that survived system test into the delivered system were requirements or specification faults.

Most interesting is that none of this good news cost us anything — our productivity on the project was as good or better than if we had done it conventionally. I believe that one reason is that the work we put in at the early stages was effective in finding lots of errors that would, if we had not found them, have proved very expensive to correct later. The formal specification enabled us to find these errors effectively.

An independent study attempted to verify the claim of higher quality, using post-delivery fault data and other objective data that could be retrieved after the fact. The researchers found the number of failures, 0.81 per thousand lines, "remarkably low". They found it hard to isolate the effects of formal methods from the effects of other technology used on the project, team composition, and other factors. However, they cautiously concluded that "formal design, combined with other techniques, yielded highly reliable code" and that "the formal *specification* is what most likely led to relatively simple and independent components."

12.3   What Have We Accomplished?

These are some promising areas for further study, but let us return to the Cleanroom-style methods that we have been studying, and pause to consider what we have accomplished.

If you have been practicing the use of the methods presented in the previous chapters, you should already be writing programs with many fewer bugs than before: the defect density that you observe should already be well below 10 per thousand lines of code. You should be spending much less time than before on debugging. The few bugs in your programs should show up very early in testing, and most of them should be very easy to find and fix. And your performance should continue to improve with practice.

You may still be spending more time than you think you should be spending in verification reviews, but practice will help here too. As much as anything else, success will depend on your skill at writing really good intended functions so that the verifications are not only possible but also easy and obvious, and this is something that takes practice to learn. So you might not find that programming the Cleanroom way is taking less overall time than normal for you yet — in fact, it might be taking more. But other people have found, once they master the methods, that doing a project using Cleanroom-style methods takes no more time than doing it the traditional way, and can even take less. Before long, this should be your experience too.

If we can get results like these consistently, we have accomplished something really substantial. But where does all this fit into the larger picture?

The methods of this book are not all you need to be a skilled programmer who produces work of the highest quality — not by any means. There is a great deal that you already know, or should eventually learn, that will contribute to the quality of your work. Consider some of the topics: data structures, patterns of code, and other programming techniques; algorithms, and how to analyze and compare them; conceptual structures, such as finite-state machines, grammars, and dataflow relationships; programming languages and the other tools of our trade; the operating systems, file systems, networks, and other systems that support our activities; the arts of speaking, writing, and collaborating with others in team efforts; and the many and diverse application areas in which you may be called upon to work. And we could identify many others. Your knowledge and skills in all areas — including our new methods of specification, verification, testing, and the rest — should work together and reinforce each other.

*   *   *   *   *

In his well-known paper of 1987, "No Silver Bullet: Essence and Accidents of Software Engineering," Frederick Brooks wrote:

> Of all the monsters that fill the nightmares of our folklore, none terrify more than werewolves, beause they transform unexpectedly from the familiar into horrors. For these, one seeks bullets of silver that can magically lay them to rest.

> The familiar software project, at least as seen by the nontechnical manager, has something of this character; it is usually innocent and straightforward, but is capable of becoming a monster of missed schedules, blown budgets, and flawed products. So we hear desperate cries for a silver bullet — something to make software costs drop as rapidly as computer hardware costs do.

> But, as we look to the horizon of a decade hence, we see no silver bullet. There is no single development, in either technology or in management technique, that by itself promises even one order of magnitude improvement in productivity, in reliability, in simplicity.

Was Brooks wrong? Is the Cleanroom process the "silver bullet" that will slay all of the monsters of software development?

Not really.

We have seen that we can expect an order of magnitude improvement in reliability by using Cleanroom-based methods, if we measure the improvement by the number of bugs left in the code when it is put into service. And, since our testing methods detect the most frequently encountered bugs first, this should correspond to at least that much improvement in the frequency at which our users encounter any remaining bugs. This is a substantial step forward, make no mistake about that. But it doesn't mean that all of our problems are now solved.

For example, "bugs," as we have been using the term, are places in which the code fails to meet its specification. But what if the specification doesn't accurately express what the user wants or needs? What if we simply got the specification wrong?

Cleanroom methods don't really give us any new solutions to the problems of requirements gathering, analyzing the new requirements and the current situation, and deciding what should be in the specification for the new software. We have some new notation for writing the specification, and some criteria for judging whether a specification is expressed well, but not much more. And getting the specification right is certainly as important as building a program to match the specification.

What about productivity? We have seen that we usually have some gain in productivity using our methods. Gains by factors of 1.5 to 5 have been observed on some projects, and this is significant. But the amount of the gain doesn't seem to be as consistent as the amount of improvement in bug rates. Certainly we can't claim a consistent improvement of an order of magnitude.

What about simplicity? Cleanroom methods can't really guarantee that our designs or programs will be a lot simpler than they would be otherwise. Of course, we can look at our intended functions to see whether they seem to be too complicated, and simplify them where possible, before going on to develop designs and code from them. And the other participants in our review meetings will often spot excessive complexity in our programs, and suggest simpler alternatives. But the process itself only helps us somewhat in spotting complexity; it doesn't do much to lead us toward simplicity.

Later in the "silver bullet" paper, Brooks says:

> Great designs come from great designers. Software construction is a *creative* process . . . . Study after study shows that the very best designers produce structures that are faster, smaller, simpler, cleaner, and produced with less effort. The differences between the great and the average approach an order of magnitude.

Brooks recommends that organizations should

> . . . spend considerable effort . . . in finding and developing the great designers upon whom the technical excellence of their products will ultimately depend . . .

each software organization must determine and proclaim that great designers are as important to its success as great managers are, and that they can expect to be similarly nurtured and rewarded.

But what about us as individuals? We should strive to become those great designers. We should continue to learn and to practice our skills. Perhaps not all of us will ever be truly great, but we can strive to achieve the best that we can be.

And if there is no silver bullet, what are the implications for our profession? No, we shouldn't give up. Brooks says:

> Even though no technological breakthrough promises to give the sort of magical results with which we are so familiar in the hardware area, there is both an abundance of good work going on now, and the promise of steady, if unspectacular progress.

That slow, steady progress is what we will need. Yes, we have made substantial progress already, but much remains to be done.

12.4   Prospects for the Future

What are the implications of all this? Where is the field going in the next few years, and where would we like it to go? What further work should be done, and what should we hope to accomplish?

Here are some of my personal opinions. In expressing them, I will quote from several recent statements from eminent people in the software field. I will do this, not to try to prove that I am right by appealing to authority, but because other people said these things first, and better than I could.

First, we are on the right track. With the advances that have been made in both Cleanroom methods and other formal methods, we have very good foundations on which to build. We don't need to start over and try to invent a completely new but even more powerful approach to program development. From David Parnas:

> We have all of the "fundamental models of programming" we will ever need . . . the ground is littered with sound foundations on which nobody has erected a useful edifice.

The time is still right to build on what we have already achieved; there is still plenty of benefit to be gained by doing so.

The Cleanroom approach derives much of its power from the use of formal reasoning, but only as much formality as is necessary in each individual situation. Strict formality is not necessary to achieve high quality, and excessive formality is even detrimental. Increasingly, many people in other parts of the formal methods community have been recognizing this as well. From Daniel Jackson and Jeannette Wing:

> By promoting full formalization . . . formalists have unwittingly guaranteed that
> the benefits of formalization are thinly spread. A lightweight approach, which in
> contrast emphasizes partiality and focused application, can bring greater benefits
> at reduced cost.

From Michael Hinchey and Jonathan Bowen:

> Formality should be used appropriately and judiciously at the weakest links in
> the chain of development, in tandem with other techniques of proven benefit for
> improved computer-based systems.

In the same spirit, we will often want to choose different notations and techniques to use as appropriate in different situations. We saw that Praxis used a
variety of formal and semiformal notations on different parts of the CDIS project.
This approach was apparently successful, and it would not be surprising to see the
same approach used on other projects of similar scale.

It appears that different notations and techniques will often be appropriate in
different phases of the development process. In some of the projects mentioned
above, the most obvious benefits of formal methods came from using formal specification notations like Z early in the process — in developing, expressing, and
validating a specification. If used appropriately, the notation can increase clarity
and reduce ambiguity in the specification, and so increase the effectiveness of such
normal parts of the development process as inspections. From Cliff Jones:

> I remember when I worked for IBM that — with traditional development meth-
> ods — those inspections conducted late in a development cycle tended to be
> crisp and useful in locating errors, whereas inspections conducted earlier in the
> project tended to be woolier and not so useful in locating errors. I believe the
> reason for this was clearly the lack of formal material available in a product's
> early stages — the later reviews had the formality of the code to ensure pre-
> cision. We all know that the expensive mistakes are made in a project's early
> stages: Undetected errors in the specification and overall design are very expen-
> sive to fix. What I have found with specification and design inspections based
> on formal documents is that they achieve the same level of precision as code
> inspections and, with that, a considerably greater level of confidence. Further-
> more, it is precisely in the review process that the virtue of formalizing rigorous
> development becomes clear: Doubts raised in an inspection can be resolved by
> going to another level of formalization.

The really formal methods such as VDM and Z have apparently not been as
helpful in later stages of the process: formal development of code from specifications still does not seem to be practical on a large scale, given the current state of the
art, and neither does completely formal verification, whether automated or manual.
But it is in these later stages that our Cleanroom-based methods have proven to be
particularly effective.

Clearly, then, a promising approach might be to use a specification notation like Z in the early phases of a project, to write the overall specification, then to proceed in the Cleanroom style for the remainder of the development. It is possible to constrain the use of the Z notation so that the assertions are similar in form to our intended functions, and this would probably help to make the transition between notations easy. Conversely, we would probably want to retain some of the Z set-theoretic notation in our lower-level intended functions, and this would be quite appropriate too.

This is not a completely new idea, but (to the best of my knowledge) no one has yet found a really effective way to combine Cleanroom-style methods with the use of a notation like Z. But, in my opinion, this is an endeavor that would be well worth more effort.

Finally, whether or not we use a particular formal method, or the specific mathematical notation that goes with any particular formal method, there are benefits to be gained simply by using mathematical concepts in our specifications and designs. From Daniel Jackson and Jeannette Wing again:

> The precision of mathematical thinking relies not on formality but on careful use of mathematical notions. You don't need to know Z to think about sets and functions.

From David Parnas again:

> We are discussing the use of mathematics in engineering, which is nothing new.... Engineers use mathematics routinely in much of their work. Software designers should do the same.

In some programming groups the language of mathematics, or some specific mathematical notation like that of Z, is something of a *lingua franca*: everyone understands the vocabulary, and everyone uses it routinely in conversations, presentations to others in the group, documents, and so on. This can make communication easier, if nothing else, but also more precise. And then it is only a small step to using common-sense mathematical intuition and informal mathematical reasoning to draw inferences and spot inconsistencies. From C. A. R. Hoare:

> Informal reasoning among those who are fluent in the idioms of mathematics is extremely efficient, and remarkably reliable. It is not immune from failure; for example simple misprints can be surprisingly hard to detect by eye. Fortunately, these are exactly the kind of error that can be removed by early tests. More formal calculation can be reserved for the most crucial issues....

which, of course, is exactly the approach that we have been taking throughout this book, and exactly our experience with it.

Regardless of whether all of the opinions that I have just expressed are correct, it is a good bet that the use of formal methods of all kinds, including Cleanroom-style methods, will grow and spread in the coming years, slowly but steadily, as it has been doing. Formal methods may even become common practice; this remains to be seen. But the field will continue to develop. Notations and techniques will be refined, and occasionally a brilliant insight may lead to a really significant advance.

In any case, you now know techniques for producing software of much higher quality than the software most of the world produces. Use what you know. Feel free to adapt these methods to whatever situation you may be in and according to your experience. Practice, and sharpen your skills every chance you get. And keep striving for zero defects.

Notes

For a summary of the complete Cleanroom process, including box structures and statistical quality certification, see [Ling94]. [Haus94] gives more detail on how a full-scale Cleanroom process works in the context of an organization, and discusses how Cleanroom methods can be adopted in phases, at increasing levels of rigor. For further details on box structures and how they are used in development, see [Mill87b] and [Deck97]. Box structures fit nicely into object-oriented methods, and there is a natural correspondence between boxes and objects; see [Hevn93]. For further details on statistical quality certification, see the references cited in the "Notes" section at the end of Chapter 10.

The paper "Seven Myths of Formal Methods" is [Hall90]. The seven myths are that:

1. Formal methods can guarantee that software is perfect.
2. Formal methods are all about program proving.
3. Formal methods are useful only for safety-critical systems.
4. Formal methods require highly trained mathematicians.
5. Formal methods increase the cost of development.
6. Formal methods are unacceptable to users.
7. Formal methods are not used on real, large-scale software.

Some references for the formal methods mentioned are

- VDM: [Jone86b].
- Z: [Spiv92].
- CCS: [Miln80].
- CSP: [Hoar85].

For brief examples of the notations of Z, VDM, CSP, and several others, see [Wing90].

An attempt to combine Z with Cleanroom methods is described in [Norm93].

The results of using Z in CICS are reported in [Hous91]; the quotations are from pages 589 and 591. The survey by Craigen, Gerhart, and Ralston is discussed in [Crai93] and [Crai95]; the quotations are from the former document, pages iv and ii, and the latter paper, page 417. The CDIS project is described in detail in [Hall96]; the quotations are from [Hall96] pp. 66–67 and [Saie96] p. 22. The independent study of this project is described in [Pfle97]; the quotations are from pages 40 and 42. A number of other recent applications of formal methods in industry are presented in [Hinc95].

The productivity gain numbers quoted for Cleanroom methods (factors of 1.5 to 5) are from [Haus94] p. 91.

The sources of the other quotations are

- Frederick Brooks: [Broo87], pp. 10, 18, 16.
- David Parnas: [Saie96], p. 28.
- Michael Hinchey and Jonathan Bowen: [Saie96], p. 18.
- Daniel Jackson and Jeannette Wing: [Saie96], p. 21.
- Cliff Jones: [Saie96], p. 20.
- C. A. R. Hoare: [Hoar96], p. 4.

Hints for Selected Exercises

Chapter 2

Exercise 1c: You should start with a conditional concurrent assignment with four cases. Now, are any of these cases redundant?

Exercise 3b: What happens if a programmer takes this specification literally, and writes code that first performs a sort on the last name and then performs a sort on the first name?

Exercise 3c: You should be able to find at least two quite different things wrong with this intended function, one in each phrase on the right-hand side of the assignment.

Exercise 4: Yes, of course the elements of b must be in ascending order. But what else must we know about the values in b?

Chapter 3

Exercise 1a: Be sure to simplify the final values of x and y. You may be surprised at the result!

Exercise 3a: Yes, the conditions in the intended function and the if-statement are different, but this may or may not mean that the if-statement computes a different function.

Chapter 4

Exercise 1d: Suppose that d is a number that divides both m and n evenly. Does it also divide m mod n evenly?

Exercise 3: This is an instance of the pattern in which a variable accumulates a value. Look again at the intended function for the while-loop in the array-sum example of Section 4.4; your solution will have a similar form.

Exercise 6: Suppose there is such a while-loop. If you can increment *x* with this code once, you should be able to increment it twice, but what happens if you try?

Chapter 5

Exercise 1c: Let us assume that your program will operate by reading and examining each character of the input in a loop, as in the "lettercount" program of Section 5.2. (Depending on your programming language, this may be the only reasonable way to do it.) The key to this exercise is the intended function that you use for the body of the loop. How you write this will determine how complicated the verification will be.

For each character, you will increment your character count, and you may also increment your word count, your line count, or both. Remember that you must write a single intended function to cover all the computation done in the loop body; therefore, this function will be a conditional.

Try to write this conditional so that it has as few cases as possible. Think especially about when you will increment your word count. One obvious way is to do it when you have detected the beginning of a word, and another is to do it when you have detected the end of a word. You will probably find that one of these choices leads you to a solution with fewer cases in the conditional than the other choice.

Chapter 7

Exercise 2: What if the loop body explicitly refers to the constant "a" in some place where you might expect it to refer to the value of *v*?

Chapter 9

Exercise 4c: Think of the characteristic function of a set, represented as a bit string containing 1 if an element is in the set and 0 if not. Then use `bitstrings`, from Section 9.4, as a guide.

Chapter 10

Exercise 1: Look back at Section 6.5. Alice, Ben, and Chris have already written some key parts of the program for you. If you are writing in C, you can use their code directly; otherwise, you can use their design and adapt it to your preferred language.

References

[Abel85]   Harold Abelson and Gerald Jay Sussman with Julie Sussman. *Structure and Interpretation of Computer Programs.* Cambridge, Mass.: The MIT Press, 1985.

[Aho86]   Alfred V. Aho, Ravi Sethi, and Jeffrey D. Ullman. *Compilers: Principles, Techniques and Tools.* Reading, Mass.: Addison-Wesley, 1986.

[Basi84]   Victor R. Basili and Barry T. Perricone. "Software errors and complexity: an empirical investigation." *Commun. ACM 27,* 1, pp. 42–52, January 1984.

[Beck97]   Shirley A. Becker and James A. Whittaker. *Cleanroom Software Engineering Practices.* Harrisburg, Pa.: Idea Group Publishing, 1997.

[Beiz90]   Boris Beizer. *Software Testing Techniques.* London: International Thompson Computer Press, 1990 (second edition).

[Boeh88]   B. W. Boehm. "A spiral model of software development and enhancement." *Computer 21,* 5, pp. 61–72, May 1988.

[Broo87]   Frederick P. Brooks, Jr. "No silver bullet: Essence and accidents of software engineering." *Computer 20,* 4, pp. 10–19, April 1987.

[Cobb90]   Richard H. Cobb and Harlan D. Mills. "Engineering software under statistical quality control." *IEEE Software 7,* 6, pp. 44–54, November 1990.

[Coop83]   Doug Cooper. *Standard Pascal: User Reference Manual.* New York: Norton, 1983.

[Crai93]   Dan Craigen, Susan Gerhart, and Ted Ralston. *An International Survey of Industrial Applications of Formal Methods,,* Volume 1. NISTGCR 93/626, U.S. Department of Commerce, National Institute of Standards and Technology, 1993. At the time of this writing, available for FTP at `hissa.ncsl.nist.gov`, in directory `pub/formal_methods`.

[Crai95]   Dan Craigen, Susan Gerhart, and Ted Ralston. "Formal methods transfer: impediments and innovation." In [Hinc95], pp. 399–419.

[Curr86]   P. Allen Currit, Michael Dyer, and Harlan D. Mills. "Certifying the reliability of software." *IEEE Trans. on Software Engineering*, vol. SE-12, no. 1, pp. 3–11, January 1986.

[Cusa95]   Michael A. Cusamano and Richard W. Selby. *Microsoft Secrets*. New York: The Free Press, 1995.

[Deck97]   Michael Deck. "Development practices." In [Beck97], pp. 37–82.

[DeMa82]   Tom DeMarco. *Controlling Software Projects: Management Measurement & Estimation*. Englewood Cliffs, N.J.: Prentice-Hall, 1982.

[Dijk75]   Edsger W. Dijkstra. "Guarded commands, nondeterminacy and formal deriviation of programs." *Commun. ACM 18*, 8, pp. 453–457, August 1975.

[Dijk76]   Edsger W. Dijkstra. *A Discipline of Programming*. Englewood Cliffs, N.J.: Prentice-Hall, 1976.

[Dunl82]   Douglas D. Dunlop and Victor R. Basili. "A comparative analysis of functional correctness." *Computing Surveys 14*, 2, pp. 229–244, June 1982.

[Dunl85]   Douglas D. Dunlop and Victor R. Basili. "Generalizing specifications for uniformly implemented loops." *ACM Trans. on Programming Languages and Systems 7*, 1, pp. 137–158, January 1985.

[Dyer92]   Michael Dyer. *The Cleanroom Approach to Quality Software Development*. New York: Wiley, 1992.

[Faga76]   Michael E. Fagan. "Design and code inspections to reduce errors in program development." *IBM Systems Journal 15*, 3, pp. 182–211, 1976.

[Faga86]   Michael E. Fagan. "Advances in software inspections." *IEEE Trans. on Software Engineering*, vol. SE-12, no. 7, pp. 744–751, July 1986.

[Fisc91]   Charles N. Fischer and Richard J. LeBlanc, Jr. *Crafting a Compiler with C*. Redwood City, Calif.: Benjamin/Cummings, 1991.

[Floy67]   Robert W. Floyd. "Assigning meanings to programs." Proc. Symposia in Applied Mathematics, vol. 19, pp. 19–32. Providence, R.I.: American Mathematical Society, 1967.

[Gamm95] Erich Gamma, Richard Helm, Ralph Johnson, and John Vlissides. *Design Patterns: Elements of Reusable Object-Oriented Software*. Reading, Mass.: Addison-Wesley, 1995.

[Gibb94] W. Wayt Gibbs. "Software's chronic crisis." *Scientific American 271*, 3, pp. 86–95, September 1994.

[Gris90] Ralph E. Griswold and Madge T. Griswold. *The Icon Programming Language*. Englewood Cliffs, N.J.: Prentice Hall, 1990 (second edition).

[Guy94] Richard K. Guy. *Unsolved Problems in Number Theory*. New York: Springer-Verlag, 1994.

[Hall90] Anthony Hall. "Seven myths of formal methods." *IEEE Software 7*, 5, pp. 11–19, September 1990.

[Hall96] Anthony Hall. "Using formal methods to develop an ATC information system." *IEEE Software 13*, 2, pp. 66–76, March 1996.

[Haus94] P. A. Hausler, R. C. Linger, and C. J. Trammell. "Adopting Cleanroom software engineering with a phased approach." *IBM Systems Journal 33*, 1, pp. 89–109, 1994. Also in [Poor96], pp. 5–35.

[Head94] Grant E. Head. "Six-sigma software using Cleanroom software engineering techniques." *Hewlett-Packard Journal 45*, 3, pp. 40–50, June 1994. Also in [Poor96], pp. 231–258.

[Held91] Gilbert Held. *Data Compression: Techniques and Applications: Hardware and Software Considerations*. Chichester, England: Wiley, 1991 (third edition).

[Hevn93] A. R. Hevner and H. D. Mills. "Box-structured methods for systems development with objects." *IBM Systems Journal 32*, 2, pp. 232–251, 1993.

[Hinc95] M. G. Hinchey and J. P. Bowen, eds. *Applications of Formal Methods*. Hemel Hempstead, England: Prentice-Hall International (UK) Ltd., 1995.

[Hoar69] C. A. R. Hoare. "An axiomatic basis for computer programming." *Commun. ACM 12*, 10, pp. 576–583, October 1969.

[Hoar72] C. A. R. Hoare. "Proof of correctness of data representations." *Acta Informatica 1*, pp. 271–281, 1972.

[Hoar85] C. A. R. Hoare. *Communicating Sequential Processes*. Englewood Cliffs, N.J.: Prentice-Hall, 1985.

[Hoar96]   C. A. R. Hoare. "How did software get so reliable without proof?" In *FME '96: Industrial Benefit and Advances in Formal Methods,* pp. 1–17. Berlin: Springer-Verlag, 1996.

[Hopc79]   John E. Hopcroft and Jeffrey D. Ullman. *Introduction to Automata Theory, Languages, and Computation.* Reading, Mass.: Addison-Wesley, 1979.

[Hous91]   Iain Houston and Steve King. "CICS project report: Experiences and results from the use of Z in IBM." In *VDM '91: Formal Software Development Methods,* pp. 588–596. Berlin: Springer-Verlag, 1991.

[John84]   W. Lewis Johnson and Elliot Soloway. "PROUST: Knowledge-based program understanding." Proc. Seventh International Conference on Software Engineering, March 26–29, 1984, Orlando, Fla.. Long Beach, Calif.: IEEE Computer Society Press, 1984.

[Jone86a]   Jones, Capers. *Programming Productivity.* New York: McGraw-Hill, 1986.

[Jone86b].   C. B. Jones. *Systematic Software Development Using VDM.* Englewood Cliffs, N.J.: Prentice-Hall, 1986.

[Jone91]   Jones, Capers. *Applied Software Measurement: Assuring Productivity and Quality.* New York: McGraw-Hill, 1991.

[Kern88]   Brian W. Kernighan and Dennis M. Ritchie. *The C Programming Language.* Englewood Cliffs, N.J.: Prentice Hall, 1988 (second edition).

[Leve93]   Nancy G. Leveson and Clark S. Turner. "An investigation of the Therac-25 accidents." *Computer 26,* 7, pp. 18–41, July 1993.

[Levi92]   John R. Levine, Tony Mason, and Doug Brown. *Lex & yacc.* Sebastopol, Calif.: O'Reilly & Associates, 1992.

[Ling79]   Richard C. Linger, Harlan D. Mills, and Bernard I. Witt. *Structured Programming: Theory and Practice.* Reading, Mass.: Addison-Wesley, 1979.

[Ling94]   Richard C. Linger. "Cleanroom process model." *IEEE Software 11,* 2, pp. 50–58, March 1994. Also in [Poor96], pp. 111–131.

[Lisk77]   Barbara Liskov, Alan Snyder, Russell Atkinson, and Craig Schaffert. "Abstraction mechanisms in CLU." *Commun. ACM 20,* 8, pp. 564–576, August 1977.

[Lisk86]   Barbara Liskov and John Guttag. *Abstraction and Specification in Program Development.* Cambridge, Mass.: MIT Press, 1986.

[Meye88]   Bertrand Meyer. *Object-oriented Software Construction.* Hemel Hempstead, England: Prentice-Hall International (UK) Ltd., 1988.

[Mill75]   Harlan D. Mills. "The new math of computer programming." *Commun. ACM 18,* 1, pp. 43–48, January 1975.

[Mill84]   Harlan D. Mills. Remarks in a panel session, "Software development paradigms". Seventh International Conference on Software Engineering, March 26–29, 1984, Orlando, Fla..

[Mill86]   Harlan D. Mills, Richard C. Linger, and Alan R. Hevner. *Information Systems Analysis and Design.* San Diego: Academic Press, 1986.

[Mill87a] Harlan D. Mills, Victor R. Basili, John D. Gannon, and Richard G. Hamlet. *Principles of Computer Programming: a Mathematical Approach.* Boston: Allyn and Bacon, 1987.

[Mill87b] Harlan D. Mills, Victor R. Basili, John D. Gannon, and Richard G. Hamlet. "Box structured information systems." *IBM Systems Journal 26,* 1, pp. 395–413, 1987. Also in [Poor96], pp. 139–167.

[Mill87c] Harlan D. Mills, Michael Dyer, and Richard C. Linger. "Cleanroom software engineering." *IEEE Software 4,* 5, pp. 19–24, September 1987. Also in [Poor96], pp. 41–53.

[Mill88a] Harlan D. Mills. *Software Productivity.* New York: Dorset House, 1988.

[Mill88b] Harlan D. Mills. "Stepwise refinement and verification in box-structured systems." *Computer 21,* 6, pp. 23–36, June 1988.

[Mill88c] Harlan D. Mills and J. H. Poore. "Bringing software under statistical quality control." *Quality Progress 21,* 11, pp. 52–55, November 1988.

[Mill89]   Harlan D. Mills, Victor R. Basili, John D. Gannon, and Richard G. Hamlet. "Mathematical principles for a first course in software engineering." *IEEE Trans. on Software Engineering,* vol. SE-4, pp. 478–486, November 1978.

[Mill95]   B. A. Miller and M. G. Pleszkoch. "A Cleanroom test case generation tool." *Proceedings of the Second European Industrial Symposium on Cleanroom Software Engineering.* Berlin, March 28–29, 1995. Also in [Poor96], pp. 269–286.

[Miln80]   Robin Milner. *A Calculus of Communicating Systems.* Lecture Notes in Computer Science, 92. Berlin: Springer-Verlag, 1980.

[Misr78]   Jayadev Misra. "Some aspects of the verification of loop computations." *IEEE Trans. on Software Engineering, 15,* 5, pp. 550–559, May 1989.

[Mitc98]   Brian Mitchell and Steven J. Zeil. "An experiment in estimating reliability growth under both repesentative and directed testing." In [Youn98], pp. 32–41.

[Myer76]   Glenford J, Myers. *Software Reliability: Principles and Practices.* New York: Wiley, 1976.

[Neum95]   Peter G. Neumann. *Computer Related Risks.* New York: ACM Press, 1995.

[Norm93]   Glyn Normington. "Cleanroom and Z." In *Z User Workshop, London 1992,* Proceedings of the Seventh Annual Z User Meeting, London, 14–15 December 1992. London: Springer-Verlag, 1993.

[Parn72]   D. L. Parnas. "On the criteria to be used in decomposing systems into modules." *Commun. ACM 15,* 12, pp. 1053–1058, December 1972.

[Paul91]   Laurence C. Pauldon. *ML for the Working Programmer.* Cambridge: Cambridge University Press, 1991.

[Pfle87]   Shari Lawrence Pfleeger. *Software Engineering.* New York: Macmillan, 1987.

[Pfle97]   Shari Lawrence Pfleeger and Les Hatton. "Investigating the influence of formal methods." *Computer 30,* 2, pp. 33–43, February 1997.

[Poly45]   G. Polya. *How to Solve It.* Princeton, N.J.: Princeton University Press, 1945.

[Poor93]   J. H. Poore, Harlan D. Mills, and David Mutchler. "Planning and certifying software system reliability." *IEEE Software 10,* 1, pp. 88–99, January 1993. Also in [Poor96], pp. 83–110.

[Poor96]   Jesse H. Poore and Carmen J. Trammell. *Cleanroom Software Engineering: A Reader.* Oxford: NCC Blackwell, 1996.

[Prat96]   Terrence W. Pratt and Marvin V. Zelkowitz. *Programming Languages: Design and Implementation.* Englewood Cliffs, N.J.: Prentice Hall, 1996 (third edition).

[Saie96]   Hossein Saiedian, ed. "An invitation to formal methods." *Computer 29,* 4, pp. 16–30, April 1996.

[Scha90]   Stephen R. Schach. *Software Engineering*. Homewood, Ill.: Irwin, 1990.

[Sebe93]   Robert W. Sebesta. *Concepts of Programming Languages*. Redwood City, Calif.: Benjamin/Cummings, 1993 (second edition).

[Solo83]   Elliot Soloway, Jeffrey Bonar, and Kate Erlich. "Cognitive strategies and looping constructs: An empirical study." *Commun. ACM 26*, 11, pp. 853–860, November 1983.

[Spiv92]   J. M. Spivey. *The Z Notation: A Reference Manual*. Englewood Cliffs, N.J.: Prentice-Hall, 1992 (second edition).

[Stav93]   Allan M. Stavely. "An empirical study of iteration in applications software." *Journal of Systems and Software 22*, pp. 167–177, September 1993.

[Stav95]   Allan M. Stavely. "Verifying definite iteration over data structures." *IEEE Trans. on Software Engineering, 21,* 6, pp. 506–514, June 1995.

[Stev74]   W. P. Stevens, G. J. Myers, and L. L. Constantine. "Structured design." *IBM Systems Journal 13,* 2, pp. 115–139, 1974.

[Stro94]   Stroustrup, Bjarne. *The C++ programming language*. Reading, Mass.: Addison-Wesley, 1994.

[Tram94]   C. J. Trammell and J. H. Poore. "Experimental control in software reliability certification." *Proceedings of the Seventeenth Annual NASA/Goddard Software Engineering Workshop,* Greenbelt, Md., November 30–December 1, 1994. Also in [Poor96], pp. 361–372.

[vanR97]   Guido van Rossum. *Python Reference Manual*. Corporation for National Research Initiatives, 1895 Preston White Drive, Reston, Va. 20191, USA, December 31, 1997 (Release 1.5). At the time of this writing, available on the World-Wide Web at
`http://www.python.org/doc/ref/`

[Wait93]   William M. Waite and Lynn R. Carter. *An Introduction to Compiler Construction*. New York: HarperCollins College Publishers, 1993.

[Walt95]   G. H. Walton, J. H. Poore, and C. J. Trammell. "Statistical testing of software based on a usage model." *Software — Practice and Experience 25,* 1, pp. 97–108, January 1995. Also in [Poor96], pp. 331–344.

[Wein71]   Gerald M. Weinberg. *The Psychology of Computer Programming*. New York: Van Nostrand Reinhold, 1971.

[Whit94]   J. A. Whittaker and M. G. Thompson. "A Markov chain model for statistical software testing." *IEEE Trans. On Software Engineering 20,* 10, pp. 812–824, October 1994. Also in [Poor96], pp. 303–330.

[Wing90]   Jeannette M. Wing. "A specifier's introduction to formal methods." *Computer 23,* 9, pp. 8–24, September 1990.

[Wirt71]   Niklaus Wirth. "Program development by stepwise refinement." *Commun. ACM 14,* 4, pp. 221–227, April 1971.

[Youn98]   Michal Young, ed. *ISSTA 98: Proceedings of the ACM SIGSOFT International Symposium on Software Testing and Analysis,* Clearwater Beach, Fla., March 2–5, 1998. New York: Association for Computing Machinery, 1998.

Index

abstraction, 86, 90–96, 97
    data, 149–167
    See also specification function
accumulating-value pattern, 62, 68, 79, 85, 225
"anything", in intended functions, 22–23, 70, 74
arithmetic progression, 131–133
assertion, 29
    loop invariant, 68
assignment statement, *See* under control constructs
Axiom of Replacement, *See* Substitution Principle
axiomatic specification and verification, 29, 68
    See also Vienna Development Method; Z

basis (base) case of a recursive definition, 172–174
black box, 209–211
Bowen, Jonathan, 220, 223
box structures, 102, 167, 209–211, 222
break statement, *See* under control constructs
Brooks, Frederick, 102, 208, 217–219
bugs (defects)
    attitude toward, x
    density (bugs per thousand lines), 2, 5–7, 9, 188, 195, 198, 216
    eliminated before testing, 3–5, 103–108, 119, 188–189
    found by testing, 4–5, 9, 104–105, 119, 187–190, 195–197, 202, 216, 218

harm caused by, 1–2, 8–9, 196
    See also debugging; syntax errors

case-statement, *See* under control constructs
cases
    in recursive definitions, 172–174, 181–182
    in specifications, 15–16, 45–46, 172–174
    minimizing number of, 97–100
    verification by, 42–46, 188
CCS, 213, 215, 222
CDIS, 215–216, 220, 223
certification of reliability, 196, 198, 211
CICS, 213–214, 223
Cleanroom, vii–viii, ix, x, 3–7, 9, 102, 104–105, 196, 198, 208, 209–212, 216–223
clear box, 210–211
cohesion of modules, 102
Collatz $3n + 1$ algorithm, 57, 68, 175
comment, 18–19, 24, 57, 74, 81, 88, 156, 158, 188
    See also documentation
complexity in programs, 90, 96–100, 102, 107, 142, 149, 166, 215, 218
    See also simplicity
concurrent assignment, 12–14, 24–25, 29, 39, 41, 77–78, 178
    conditional, 15–16, 24, 29, 33, 48–49, 74, 171, 172
    nested conditional, 92
control constructs, 31–38
    assignment statement, 12–14, 31–33
    case-statement, 31, 45, 45n

control constructs *(continued)*
    exit (break, return, stop) statement, 31–
      32, 45n, 65, 67
    exit-in-the-middle (do-while-do, $n\frac{1}{2}$
      times) loop, 65
    for-each statement, 31, 121–147
    goto-statement, 32
    if-expression, 178–179
    if-statement, 16, 31, 35, 42–47
    initialized loop, 57–63
    loop, 31, 32, 53–68
    procedure call, 31, 33, 118
    procedure definition, 84, 169–174
    repeat-until loop, 63–65, 67
    sequence of statements, 31, 32, 34, 38–
      42, 65
    switch-statement, 45n
    while-statement, 31, 32, 34, 53–63, 67,
      145
control state, 12
correctness, 19–20, 36–38, 39, 103
    questions, *See* verification conditions
      and correctness questions
cost, *See* productivity and cost
coupling between modules, 102
coverage in testing, 190, 195, 197, 198
Craigen, Dan, 214–215, 223
CSP, 213, 215, 222

data abstraction, 149–167
    See also data abstraction
data compression, 83–89, 102
data encapsulation, 150, 166
data invariant, 155–161, 166
data state, 12, 40, 125
data structure, 99, 121–147, 170, 172,
    175
    grouping values into, 99
    infinite, 172, 185
    iteration over, 121–147
    recursive definition and processing of,
      170–175, 185
    See also data abstraction; data invariant;
      names of specific data structures
debugging, 2, 3, 5, 7, 103, 104, 187, 188,
    189, 216
declaration, 81, 117, 150, 155, 169–170
    See also scope; type information

defects, *See* bugs
definite iteration, 121–147
design, 3, 5, 96–100, 104, 142–145, 149,
    166–167, 208, 209–221
Dijkstra, Edsger, 29
directed graph, 133, 135, 177
do-while-do loop, *See* under control
    constructs
documentation, 23–24, 26, 33, 35, 74,
    104, 106, 118, 142, 151
    See also comment
domain of a function, 15, 19–22, 37
    in verification conditions, 39, 54, 64,
      65, 124
    suffix of a sequence in, 125–131

else, as a precondition, 15, 50, 74
empty (predicate on data structures), 122,
    124, 131, 134, 138–139
Ericsson Telecom, 6
examples
    all possible bit strings, 182–183
    appending lists, 178–179, 182
    big strings, 157–159, 161–163
    comparing attributes of files, 162–165
    counting letters and digits, 77–83, 97,
      121, 144–145, 160–161
    fields of a line, 135–136, 141, 160
    length of the longest line, 69–76
    median value in a list, 180–181
    registrar's program, 90–96, 99–100,
      108–111
    rehearsal scheduling, 203–207
    test-data generator, 111–117
    uncompressing a string, 83–89
examples, by programming language
    C, 77–83, 90–96, 97, 99–100, 108–
      117, 143–145, 157–161
    C++, 161–163
    Icon, 83–89, 121, 135–136, 141, 160
    ML, 181–183
    Pascal, 69–76
    Python, 162–165
    Scheme, 178–181
exit statement, *See* under control constructs
exit-in-the-middle loop, *See* under control
    constructs

finite-state machine, 192, 217
first (function on data structures), 121–122, 124–125, 131, 138–139
Floyd, Robert, 29
for-each statement, *See* under control constructs
formal methods, 212–216, 219–223
function
  abstraction (meaning) function, 152–155, 166
  as a programming-language construct, *See* routine
  computed by programs or parts of programs, 11–20, 35, 36–42, 47–49, 53–54, 118, 170, 174
  intended, *See* intended function
  notation conventions for, 12–16, 20–27, 29, 74, 77–79, 81, 84, 92, 118, 137, 156, 182–184
  specification function, 25–26, 83, 85–86, 97, 151, 188, 206

generator (programming-language construct), 122–123
procedure, 135–136, 140–141, 147
Gerhart, Susan, 214–215, 223
goto-statement, *See* under control constructs
grammar, context-free, 191–195, 198, 217
group (team)
  programming (development), 4, 6–7, 104–105, 118, 189, 195, 200–203, 221
  testing, 4, 7, 105, 189, 195, 202
  verification, 4, 7, 103–120, 187

Hall, Anthony, 213, 215–216
Hinchey, Michael, 220, 223
Hoare, C. A. R., 29, 221, 223

I, See identity function
IBM, vii, ix, 3, 5, 6, 119, 190, 198, 213–214, 220
identity function (*I*), 16, 44, 54, 62, 74, 124, 134
if-expression, *See* under control constructs
if-statement, *See* under control constructs
incidental variable, 23, 70, 74

incremental development, 4, 6, 199–208, 212
  See also stepwise refinement
indefinite iteration, 53–68
infinite data structure, 172, 185
information hiding, 158, 166
inheritance, 161, 162, 166
initialization, 156, 161, 195
  by declarations, 81
  of loops, 57–63
input, 18, 31, 121, 142, 201
  as a state variable, 11, 32, 56, 70, 175
  data, for testing, 4, 40, 190–197, 200
  in the C language, 77–78, 143–145
  See also interface, user
inspections, 104, 106, 107, 119, 211–212, 214, 220
  See also verification reviews
intended function, 18–29, 33–47, 106, 107, 137, 188, 216, 218, 221
  correctness with respect to, *See* correctness; verification conditions and correctness questions
  domain of, *See* domain of a function
  for specific control constructs, *See* control constructs
  inner versus outer, with data abstractions, 153–154
  placement of, in programs, 33–36, 84, 151
  programming with, 69–100
  writing, 23–27, 59–63, 67–68, 118; *See also* function, notation conventions for
intended value, 178–185
interfaces
  among parts of a program, 98–100, 102, 118, 120, 150
  to other software, 102, 189
  user, 189, 199, 201
invariant
  data, 155–161, 166
  implementation (representation), 155
  loop, 68
iteration
  definite, 121–147
  indefinite, 53–68
  mechanism, 136–142

iteration *(continued)*
    See also control constructs

Jackson, Daniel, 219, 220, 223
Jones, Cliff, 220, 223

list (data structure), 55–56, 121, 143
local variables, 17–18
long-form correctness questions for definite
        iteration, 126, 128, 131–133
loop, *See* under control constructs

Markov chain, 192, 194–195, 198
mean time to failure (MTTF), 190, 196
meetings, *See* inspections; verification
        reviews
Mills, Harlan, 3, 29, 54, 104, 119–120,
        190, 210n
MTTF, *See* mean time to failure
mutual recursion, 176–177

$n\frac{1}{2}$ times loop, *See* under control constructs
NASA, 5, 120
nonterminal symbol of a grammar, 191–
        192, 195
nonterminating computation, 172

object-oriented programs and program-
        ming, 149, 161–167, 215, 222
output, 11, 18, 31, 142
overloading, 158, 162, 166
Oxford University, 213

Parnas, David, 219, 221, 223
patterns of code, 62, 68, 79, 85, 122, 143–
        144, 225
postcondition, 29, 213
Praxis, 215, 220
precondition, 15–16, 20–21, 33, 188
        implicit, 20–21, 188
        in axiomatic specifications, 29, 213
        manipulating in verification, 43, 45–
                46, 48–50, 129–130
        type information in, 84–86, 164, 179
        See also domain of a function
procedure, *See* routine
production of a grammar, 191–192, 195

productivity and cost, effects of develop-
        ment practices on
        Cleanroom methods, viii, 5–6, 217–
                218, 223
        formal methods, 213–216, 220, 222
        incremental development, 202–203
        testing, 197
programming languages, properties and
        details of
        C, 17, 27, 32, 45n, 77, 78, 80, 81, 92,
                102, 136–139, 143–145, 146
        C++, 161, 167
        CLU, 135, 147, 150, 154, 166
        FORTRAN, 131
        Icon, 84, 85, 87, 102, 122–123, 133–
                135, 140–141
        ML, 181–182, 185
        Modula, 45, 150
        Pascal, 63, 72–74, 102, 131
        Python, 122, 147, 164
        Scheme, 178–181, 185
        See also examples, by programming
                language
prototype, 189, 200, 201

quality of software
        assessing and improving, 104, 107, 108,
                190, 213, 215, 216, 217
        control of, 4, 187–189, 197
        statistical certification of, 196, 198,
                211, 222

Ralston, Ted, 214–215, 223
ranges of integers, 131–133
recursion, 169–185
        mutual, 176–77
recursive definition of data, 172–174, 183,
        185
recursive descent, 176–177, 185
relation, 22, 23, 29, 153
repeat-until loop, *See* under control
        constructs
requirements
        determining, 97–98, 201–202, 212,
                215, 218
        effects of, 2, 102
        errors in, 216, 218
        safety and security, 6, 215

simplification of, 97—98

response to stimulus, 209—211

rest (function on data structures), 121—122, 124—125, 127—128, 131, 138—139

return, in intended functions, 84, 183

return statement, *See* under control constructs

review meeting, *See* verification reviews

routine (procedure, subroutine, function)
    development of, examples, 69, 83—99
    generator, 135—136, 140—141, 147
    in functional languages, 178—184
    interfaces between, 118, 120
    recursive, 169—185
    testing of, 4, 104
    See also control constructs (exit statement; procedure call; procedure definition); type information

run-length encoding, 83—89, 102

scope, 17—18, 21, 150

sequence
    data structure, 121—136, 142—143, 147, 213
    of statements, *See* under control constructs

set
    iteration over elements of, 133—134
    in specifications and designs, 118, 142—143, 147, 149—150, 213, 221
    representation of, specifying and verifying, 150—156

short-form correctness questions for definite iteration, 126, 133

side effect, 32—33, 144, 178

simplicity, 96—100, 107, 118—119, 217—218
    See also complexity in programs

specifications, 2, 6, 70, 83, 212, 218
    axiomatic, 29, 68
    box structures, 209—211
    definition of, 18
    formal methods for, 212—216, 220—221
    functional, 3, 18—29, 69—102, 178, 211; *See also* function, intended; function, notation conventions

of increments, 200—203

of test data, 191—195, 198, 200

use of discrete mathematics in, 142, 221

weakest-precondition, 29

specification function, 25—26, 83, 85—86, 97, 151, 188, 206

state box, 210—211

state of a program, 11—18, 21, 38, 40, 58—59
    See also domain of a function; state variable

state variable, 11—14, 17—18, 39—40, 97—98, 178
    input as, 11, 32, 56, 70, 175
    other quantities treated as, 11, 56, 125, 140, 159
    See also trace tables

statistical inference from testing, 196—198, 222

stepwise refinement, 36, 52, 69, 102, 209, 211
    formal derivation, 212—213
    See also top-down development

stimulus, 209—211

stop statement, *See* under control constructs

stub, 5, 199—200

subroutine, *See* routine

Substitution Principle, 36—38, 40, 52

suffix of a sequence, 125, 129—131

switch-statement, *See* under control constructs

syntax errors, 7, 105, 119—120, 188

team, *See* group

terminal symbol of a grammar, 191—192, 195

termination
    of loop, 31, 54—58, 62, 63—64, 124—125
    of recursion, 169, 172, 174—177

testing, 120, 187—198, 216, 218
    boundary conditions, 195, 197
    coverage, 190, 195, 197, 198
    data generators, 111—117, 191—195, 197, 198, 200
    directed, 195—198
    effectiveness of, 2—3, 9, 101

testing *(continued)*
  in incremental development, 199–200,
    202, 208
  input data for, 4, 40, 190–197, 200
  integration, 4, 105, 120, 200
  plans, 202, 212
  private, 189
  random, *See* usage-based
  role of, vii, 3–5, 103–105, 187–189
  special cases, 195, 197
  statistical inference from results of,
    196–198, 222
  structural, 190, 198
  team, 4, 7, 105, 189, 195, 202
  unit, 4–5, 104–105, 119–120, 189,
    197, 198
  usage-based, 190–198
  "white-box", 210n
time to market, 5, 215
top-down development of programs, 36,
  199
  See also incremental development;
    stepwise refinement
trace tables, 41–42, 52, 106, 181, 188
  conditional, 47–51, 52, 181
tree (data structure), 133, 135, 183
true, as a precondition, 15, 16, 49, 50, 74
Turing machine, 53, 56
type information, 21, 83–86, 94, 112,
  155, 179

undecidable problem, 53, 56, 175
undefined function or computation, 15–
  16, 20, 22, 50
  See also domain of a function

undefined, in intended functions, 22, 50
uninitialized loops, 59–63, 68, 129–130

value, intended, 178–185
  conditional, 178
VDM, *See* Vienna Development Method
verification conditions and correctness
    questions
  data invariant, 156
  exit-in-the-middle (do-while-do, $n\frac{1}{2}$
    times) loop, 65, 67
  for-each statement, 124–126, 131, 133,
    134, 138–139
  if-statement, 43–45
  iteration mechanism, 138–139
  repeat-until loop, 63–64, 67
  sequence of statements, 39
  while-loop, 54, 67
verification reviews
  effectiveness of, 119, 195
  how to conduct, 105–120, 187–188
  role of, vii, 3–4, 7, 103–105, 189, 200,
    211–212, 216, 218
  See also inspection
Vienna Development Method (VDM), 213,
  215, 222

while-statement, *See* under control con-
    structs
"white box", 210n
Wing, Jeanette, 219, 220, 223

Z, 213–214, 220–223